SPIES AND TRAITORS
of WORLD WAR II

by

KURT SINGER

Author of
Duel for the Northland
Göring
and other books

New York **PRENTICE-HALL,** *Inc.* *1945*

Copyright, 1945, by
PRENTICE-HALL, Inc.
70 Fifth Avenue, New York

To my friends

HARLOWE R. HOYT
JOSEPH ROOS
ROWENA WILSON TOBIAS

IN *Spies and Traitors of World War II* I have attempted to portray the workings of modernized espionage during the second great World War. I have tried to lay bare the network of espionage that was thrown around all lands from Greenland to Africa, from Finland to Hawaii, from Tokyo to Montreal.

For obvious reasons, many facts could not, at the time of writing, be revealed; many others are state secrets of whose existence I have only the barest hints. But there are many facts that I do know because, as a newspaper man, I have concerned myself with matters of espionage since 1933. I actively participated in exposing Axis agents, and I have had the honor of being consulted by Allied military and civilian governmental agencies.

Ninety-five per cent of the names and incidents mentioned in this book are taken from well-substantiated documents. A few names had to be changed or suppressed in order to protect Allied agents still at work. Here and there, for the sake of smooth presentation, I have reconstructed incidents or dialogue because documentary proof from court records, newspapers or the statements of government officials was not available. In the very few cases where this method is used, I have tried to conform as closely as possible to the facts as they logically must have been.

Ideas and people remain basically the same. We may speak of Delilah as the first woman spy in history; she spied on Samson for the Philistines. You may be sure that the Mata Haris of World War II employed wiles similar to those that brought such bitter success to Delilah.

Military principles have also remained unchanged for generations. Every military academy in the world still teaches the maxim formulated by German General Karl von Clausewitz, that war is only the continuation of politics by other means. Conversely, peace politics are but the continuation of war by other means. This basic principle will continue to be applied even after World War II, and as its logical corollary global espionage will survive. Victors and vanquished, not daring to trust one another, will build up new Secret Services.

There will always be human material for spies and traitors. The Delilahs and Mata Haris, the Benedict Arnolds and Major Andrés can always be found. For the sake of money, adventure, love or idealism, spies and informers will always be ready to serve their devious masters.

It is my hope that this book may serve as a warning to friend and foe in a postwar world: as a warning to the United Nations that the spirit of vengeance will continue to lurk in the Axis nations and that the Secret Service in peacetime has but one mission—to prevent future wars; and as a stern warning to the Axis countries and to those lands which offer Fascism a chance to survive that the United Nations will be on their guard. For one branch of the Allied armies will never be dismissed—the Secret Service; never, that is, until some remote generation finds that Utopia can be realized. It was once considered Utopian to think that man would realize the dream of Icarus and fly toward the sun; but men are actually flying today. It is still considered Utopian to believe that the human world can live without wars, without Secret Services and spies. That is still Utopian and will be Utopian tomorrow. But the day may come when our great-grandchildren will fight all their battles on the playing fields of Eton and the sandlots of America, instead of at Tarawa, Sedan, Stalingrad, Manila or along the bloodstained Rhine. Let us pray that World War III may be prevented!

KURT SINGER

Bronxville, N. Y.

CONTENTS

CONTENTS

"I am not what I am!"

—Iago in *Othello*.

CHAPTER I

The Admiral Who Never Wears a Uniform

O_N THE historic morning of September 1, 1939, a neatly dressed little man of most unhistoric appearance walked down Berlin's Wilhelmstrasse. World War II was but a few hours old; at dawn German troops had poured across the border into Poland. The Berlin police had closed the Wilhelmstrasse against all traffic. They wanted no demonstrations, patriotic or otherwise, in front of the government buildings. But the little man walked through their lines without hindrance toward the fabulous Reich Chancellory, a structure as grandiose and impious as the Tower of Babel.

He entered the building, passing Hitler's personal guard at the door, who was obviously a high officer, with many ribbons and cords bedecking his dark-blue uniform. The officer stiffened his arm and cried, "Heil Hitler, Admiral."

The privileged little man in civilian dress was, of course, no civilian. He had just been promoted to the rank of Admiral, and he had come to thank Hitler for the promotion. He knew his way around the tremendous building; he knew how to thread the labyrinth of stairways and corridors. The pillars gleaming with silver and gold did not dazzle him, nor did the marble floors and the galleries of monstrous war paintings impress him; they were familiar sights.

This civilian, whom the officer at the door addressed as Admiral, was the new chief of all German espionage, the head of the German Secret Service in World War II.

Admiral Walter Wilhelm Canaris is the mystery man of German espionage. He himself may well be judged by future historians to have been the greatest spy of our time; certainly he is the greatest *organizer* of espionage the world has ever known. He, more than any other important Nazi, has cultivated obscurity. Deliberately he has reduced his personality to a cipher. Few cameras have ever caught his likeness. He has chosen to renounce all public glory. He has never been seen at any of the

1

great Nazi mass meetings in the Berlin Sportpalast. He has never spoken on the air. Though one of the mightiest and deadliest men of Hitler's Germany, he has never been mentioned in the German press.

His headquarters, however, could not be concealed so successfully. He shared quarters with the War Department at 14 Bendlerstrasse, in the very heart of Berlin. Of the thousands who frequented this enormous building, only a few ever saw him face to face. Those who caught a glimpse describe him as small and of slight build. His skin is colorless and sallow, like that of men who work at night. His cheekbones are prominent and lend his face a more Slavic than Teutonic cast. But the name Canaris is Greek; his grandparents were of Greek stock and had emigrated to Germany.

The Admiral does not carry himself well; he walks with a slight hunch of the shoulders and furtive droop of the head. His fair thin hair is gradually shading into white. As he nears his sixties, he is putting on weight. How he would look in an admiral's uniform no one can say, for he invariably dresses as a civilian.

His home address during the War has been a close secret. A handful of his assistants knew that he lived somewhere in the suburb of Zehlendorf, and that his house was surrounded by a flower garden of which the Admiral was very fond. However, the War kept the Admiral excessively busy and permitted no time for his hobby of gardening. The garden became the responsibility of his wife and daughter. Finally, Frau Canaris had to take care of it by herself, for with the Allied invasion of France in 1944 the Admiral decided to send his daughter to school in Switzerland. His parental concern is understandable. Fräulein Canaris, who is nineteen, is enrolled under another name in a school near Lake Geneva.

One might have trudged down every corridor in the building at 14 Bendlerstrasse without finding a door bearing the Admiral's name. Indeed, few could have directed you even to the part of the building where his offices were located. In March, 1935, Canaris had a private entrance constructed, and he entered and left by a staircase exclusively his.

A big Mercedes, one of the staff cars, brought him daily from his estate in Zehlendorf. The automobile was armored and had bullet-proof windows.

For years the committing of "perfect crimes" has been all in his day's routine. In consequence, the Admiral's demeanor became that of the perfect criminal or the perfect detective. It is significant that the few men who have met him all allude to his neurotic alertness.

"He considers no situation harmless. He is obviously afraid to turn his back to you; he takes care to face you and let the wall guard his back. His voice and his uncanny poise also indicate a perpetual fear." Such was the comment of an Allied Intelligence agent who met the Admiral.

The combination of power over others and fear for oneself produces a definite type. It gives rise to a merciless character fitted to perform the scientific crimes of the brutal Nazi system. Canaris most certainly filled the specifications for ruthlessness, else he would not have been chosen by Hitler for his role.

His career as a spy started back in 1914. At the age of twenty-five years, he was a naval officer of great promise, already the commander of the cruiser *Dresden*. The outbreak of war found him on the high seas. There was no hope of returning to a German port, so he brought his ship to neutral Chile, where he and his crew were interned.

A German Secret Service officer in the guise of a Red Cross visitor made contact with him in the internment camp. He outlined a plan for a daring escape that would enable Canaris to go on serving the Fatherland. Once free, Canaris was to enter the Imperial Intelligence Service. He would then go to the United States and work under Franz von Papen, organizing anti-American espionage and sabotage.

The escape was managed with ease. And in 1916 an unprepossessing, smallish man with prominent cheekbones came to New York. He called himself Otto Seliger, a Polish Jew. The American and Canadian Intelligence Services possess huge dossiers on Otto Seliger, who was in charge of dangerous sabotage assignments under the leadership of the reckless spies and saboteurs of the Imperial German Secret Service, headed in America by Franz von Papen and Franz von Rintelen.

The American dossiers also mention the alias of Moses Meyerbeer. Under this name Canaris gave his occupation as music dealer and even dared to pretend that he was a nephew of the famous composer Meyerbeer. As Moses Meyerbeer he organized the dynamiting of the Canadian Car and Foundry Company. Was it some masochistic impulse which made Canaris twice pose as a Jew? Throughout his life Canaris has been pathologically anti-Semitic.

A few weeks before the United States entered World War I, Canaris received orders for precipitate action. He was to clear out of the United States, go to Spain and there organize a naval espionage unit. It was in Spain that he met a woman whom he would never forget, a woman who was to play a fateful role in his life. This woman, as we shall see, was to give her life to purchase advancement for the career of Walter Wilhelm Canaris.

For her beauty alone she was unforgettable, as many have testified. Her name was Margarete Gertrude Zelle. She was dark, exotic, fascinating, a passionate and inspired dancer. Born in Java of Dutch parents, she had taken the stage name "Mata Hari," Arabic words meaning "Eye of the morning."

Young Canaris first saw her at the famous Madrid night club, Trocadero. As he entered she was dancing an authentic Javanese Temple dance. Afterward Canaris invited the dancer to his table. He was never good-looking, but his Prussian formality and the forcefulness of his vaulting ambition gave him power over women. It began as a light-hearted flirtation, with Canaris coming to the Trocadero night after night, but soon it developed into a passionate love affair.

The passion did not last long. Canaris had other uses for Mata Hari. His immediate superior, the German Ambassador to Spain, Baron Eberhard von Stohrer, wanted a woman spy to be sent to Paris as soon as possible. This Baron von Stohrer, by the way, was again to be German Ambassador to Spain during World War II.

Canaris was ostensibly a military attaché to Spain. His real duties, however, were not so ornamental. What he was actually doing was preparing bases for German submarines along the neutral Spanish coast, conducting harbor espionage against Allied shipping and planting agents at the Spanish court to offset Allied influence over the Spanish royal house.

Above all, Canaris's job was to smuggle German agents into France across the Pyrenees. It was here that Mata Hari came in. She was to go to Paris on a Dutch transport, dance at the Moulin Rouge and become his key agent in France. It was anticipated that her beauty and artistry would conquer all Paris, especially—and this interested Canaris most—high-ranking officers of the army and navy.

Mata Hari was reluctant to go. But Canaris promised that he would see her soon. He turned her head with promises and with flattery, and he swore he would arrange splendid engagements. She would become the greatest dancer in Europe.

Canaris's prediction came true. Mata Hari fascinated Paris. The most sophisticated roués worshipped at her feet. Money poured in, and Mata Hari loved money. She purchased a small estate near the Bois de Boulogne. There she held open house every Sunday evening. Forty or fifty men would come to vie for her favors, among them members of the French General Staff.

In Spain, her lover Canaris grew negligent; his letters became less frequent. His duties were too pressing to allow time for romantic attentions. After all, the girl was not a German, so marriage was out of the question. For him, Mata Hari became only Agent No. H-21.

In that capacity she did brilliant work. She learned the secrets of troop movements, of new offensives, of fortifications and defense plans. She made occasional trips to Holland, where she reported her findings to German officers.

In 1917 Agent H-21 made one of her courier trips via Holland to Cologne. There she had a prearranged meeting in the loge of the Opera with one of the highest officers of the German General Staff. She had come to inform him about important troop movements from England to France and to give him details on the Allied defense lines. By chance, French Intelligence agents saw her talking to the German.

The mission accomplished, Mata Hari set out for home. Without the slightest trepidation she took a boat which was headed for France via Denmark and England. She was about to leave it when a British customs official came up to her and whispered: "Don't touch French soil. You'd better stay on this boat. It goes to Spain."

Mata Hari thought swiftly. She instantly realized that some-one•had discovered her. She was fortunate in being on a neutral boat and she decided to stay on it and flee to Spain.

Her frequent and apparently aimless trips to Holland had aroused the suspicions of the British and French Intelligence Services, and she had been under observation for several months. The mischance that enabled French Intelligence agents to encounter her talking to the German officer at the Cologne Opera was enough to clinch the case against her. But the German counter-espionage was also on the alert, and the British customs official who warned her not to return to France was in reality a German agent.

In Spain, she went to the German Embassy. She asked for Walter Wilhelm Canaris, the man she still loved. Her lover was disgruntled at seeing her. She had no business here; her place was in Paris. She tried to tell him what had happened, but he interrupted her and made a fearful scene about her *affaires d'amour* in Paris.

They finally made up and spent a week together. It was none too blissful and at its end Canaris broke his news. New orders had come. It was regrettable but imperative. Her work had been so valuable that it was sorely missed. She had to return to Paris, *"mag es kosten was es will"*—at no matter what price.

She bade Canaris a heartbreaking adieu, for Mata Hari knew that she would never see him again. She had a foreboding of her doom, but there was no way out. A German spy could not desert.

The inevitable happened. Mata Hari was arrested by the French, court-martialed and in the fall of 1917 shot. But it was not the French who really sentenced her to death. *It was Canaris himself*. When he ordered her back to Paris on the assignment that was to be her last, he informed the German Intelligence Service in Amsterdam of her whereabouts. To send the message he deliberately used a code which had been discarded for the transmission of vital information. French Intelligence had broken it. His treachery was successful. The French intercepted the message—and that was the end of Mata Hari.

* * *

Then the German Revolution broke out. The Kaiser went; the generals remained. Nevertheless, many conscientious military men found themselves out of a job. Canaris emerged from the war with the rank of Lieutenant Commander but jobless.

During the next few years he appeared and disappeared. It is hard to say what he did in those unfavorable times. We do know that on his own initiative Canaris was extremely active in organizing counter-revolution against the Weimar Republic. He helped to conceal the arms the Inter-Allied Control Commissions were hunting for. He helped to establish the various Free Corps which were in the forefront of the numerous *Putsches* that shook the German Republic. In fact, he planned several of them. He was one of Hitler's collaborators in the famous Beer Cellar Putsch of 1923, and, had that conspiracy been successful, Canaris was to have "taken over" the northern seacoast of Germany.

Around 1926 Walter Canaris, in title still a member of the non-existent navy, sank out of sight of the general public. Only a few insiders knew that a man like Canaris would not disappear for good. Obscurely but patiently he was working in a tiny office in the War Ministry. The lettering on his door read "Department for Naval Transport," which meant exactly nothing. In these cramped quarters Canaris toiled away at Naval Intelligence, preparing for *"Der Tag."*

In 1927 the limelight was suddenly turned upon him, to his very great annoyance. At that time one of Germany's largest motion picture companies, the Phoebus Corporation, went into bankruptcy. The company had produced a number of pictures glorifying the gallantry of the non-existent Germany navy. These movies were nothing more nor less than militaristic propaganda for the navy and merchant marine. The bankruptcy proceedings turned up the embarrassing evidence that they had been financed by Canaris.

The German public was curious to know where Canaris had

secured the necessary money, for the cost of the pictures had come to some seven million marks (roughly three million dollars). Canaris answered, "Secret funds." But he would not tell the German court anything further. His excuse: to say more would give away important defense secrets. That was enough for the nationalistic judges. He was excused from further questioning. The financial crookedness was not only never punished—it was never prosecuted.

Nevertheless it created a scandal, one big enough to cause Canaris to lie very low for a while. The German navy packed him off to Spain, where much of the secret German rearmament was going on. He saw to the building of U-boats in the Echeveria shipyard. Although the treaty of Versailles prohibited Germany from having any submarines at all, construction went on quite brazenly.

In Spain, he was a frequent guest of the well-known Spanish munitions king, Juan March. They discussed purchasing weapons for the German army and storing them in Spain. Canaris's connection with Juan March turned out to be highly useful during the Spanish Civil War. For some time, it will be remembered, the Germans did not have to come openly to the aid of Franco, since they were already established in key positions in Spain.

Canaris's reports from Spain were invaluable to the German Naval Intelligence. He set up an espionage system directed against British and Italian shipping which was to be of immense value to Germany.

In 1929, Franz von Papen, who had been his superior when they worked in the United States, introduced him to Hermann Goering. The characters of Canaris and Goering had much in common, since both men were the Prussian type of Junker officer, and they liked each other from the start. Both had actively participated in the Munich Beer Hall Putsch, but had never chanced to meet. Canaris told Goering that he, Canaris, could bring some of the Intelligence facilities of the democratic German army to the aid of the Hitler movement. Goering agreed. Canaris was the very man to head an espionage apparatus for the steadily growing Nazi Party. He had proved in World War I that he was one of the best pupils of Colonel

Walter Nicolai, then the head of the German Secret Service. He had excellent connections in the navy, too. Moreover, the information he could bring in was supremely marketable; certainly Fascist Italy would be glad to buy it, and that would help swell the party's finances.

Canaris's first job for the Hitler gang was a simple personnel report. Hitler asked for a file on all German officers, indicating their political leanings, their financial situations and their moral attitudes.

It is well known that Canaris and Papen were instrumental in deposing Chancellor Kurt von Schleicher, thus leaving his post free for Hitler. The deposing came about because Canaris was able to steal an interesting document from Schleicher's private desk.

Schleicher had been secretly dallying with the idea of a new legislative measure that would cut off the Junkers' subsidies and break up the vast East Prussian estates into small farms. Certainly, the measure would have eased somewhat the dangerous unemployment problem in Germany. But Schleicher knew well that the time was not yet ripe for risking such a great reform; the reactionary forces in the country were still too strong. Quite probably Schleicher himself was none too eager to have such a law passed, but the economic predicament of the country was driving him to it.

After Canaris succeeded in stealing a copy of this secret document, he immediately turned it over to Hitler. A photostat of the stolen document was presented to President von Hindenburg, along with what amounted to an ultimatum from Hitler. Hitler accused Hindenburg of harboring Bolsheviks in his government. He threatened to arouse industry and the landowners. The doddering Hindenburg was embarrassed and dismayed. He wanted to avoid a scandal, and above all he wanted to protect his Junker friends.

The upshot was that he dismissed Schleicher from the cabinet. Germany received Hitler as her new chancellor and Fuehrer, the world in due time received a Second World War and Walter Wilhelm Canaris, the clever thief, received his high position. He climbed rapidly higher.

CHAPTER II

The Admiral's New Spy Technique

History repeats, and each generation repeats the blunders of the last. In World War II a woman inherited the title of Mata Hari. She should have pondered the tragic fate of her great idol. Had she done so, she probably would not have taken up with the fascinating Admiral in mufti.

The affair started in a simple businesslike way. In 1935 the German War Department received a letter from one of its former agents, a woman who stated that she had worked for the Secret Service in 1917, while she was still in her teens. She claimed to be an experienced agent and asked for a job under the new regime.

The letter was turned over to Canaris, who stipulated that thirty-three-year-old Baroness Reissa von Einem be accepted on probation. To test her ability she was given a simple first assignment in France and Czechoslovakia, checking on the anti-Nazi activity of some German refugees. In the course of this routine work, she discovered that an underground radio station had been set up in Czechoslovakia to broadcast to the German people suppressed news and anti-Nazi propaganda.

The radio station was wiped out in 1936 near Prague, and its operators were killed. The whole affair had been handled with such subtlety and dispatch that it was called to the attention of Admiral Canaris. He decided to see this woman who had distinguished herself on her very first assignment. He sent for her and congratulated her.

Reissa, born Maria Elizabeth von Einem, was a dark-haired aristocratic damsel. Canaris thought that she dressed extremely well, and he liked her willowy figure. He supplemented his brief congratulatory words with an invitation to dinner.

They met several times at the Horcher Restaurant in Berlin, and Canaris won her as he had won the Mata Hari twenty years before. For a brief time Reissa was his mistress; for a much longer time she remained one of his most trusted agents. He sent her to many of the capitals of Europe. Ultimately she settled in Paris, where she entertained a great deal. While not a dancer, she was a fascinating woman with a good head for business. She acted as intermediary in the international arms racket, negotiating the sale of enormous quantities of arms to the South American countries, China, Finland and the former Baltic republics. This semi-legal work placed her in an ideal position for the strictly illegal work of espionage.

Between 1936 and 1939 she became a celebrated figure in Parisian society. And she directed German espionage activities all over France. Her connections were the very best, her intimacies extending even to some members of the French government—to Minister Georges Bonnet, for example. It was through her that Bonnet was induced to become one of the most important listening posts of Admiral Canaris.

Women agents like the Baroness sapped the strength of France, prepared the way for the Lavals and other traitors. Baroness von Einem was in the lead. She scouted for and found talented traitors among members of the Paris police force and high government officials. She was the procuress in France for the Canaris espionage system.

Her activities remained undiscovered until only a few months before the outbreak of the War. Then the military authorities arrested a stenographer of the Military Commission of the French Senate. This stenographer had been supplying the minutes of all the secret sessions to Reissa von Einem. But the authorities were not quick enough to catch the real culprit. Warned by Bonnet's wife, she escaped in her private plane. She was sentenced to death *in absentia*. As soon as the German occupation was accomplished, Reissa tauntingly returned to Paris.

Yes, she could return to Paris, but the very circumstance which permitted her triumphant return meant that her usefulness to Canaris was over. That does not seem to have occurred to her. It should also have occurred to her that Canaris was a jealous man and would not like her to form gratuitous friendships with men younger than himself.

Baroness von Einem should have understood Canaris. She

might then have discouraged the advances of the former German representative in Paris, Otto Abetz. Instead, she embarked on a scandalous love affair which became the talk of the capital. A brusque order came bidding her to leave Paris and go to Brussels. On her arrival there she was arrested. That was the last time Baroness von Einem was mentioned prominently in the press. But it was not quite the last news item. A few German provincial papers in November, 1941, reported that a certain Maria Elizabeth von Einem had been sentenced to death by the People's Court. She was executed in the Ploetzensee Prison in Berlin a few days later. But the People's Court had only a formal part in the proceedings. She had already been condemned by Walter Wilhelm Canaris.

* * *

The Admiral is not a sensitive man. A cold sensualist, he needs women, but they are only minor episodes in his life. Basically he is an adventurer. Though his impassive exterior belies it, he loves to play with fire, to play with death. Especially he loves to play with money. He is the only Secret Service chief in the world who is wealthy. Canaris is in fact a millionaire. His secret information has been useful on the stock exchange, and Canaris has made some prodigious speculations.

Daring feats are meat and drink to him. He is beyond doubt fanatically chauvinistic. Like all Prussian patriots, he would see the rest of the world annihilated for the greater glory of Germany. Hitler's inner circle always was composed of such fanatically super-patriotic men. Similarities of character bind Canaris to his Fuehrer. Hitler, too, likes daring feats and surprises, so long as they have happy endings.

An air-borne surprise was planned for Hitler on February 16, 1938. It was a very cold day on the southern coast of England. At 6:30 A.M. an airplane was rolled out of its hangar at Farnborough by a specially selected ground crew. The plane was a rather special one, a brand-new Vickers-Wellesley model, a low-wing monoplane having two motors, a new wing type with a large span and unusual speed. Presently Flight Lieutenant F. S. Gardiner and Flying Officer G. D. D. Thompson boarded the plane. They took off from Farnborough Experimental Airfield at exactly 9:15 A.M.

They never came back.

Nothing more was heard of the two pilots or the airplane —although the British spared no pains in searching for it. Mine sweepers combed the Channel for days, but in vain.

About a year later audiences in Britain and America were entertained by an English-produced motion picture. The title was *Clouds Over Europe* and Laurence Olivier played the lead. It was a spy-thriller. The basis of the plot was the circumstance that for some time important new models of English airplanes had not been returning from their trial flights.

The picture revolved around a German spy center in London, which in devious ways had obtained word of these secret trial flights. The spy center had warned a German warship which was anchored somewhere near the British coast. The warship projected a kind of death ray which automatically stopped the motor of any airplane in its path and made a forced landing necessary. The pilots were taken prisoner and all the new English plane models fell into the hands of the Germans. Incidentally, the film had a happy ending: the British flyers finally overwhelmed the crew of the German warship and in turn took them prisoner.

More interesting than this silly movie plot was the story behind the motion picture. The company that released it was called Harfield Productions, a firm founded for the sole purpose of making this picture. As co-authors the names of Arthur Bloch and William Jack Wittingham were cited. But there was another author who got no credits. This third and most important author was much more than a script-writer; he was the man who had contributed the germ of the plot and who was behind the entire production. This man had no connection with the film world of Europe or America and his motive for producing the picture was a motive no ordinary producer would have.

That man's name was Sir Robert Vansittart. His title at the time was Permanent Undersecretary of the Foreign Office, and in this capacity he was also chief of the British Intelligence.

When we know this, we are no longer astonished at the

strange coincidence between the plot of the movie and the fact that one of the most important British airplane models had disappeared. Sir Robert Vansittart, when he sketched the outline for the picture, knew exactly where the lost Vickers-Wellesley model was.

He was well aware that as soon as the Vickers plants had begun experimenting with low-wing monoplanes in 1936, the Nazis had had a scare. They feared that the British innovations might be decisive weapons in the coming war. Consequently they did their best to seize blueprints of the new Vickers-Wellesley (a forerunner of the Wellington). But their efforts failed. As a last resort Admiral Canaris resolved to get hold of a real model.

On February 12, 1938—that is, four days before the trial flight—a sealed envelope was sent from the Air Ministry in London to Farnborough. It gave a chart of the route the model was to take. The envelope was not to be opened until the two officers were actually seated in the machine.

Nevertheless, the contents of the envelope were known in Berlin within twenty-four hours. This was the kind of game Admiral Canaris liked. It was, remember, 1938, still peacetime with its unlimited possibilities for espionage. Europe was still praying for peace when Canaris ordered a 600-ton German submarine anchored at a point in the North Sea over which the airplane was scheduled to fly.

The U-boat was armed with three-inch guns which could have knocked the plane out of the sky at a height of twenty thousand feet. According to instructions, however, the plane flew no higher than six thousand feet.

There were a number of other German U-boats near by and on the alert.

When the plane appeared, the submarine shot it down. The German commander was instructed to kill the pilots, should they be alive. Whether or not they survived the crash will probably never be known. But the prize, the Vickers-Wellesley, was taken apart, stowed away in the submarines, and brought to Germany a few hours later. British Military Intelligence traced it without any trouble in Kiel and Berlin. The capture of the model, however, was a waste of effort as far as the German

Luftwaffe was concerned, for after studying the model their experts decided that such planes could never be manufactured by mass production.

The British Intelligence Service also found out who had been behind the daring theft. On learning the name of the man, Sir Robert Vansittart asked Prime Minister Neville Chamberlain to take some action. But Chamberlain, wary of irritating the Germans, preferred to let the matter rest. Since there was no other way of administering a rebuke, Vansittart conceived the idea of producing the movie. By it, he would make plain to the German military espionage that he was not being fooled. He was very forthright. He cast for the role of chief German spy an actor who looked very much like the real spy, Admiral Canaris.

This was only one of the numerous times that British Intelligence was pitted against Admiral Canaris. Another incident was closely related to the capture of the Vickers model. Canaris himself took a trip to London a few weeks before launching this plot. He arrived in London on January 21, 1938, and stopped at 28 Cleveland Terrace, Bayswater. The exact day he left is not known.

Though Canaris entered on a false passport, the British Intelligence Service knew of his presence almost immediately. The information had been secured from another German agent whom the British had arrested, a man with two names and two passports, a certain Ludwig, alias Winkler.

Canaris spent January and part of February trying to lay his hands on certain items, aside from the Vickers-Wellesley model about which he was most keen. The items were a new 14-inch gun, a new depth charge, a new detonator testing apparatus and a confidential bulletin on explosives used in naval warfare.

The gun, the depth charge and the testing apparatus were produced in the Woolwich arsenal. Canaris had a number of agents planted there, the most important being P. E. Glading, who had worked there since 1928, and Albert Williams, an armament inspector; also there were George Womack, foreman of the gun section, and C. W. Munday, assistant chemist at the arsenal.

British Intelligence knew pretty well what was going on. It

knew, for example, that Glading had met Canaris through a certain woman. For that woman was a British counter-espionage agent. (The dossiers always alluded to her as Miss X. Her real name cannot be mentioned.)

The purpose of Canaris's trip was the delicate work of preparing the ground. Later that year, Canaris and Glading met in Holland. Also present was an Englishman named Kelly. The rendezvous took place in the office of the German Military Attaché at the Hague.

Kelly was an employee of the Euston Shell factory in Lancashire, which at that time employed fourteen thousand workers. Canaris offered Kelly thirty pounds a week, in return for gathering valuable information.

Kelly, however, had been under surveillance before he left England. A Scotland Yard man followed him throughout his trip, and upon his return he was arrested. Kelly proved quite amenable to the proposals Scotland Yard laid before him. He would go on playing his part for the Nazis. He would supply them with bogus material which the British authorities would give him, and he would let the British authorities know everything he could discover about German espionage. This bit of counter-espionage can now be disclosed, but apparently Canaris never caught on.

The British Secret Service nevertheless could not plume itself on a complete triumph over Canaris. They had had their man successfully shadowing Canaris and his agents in Holland, but four years later they learned that they had been outwitted in some respects.

The watchful eyes of Scotland Yard had missed some other important meetings and conferences. Two agents from Ireland had their first conference with Canaris at the German Embassy. They discussed neutrality and espionage in Ireland, received instructions, codes and orders for action whenever war broke out.

Had the British known this in 1938, much underground work in neutral Ireland might have been prevented. But Canaris won that round.

* * *

During the Munich conference in September, 1938, Canaris succeeded in putting over a coup which ranks among the most daring in modern espionage. He got hold of the complete mobilization orders of the French navy even before the orders had been signed by Admiral Darlan. The deed was done by a Second Class Ensign, Elophe Marc Aubert, who was in touch with Canaris through his pretty blonde mistress, Marie Jeanne Maurel.

Later the Nazi press openly boasted of Germany's efficiency in espionage and the *Voelkischer Beobachter* emphatically applauded this daring coup.

Canaris's evil genius functioned perfectly in the months just preceding World War II. Among other feats, he was able to seize the complete British plans for the co-ordination of the air force and the army.

Admiral Canaris's record for the espionage preparation of World War II is almost without a flaw. He wove a huge web of spy centers all over the world. His machinery worked smoothly and swiftly during the spring and summer of 1939, and gathered great momentum after the War broke out.

It was, for instance, not a coincidence that many German consuls in cities and towns strategically situated near the sea were men who had been submarine commanders. There were, for example, Baron Eduard von Spiegel, Consul General in New Orleans, and Franz Nolde, Consul in Le Havre, later Consul in Narvik.

The Stockholm Legation and nearly all the German consulates in Sweden were located in harbors or on the waterfront. The same scheme operated in Finland and Denmark. Many of the German consuls or ministers, whose offices strangely happened to be near the harbors, were members of the Naval Intelligence Service. Under them worked hundreds of subagents, who were all on Canaris's pay roll. Nor were the salaries of this pay roll stingy. Canaris was a firm believer in the modern invention of mass espionage and of the adage that the laborer is worthy of his hire.

* * *

About this time the Baroness von Einem, whose fate we

glanced at earlier in this chapter, was at the height of her glory in France. Another event which falls into this period was the sinking in October, 1939, of the British battleship *Royal Oak* at its base in Scapa Flow. At the time it was both a mystery and a scandal. A German U-boat had been impertinent enough to enter Scapa Flow! Today we recognize it as a clear case of clever espionage. An alleged Swiss watchmaker who signalled the German submarine and engineered the sinking of the *Royal Oak* had been one of Canaris's trusted agents for years. The full story of this is related in a later chapter.

Canaris did not concentrate on Europe alone. His hand reached out to the Near East. His chief agent in Iran was the well-known archeologist, Max von Oppenheim, who in his frequent trips around the country engaged in anti-British propaganda among the Arabs. Canaris had his spies in Palestine, who furnished the Arabs with arms and urged revolt against England. Canaris's most trusted agent in this region was a certain Dr. Fritz Grobba, an expert on Arabian affairs who had been German Minister to Afghanistan. Later Grobba was made Minister to Iraq, where he poisoned the country with anti-British propaganda and assembled an army of fifth columnists. After the outbreak of the War, Grobba settled some agents comfortably in Bagdad in the Italian Legation, while he himself shuttled between Saudi Arabia, Syria and Iran. The Iraq uprising in 1941 was his personal achievement, and thus can be credited to Canaris's books. It caused the British no small trouble to put down.

Still later—during the latter part of 1941 and on into 1942—Canaris set up new espionage headquarters in Athens. From this vantage point his agents covered British-controlled territory from Syria far into the Mongolian desert. He thus spread an espionage net which was soon reputed to encompass advanced positions on the Japanese side of Burma and in northern Indo-China. Communication was maintained by desert caravans equipped with modern ultra-short-wave receivers and transmitters. Such instruments employ waves so weak that only a post very close by can pick up the code messages. By these means intelligence was transmitted in short jumps over the desert until it finally reached Berlin or Tokyo.

It certainly seems a fantastic achievement, which we would have difficulty in believing but for the fact that it is attested to by the branches of the British and U.S. Intelligence Services; working independently, both of them caught onto this smart trick of Admiral Canaris.

* * *

Up to November, 1942, Admiral Canaris was one of the most successful figures in World War II. Occasionally a rumor would crop up that Canaris had fallen into disfavor with Hitler, that he had been retired or that his job had been taken over by a close collaborator and friend of Professor Karl Haushofer. These rumors invariably proved to be lies and it may be suspected that they originated with Canaris himself. He has always endeavored to screen his affairs, and he would certainly enjoy making the world think him dead, since then his work and Werewolf organization would go on more merrily than ever.

When it became evident that the Germans were destined to lose this War, when after the African debacle came Italy, France, Belgium and Holland, Canaris grew more and more desperate. The German army ran into defeat after defeat. Hitler decided that Canaris had made a bungle of Africa, where Marshal Rommel had previously been so successful. And certainly he seems to have slipped up on the job. German Intelligence officers who were taken prisoner told their captors, "Our office hadn't the slightest idea that the American General Mark W. Clark had visited Africa to look the ground over before the invasion."

The head of the German espionage must have felt very chagrined. Canaris rushed to all the battle fronts and took hasty measures. He went to Italy during the campaign and frantically tried to organize a network of spies reaching into the liberated parts of Italy. He hoped that by this transmission-belt of spies the Germans who were fighting doggedly in Northern Italy would be tipped off on Allied movements.

The successful organization of a network of global espionage is a considerable achievement. What sort of life lies behind that achievement? What principle does Canaris follow? If he follows any, it is certainly the principle of ruthlessness. "The art of espionage," as Canaris calls it, is a cruel art. The capture of the Vickers-Wellesley model involved murder; so did most of his plans. It was, for example, a cruel inspiration of the Admiral's to shoot down a Swedish courier plane in 1940 on its way from Stockholm to Moscow. The plane was carrying an outline for a Finnish-Russian armistice, as well as secret maps of Baltic defenses. Besides, it carried hundreds of pounds of mail and a few diplomats as passengers. It plainly displayed the signs of the Swedish three crowns, and the neutral colors of blue and yellow. But the German fighter planes pretended not to see all this when they attacked the courier plane as it was crossing the Baltic Sea. The fighters were in communication with German submarines. When his spies at the Bromma Airfield in Stockholm radioed Germany that the courier plane was leaving, Canaris mustered all his weapons.

Two fighters shot down the unarmed neutral courier plane. That passengers were killed was incidental; the next day the mail and precious documents were at 14 Bendlerstrasse in Berlin. Canaris scanned them quickly. He learned what Russia and Finland were planning for the near future. New and drastic instructions were immediately sent to the German Ambassador to Finland, von Bluecher.

Meanwhile the Russian Foreign Office was waiting for the courier plane; insistently the Russians queried the Swedish government to find out what was holding it up. They sent out reconnaissance planes, but the courier plane had vanished from the face of the earth.

Canaris had outwitted the Russians.

In Moscow a man sat flushed with anger. He smoked one cigar after another, and his assistants, members of the Russian Secret Service, with headquarters at Lubianka Street, whispered anxiously to each other. They knew that the person who had so profoundly irritated their boss, Laurenti Beria, was headed for trouble. You might outwit the Soviets once, but the OGPU had turned the tables more than once.

CHAPTER III

The Master Mind of Lubianka Street

Laurenti Beria looks oddly like a mild old bear and is certainly not the type one expects to find as chief of the famous OGPU, now called NKVD. He smiles readily and is very human. He is by no means the man of cruel eyes and rapacious mouth whom the Nazis and other enemies have tried to paint.

Laurenti Pavlovich Beria works in a cheerful office on Lubianka Street. Thousands of men work under him, all of whom praise his friendliness, his amazing capacity for work and his consistent fairness to his associates. Legends have of course sprung up in wild profusion around the OGPU, to use the initials more familiar than NKVD to the English-speaking world. The truth is much more sober. The OGPU (*Obejedinenonnoe Gosudarstennoe Politicheskoye Upravlenie*) is no doubt one of the world's most efficient espionage and counter-espionage organizations. Its head has to match wits with cunning murderers like Admiral Canaris and the brains of the Japanese Secret Service. He has to keep a sharp eye on the rest of the world as well.

Beria seems to have proved himself the most talented man the OGPU has ever had. Certainly he has attained a position of great trust. Because of his reliability and his long-standing personal friendship with Marshal Joseph Stalin, he has held office longer than any of his predecessors. A good many of those predecessors are no longer among the living. They became involved in scandals and were accused of bribery or high treason.

Beria smokes cigars at a greater rate than Winston Churchill. He wears old-fashioned quaint pince-nez, which are of course constantly breaking. A visitor once counted twenty pairs littered about his desk, to be snatched up whenever Beria required spectacles. Men who have worked for Beria have commented that he always looks tired, for his working day is often sixteen to twenty hours. He needs very little sleep and in general is endowed with great strength and endurance.

He gives the impression of being disillusioned and a little sad about his own disillusionment. In his early youth in Czarist Georgia he was a confirmed, God-fearing idealist who wanted to redeem the world and cast out all evil. He is now an agnostic on philosophical grounds. But he speculates much and he stops far short of militant atheism. He is well educated, speaks many languages and quite casually quotes Persian poetry or bits of Heinrich Heine, Longfellow and Elizabeth Browning.

Two men more different from each other than Canaris and Beria are not easy to conceive. Beria claims to despise women, contending that they would distract him from his socially useful work. He believes that a man succeeds in the measure he is able to eliminate women from his life. He likes to refer to the story of Samson, interpreting it to mean that the Philistines sent the woman spy Delilah to destroy Samson. One suspects that Beria is really very shy and rather afraid of women. But there are a few women who are his good friends, and Beria sets friendship very high in his scale of values.

His character is extremely complex. His imagination and his deft technique proved as good as those of Admiral Canaris or the Gestapo. He would go through fire for a friend or co-worker. At the same time, he can be ruthless and cruel to a degree which might make even the Gestapo falter.

He would often abstain from killing a woman agent or from beating her; he does not favor the Inquisition-like methods of the Gestapo. On the other hand, he has subjected women to hearings lasting fifty hours without a pause. One officer conducting the hearing would be replaced by another, the relieved officer would eat in the presence of the famished prisoner—and after fifty hours Beria would very likely have his confession. Or the woman agent might be set at liberty. Beria would drive her through the streets of Moscow. He would go to a shop with her to choose a beautiful dress, the way to the heart of a woman emerging from six months' imprisonment during which she has not changed her dress or underclothes. Beria might treat her to drinks or to the theatre. Then, after she had made her confession, she might be imprisoned again, and later led off to be shot or hanged.

In short, Beria is a master of psychology. In the presence of this mild-mannered and cultivated man, the cleverest spy is perplexed and does not know where he stands. Beria is a cross between a Dostoievsky detective and Heinrich Himmler. His amazing past has fitted him exactly for the role he now plays.

Beria was born in Tiflis in 1888, of good family. In his student days he became infected with the prevalent spirit of revolution. When he was twenty-seven, a Czarist court-martial sentenced him to death for the crime of spreading revolutionary propaganda within the Caucasian army. That was in 1915. While in prison awaiting execution, he managed to escape. He took to the mountains and lived the hard life of a fugitive. Then he became a partisan, and as such kept in steady contact with the leader of the Russian underground, Stalin. He studied the treatises of Lenin, and read Pushkin and Karl Marx. He obtained weapons from the army and took a hand in getting money for the Communist Party. Like Dostoievsky he cried for abstract justice and truth in Russia. With the Bolsheviks, he prepared for the coming revolution.

Finally the great storm broke. Beria joined the workers in the Baku oilfields. After some time the private detectives of the Nobel Oil Refinery discovered what he was up to, and to stay longer meant death. Beria dressed himself in the cumbersome costume of a Tartar woman, sneaked through the enemy lines and escaped death a second time. He reached the ancient Balkan city Albana, the old capital of what is now Albania. There he met other revolutionaries who helped him. One was a young Communist who, like Beria, thirsted for adventure and was willing to stake his life, if the cause were high enough. He was a handsome, bold young man named Josip Broz, who today is known to the world as Marshal Tito, the Jugoslav partisan leader.

In his wanderings through the Balkan cities Beria discovered how easy it was to fake passports whenever he needed a new one. They could be counterfeited or else bought from some poor worker or farmer. Armed with a new passport and a new birth certificate, he returned to Russia to take part in Lenin's revolution. In his "travels" he used various aliases, such as Vanno Tcheshivilli and Garabet Abamalek. After all, aliases were the fashion among revolutionaries. The names Lenin and Stalin were aliases, too.

As Garabet Abamalek, he commanded a group of five hundred Communists, former Austrian prisoners of war, in their fight against the White Guards. While engaged in this, Beria-Abamalek hit upon the scheme of sending some of his men as deserters to the Whites. They were to join up with the enemy and win confidence by giving them fake information about the Reds. These "deserters" were Russia's first Military Intelligence officers.

His work did not go unnoticed. The Moscow government decided that such a man should not be wasted on minor frays with the Whites. He was given greater responsibilities.

We find Beria in 1920 in Prague, ancient capital of Bohemia. He was a member of the Ukrainian Embassy in the newly established nation of Czechoslovakia. His secret business was espionage. With Prague as his seat, he organized a Russian counter-espionage system which covered the continent of Europe. Every White Russian emigré was listed and the more dangerous ones shadowed. All the Czarist officers were carefully watched, for the Russians at that time seriously feared the Czarist clique. Even nine years later, when Beria was attached to the Soviet Embassy in Paris, they still felt it necessary to keep a sharp lookout in that direction. By that time Beria had risen to be head of the Foreign Department of the OGPU.

Now Beria accomplished a masterpiece of espionage. So far as the French authorities knew, he was in France officially on diplomatic business. Unofficially he was virtually reborn. He cast off the pince-nez and even gave up his beloved cigars. He took a daily walk down the broad avenues of Paris. He did this with a stately air and he invariably dressed in a Czarist uniform. He was seen at the Café de la Paix and the Champs Elysees again always in uniform and wearing an arrogant expression which went well with his new name, Colonel Yenonlidze, who had lost his fortune in Russia and was an arch-hater of the Bolsheviks.

As Colonel Yenonlidze he made clear his interest in co-oper-
ating with anyone who would overthrow the Stalin regime.

He met Ukrainian Fascists, Japanese agents and White Russian officers who had contacts with Mussolini and were already
hand-in-glove with Hitler's young movement. To all he aired
his plans. He knew ways to smuggle agents into Russia by
way of the Estonian border. He contributed articles to the
Russian emigré press. It was not hard for him to become popular in the White Russian circles. His articles were incisive and
brilliant, as was his conversation, which was interlarded with
quotations from Persian poetry. He came to be looked upon
as quite a leader among the emigrés.

In two years he had learned whatever there was to be known
about the network of counter-revolution. It spread from Japan
to Manchuria and China, to Germany and Poland and the Baltic countries. Russian Czarist officers had established themselves in the Secret Services of all these nations and worked for
their own ends. It was Beria who exposed them—not publicly,
but very privately to the Soviet Secret Service. His investigations, begun as far back as 1929, uncovered most of Russia's
busy enemies.

That was why Russia was able to exterminate her fifth column and Stalin's personal enemies in the controversial Moscow
trials, before they had a chance to strike. The arch-enemy
Trotsky was assassinated in Mexico. Dangerous spies and Czarist generals working from Paris were kidnaped and put out
of the way. The leading spirit behind these purges was Laurenti Beria.

From 1930 to 1937 he traveled all over Europe, inspecting
and re-inspecting Russia's espionage network for possible weak
links. He had come to feel that the major problem was to
strengthen and safeguard Russia's military position, rather than
to waste time on the complicated quarrels within the various
Communist Parties of Europe. He even decided that it would
be wiser for the Soviets to employ non-Communist agents rather
than party members in the various countries. Like most Russians, he was converted during that period from an International Communist to a plain Russian.

Beria went to Spain during the civil war to study combat espionage in action. Like Canaris, who stole English models for the German general staff to copy, Beria spirited away German models of tanks and guns. He was especially interested in their anti-aircraft guns on which a new Russian model was to be based.

Beria commanded a large army of sub-agents throughout Europe. In 1938, just after he had been promoted to the head of the entire OGPU apparatus, he summoned his ten best agents to Moscow. A conference was held at Lubianka Street.

It is not known what was discussed, but it is known that in the next two months ten Soviet agents were smuggled into Hitlerite Germany. They entered from England, from Belgium, from Norway and from Italy. They had foolproof passports; some were even equipped with names of German aristocrats. Beria had a number of passport tricks. He could have them expertly counterfeited—a sub-agent of his, Rudolf Haus, had a very fine counterfeiting outfit. Another method was to get Communists in other countries to take out passports and send them to the OGPU, which distributed them to its agents. Spain was a bonanza mine for passports. Thousands of volunteers who came to fight for the Loyalists from all parts of the world lent their American, Swedish, Dutch or French passports to the OGPU which used them for a while and then returned them. Fascists taken prisoner in Spain carried passports which could be used, too.

These ten agents belonged to a secret section of the OGPU, the N.O.7, a department devoted to obtaining blueprints or models of the latest armament of the Great Powers.

These agents were exceptional. They went to Lübeck and to Dessau and to the other cities where Stukas, dive bombers and fighters were being built. They had plenty of money to work with. They opened neat diners near the armament plants, where workers in the aircraft industry went to eat. They also set up shabby little saloons with hot shows and some pretty girls to entertain the workers. They went to the hidden underground Communist cells in Germany and organized them for industrial espionage. The very same year that Hitler struck at Austria and Czechoslovakia, Lubianka Street had possession of Hitler's latest airplanes in blueprint. They were the He 70; the Ju 60; the Focke-Wulf A 43; the Junkers G 38.

Beria had not only outwitted Admiral Canaris—he had outwitted the Secret Services of all other countries. In 1939, his agents, in co-operation with the Communist underground, managed to place a woman agent, a daughter of a noble German family, in the German Degendorff Works. Before being hired, she underwent a thorough investigation by the Gestapo. They were satisfied that Fräulein von X had always been anti-Communist.

It was entirely true that she had been anti-Communist ever since her father had been wounded by the Russian Reds in the First World War. How then did she come to work for the Russians? Some British officers had saved her father's life and her family had a long-standing sympathy for the British. The Gestapo had overlooked this part of her story. Cautiously, some British friends made a proposal to her: she could help prevent the coming war by working with them. They offered her very good terms. Agent X worked for men whom she thought were British agents. But in the game of espionage one never knows precisely for what country one is working, or from what pocket one's money comes. The "British" agents were members of Beria's Secret Service. Agent X handed over to the Russians photostatic copies of plans for the Degendorff double flak gun, which was made with certain 12 mm. plates of Swedish steel.

She was not the ravishing type. She was a spinster, who was becoming more and more maladjusted and bitter. There had been a tragedy in her past, a seduction by a German officer who left her when she became pregnant. The child was stillborn. Perhaps it was this that disposed her against Prussian militarism.

Drab Agent X fooled both the Gestapo and the private detectives of the company. She carried on her person a little camera which her "British" friends had given her. Not until many years later did she learn that as soon as her photographs were received, the Kaganovitch Ball Bearing Plants started to produce identical weapons. The Germans discovered the espionage in 1941 when they captured a copy of their gun in Russia.

Fräulein von X was a hard-headed girl. She knew that if she spent all her money in Germany, the Gestapo would soon know of it. She had her "British" friends deposit all the money in a British bank. After a reasonable interval, she intended to have it transferred from that bank to banks in Switzerland and Sweden. The Russians complied. They used British names in making the deposits, and were punctilious in keeping to their agreement.

She became rich through a successful coup in an I. G. Farben subsidiary firm. Beria had drawn up what needed to be done, and it was told to her in detail by her "British" friends. Thereupon, Agent X had to leave her war job at the Degendorff Works. She wanted to join her family in Berlin. Coming from a great war plant, she found it easy to get another job. After a few months' waiting and investigation, she was given a typist's job in the technical department at the Sicherer Laboratory in Berlin-Spandau. The Laboratory, by the way, was a much-bombed target during the War.

Agent-typist X was an excellent secretary. She had quite an exceptional knowledge of technical terms and her work was praised. True, she was no beauty, but she managed to get a few dates with employees of the factory. She had always been a thrifty person and had saved about eight thousand marks. She showed her bankbook to one of the minor engineers, who thought it would not be a bad idea to marry eight thousand marks. It would enable him to start a small business of his own, which, with a few war contracts, might well prosper. He proposed to her.

Fräulein X was demure and did not accept straight off. She said she wanted to wait until they knew each other better. Still, she would lend him some money, so he could start right away. The marriage day was tentatively set for August 15, 1939. Two weeks before, Agent X paid a visit to her fiancé's apartment. Her prospective husband, who was eager to get the wedding over so he could begin his business plans, was glad to see her. In a tender mood they talked of their future life together. Agent X murmured, "If you could get hold of some of the

chemical formulas of the Sicherer Laboratory, we could produce them ourselves and make a fortune."

After all, she argued, he, Hermann, had helped develop the
latest gas. Why should the rich I. G. Farben get all the profits?
Why shouldn't they take copies of the formulas?

Hermann felt there was something wrong about it, but after
a while he admitted that she was right. A few days later, four
test tubes filled with Germany's latest poison gas were stolen
and replaced by others. The Nazis discovered their loss from
Laboratory No. 27 long afterward; by then the tubes were
safely in Beria's office in Moscow.

On August 14th, one day before the marriage day of Hermann and Agent X, there was a terrific explosion at the Sicherer
works in Spandau. Admiral Canaris's office sent three officers
to investigate. It was found that twenty-two cases of 10.5 cm.
G. high explosive shells had been touched off by T.N.T. The
explosion and the release of poison gas caused death and injury
to about forty persons.

Was it accident or sabotage? Canaris, as was his habit, assumed the worst. Beria knew! And Hermann is waiting to
this day for his wife and her eight thousand marks. Agent
X crossed the border into Switzerland. She decided that this
job had been her last. She would get out of espionage and
settle abroad as a respectable private person.

She went to England, and there she discovered that the
friends with whom she had been communicating had disappeared. World War II had just started, and it struck her that
they may not have been British after all. She knew a way of
making sure. She found that the poison gas formula of the
Sicherer Laboratory was not known to the British, for they
were very anxious to get hold of it. Whom she had sold it to,
she never found out. But Beria, her former chief, soon learned
that she had sold it a second time—to the British government!
With that, she dropped out of the picture. She is a plain, rich
old maid, with some queer ways. Nobody would suspect that
she had ever dabbled in espionage. She is one of the very few
who was able to get out while there was still time.

Beria knows what a rapid turnover there is in secret agents.
They are either unmasked and their work made useless from

then on, or they are arrested and shot. He had to replace Agent X with other N.O.7 agents. One was a girl Katia, whom he planted in the Benz Motor Plant in Munich. He sent another agent into the Daimler plant in Stuttgart.

In the very midst of the war, Beria was supplied with blueprints and details on the D.B. 37 armored car, reports on the new Diesel engine and latest submarine improvements used on U-boats intended to operate from Baltic ports.

Beria calculated as follows: the Communists had received five million votes before Hitler took power. Of the five million there should be at least five hundred left who would be willing to pretend they were good Nazis but work for Beria dressed in SA or SS Elite Guard uniforms.

The flying robot bombs which did so much damage to England were not solely discovered by British aerial photographs taken of their launching points in France. Long before that, British Intelligence officers received warnings from Beria. He knew from reports of his Communist underground that Germany was building the robot planes. He knew that workers assigned to their construction were being kept in strict isolation, segregated even from their families. Beria knew the location of the underground factories. Russia officially informed her Allies of the substance of Beria's reports.

When Beria learned much later that Canaris's men had shot down the Swedish courier plane mentioned in our last chapter and had intercepted the documents necessary for Russo-Finnish peace negotiations, Beria decided that his greatest coup had still to be performed. He had to liquidate Admiral Canaris.

CHAPTER IV

A Beautiful "Pacifist"

IN THIS chapter the author must inject a personal note, for much of it comes from personal knowledge. . . .

I lived in Sweden for about seven years, working as a correspondent for European and American newspapers. In this capacity I had a chance to observe the more intricate workings of espionage in Scandinavia, carried on by Admiral Canaris, by Laurenti Beria and by the British and American Intelligence Services, too.

Neutral countries are destined to be spy centers, and a leading spy center was what Stockholm became. For a Stockholm newspaperman it was not particularly difficult to learn when a courier plane was leaving the Bromma Airfield. One simply saw it with one's own eyes as one dined in the beautiful, glass-enclosed Airfield Restaurant.

Early in the War, in January, 1940, when I was associate editor on the newspaper *Trots Allt,* I was visited in my office by an old friend, Nils Nilson, who was a social worker. Nils had always been close to me. He was a deeply sincere person, an idealist with feet on the ground, very active in the Swedish co-operative movement and the field of adult education. He looked younger than his thirty-five years. He had been active in the youth movement, was a scout leader, was now helping refugees from various countries.

Once he had been a firm pacifist, but after the fall of Czechoslovakia he became convinced that war was inevitable and declared his willingness to fight the aggressor countries—for his ideals did not permit him to be so neutral as the rest of his countrymen.

A normally serene person, he now behaved very strangely. I had never before seen him so upset. He told me he was entangled in a love affair. But Nils had a vague but disquieting suspicion that he was somehow involved in something mysterious, perhaps something quite unsavory, something which might have to do with espionage. He had come to me as a personal friend for advice and, as a newspaper man who knew something about these things, for assistance.

He related his story, as we sat drinking our Danish aquavit. The telling took four hours in all. Outside the day was dark, and there was a heavy snow falling. I became extremely interested and pressed him for all the details.

He began: "You know me well enough to know that I hate the Nazis and am not very fond of Germans in general. I don't like their heiling and their marching, and I don't like their arrogant concept of *Kultur*. We Swedes don't have such a highly developed culture, but we're a decent people. We don't have a Goethe or a Beethoven, but neither do we have concentration camps or a Gestapo. But look at me—I've gone and fallen in love with a woman I suspect may be a Nazi, and a Nazi spy to boot. I have to put a stop to it. And I want you to tell me—is she or isn't she a spy? I think she is. If I'm right, you must help me get her arrested."

He paused and gazed moodily out the window, his lips set. Then he resumed:

"I think she is a spy, but there is no way to prove it. I can't, just on bare suspicion, set the police on her trail. I am powerless, but the more I see of her, the more I am convinced. And I've seen a great deal of Greta Kainen; I've seen her at least three times a week. Every time fear and disgust are mingled with worship. My heart pumps madly when I talk to her. It takes all my self-control to act like a normal, unhysterical human being. I've resolved again and again to stop seeing her, but now I think that I must go on meeting her till I find out the truth.

"I can't seem to break with this woman. And yet she is far from young. She is easily over forty, though still terrifyingly beautiful, with that tall blond stateliness and elegant intellectual manner that is characteristic of many of our Swedish women. Yet she is not typical at all. She possesses a unique glamor that I find irresistible.

"I made up my mind to give her no information at all. I

would sound her out, learn the truth, and then I would expose her. No, she would get nothing out of me.

"But I can never carry out my intentions. Her conversational technique is magnificent. Carelessly she will recount insignificant but interesting stories of the diplomatic underworld, and then, in connection with her stories, she will naïvely ask a harmless question. And I answer it—answer it, and a moment later I want to beat my head against the wall.

"For somehow I find that I have been giving her information about persons or things that might interest one of the Axis Secret Services. At first I thought it was chance. But it happened too often. She knew precisely when to stop, and never asked too many questions. And a moment afterward she would become wholly feminine and melting. Her eyes would soften with melancholy and she would tell me about her unhappy married life with her Finnish husband, Veino.

"She has a wonderful way of talking about her personal life, so wonderful that I sometimes am overcome with self-contempt. What a cad I am, suspecting such a frank, good-hearted woman of meddling in the filthy trade of espionage!

"It can't go on, and I know it. She is older than I, and she is too much for me. It is a rather sad blow to my ego. I always thought I could master such situations. But not this one.

"The climax came at Christmas time, and you know Christmas in snow-covered Stockholm; it's a romantic time of year. The Kungsgatan and the Regeringsgatan were gaily decked with flags and streamers; Christmas trees with their cheerful colored lights glittered everywhere. Together, Greta and I made our way down the narrow streets of the Old City"—streets at least four hundred years old, he reminded me as a foreigner —"to the Christmas Fair. It was all so beautiful, so confusing. Three months with Greta had brought me to my wits' end; I could not think clearly. I cast my doubts away.

"We crossed the bridge to the Zoo, to Skansen. The festival spirit, dancing, mulled wine, the old Swedish folk songs and the entrancing candlelight impelled me toward the climax of my relationship with Greta. I kissed her. And then we left the Gösta Berling Restaurant. I had to get out into the cold

Arctic night, to clear my head. We left Skansen, walked through the deep snow along Mälar Lake. There was no one in sight; it was as though all the lake were ours alone. I kissed her again, and then I told her how unjust I had been to her. I tried to explain.

" 'Imagine,' I said, 'I've been suspecting you—oh, how foolishly—of being a spy.'

"She was wonderful. Her eyes filled with tears, but then she laughed and laughed.

" 'You never really believed it seriously, did you?'

" 'Oh, yes, I was absolutely convinced.'

" 'And yet you went on seeing me. You still liked me.'

" 'Yes, I didn't care,' I said and my voice sounded strange to me. 'Life is short. My life has been spoiled by politics. I've had enough of it; I don't want anything more to do with it.'

"To this day I can't make up my mind whether I meant it, or whether I instinctively said what Greta wanted to hear. At any rate, I went on to tell her that there was now a bond between us that would be lasting. I was enough of an idealist, I said, to prize true friendship, because I had learned how rare a thing it was."

In words similar to these he made his confession. The man was looking for sympathy. My newspaper training asserted itself and I shook my head humorously. I said that the love angle was his own affair, but that I was surprised at him because he had fallen so easily into an enemy alien's trap. It was just like an idealist, I added, to be taken in by such elementary methods.

In a matter-of-fact way I recommended that Nils go for a week's skiing to Åre in Jämtland. I felt sure that the week would bring him to his senses and help him shake off the passion. Meanwhile I would try my wits on the espionage riddle.

Sometimes a week of snow and sunshine will transform both body and mind. Nils got over his infatuation. But two events contributed greatly to the cure. One was Greta's announcement that she was going to join the Swedish peace movement. The other was the result of an investigation.

Before Nils left for Åre I followed my journalist's instincts and asked a friend who worked on *Dagens Nyheter,* the great

Swedish liberal newspaper, to find out about Greta's past.

I knew a little about her past, but my friend found out a great deal more. Her maiden name was Greta Anna Bolander. She had served as a nurse in World War I and had married a German army officer who fell in battle after they had been wed a year. Until 1927 she lived in Germany. Then she returned to Sweden, her birthplace, where she met her present husband whom she had not yet divorced, although their marriage was reputedly very unhappy. Veino Kainen was a Finnish ship-owner.

Greta had also written a book—this was the first I had heard of it. The book was an attack upon the French Army of Occupation in the Rhineland; apparently Greta was chiefly concerned with the Negro French soldiers, who allegedly had assaulted German girls.

I felt that I was on the track of something. Nils' unwilling suspicions might possibly be right and this woman might be playing a curious game. But what could she possibly want of Nils? Why was she cultivating his friendship? The riddle was solved sooner than I expected.

Greta lived in the Grand Hotel in Stockholm, which, as the war advanced, became the city's great spy nest. She could afford it; her husband was a rich man and was generous with his money, despite their lack of marital harmony. Nils went to see her there when he returned from the skiing trip.

She suspected no change in him. She greeted him warmly, embraced him and made Nils tell her all about the skiing. Then she produced her surprise.

"I've given twenty thousand kronor to the Swedish Peace Society. And, imagine, they've made me an honorary member of the executive committee and want to send me on a lecture tour through Sweden, Norway and Finland!"

A gift of twenty thousand kronor to the Swedish Peace Society was quite an act of generosity, especially for a former nurse.

"That's wonderful," Nils said without conviction.

"Don't you like it?" she asked anxiously.

"Oh, yes, of course."

Reassured, she began to tell him about her plans.

War was on, she said. It was the duty of everyone to work

for peace. The peace movements in all countries must work hard to stop war.

"In Germany, too," Nils said.

She gave him a look of dismay, but at once recovered her composure.

"Of course, in Germany, too."

She actually believed Nils naïve enough to credit her—as though he did not know that all anti-militaristic organizations in Germany had long since been destroyed by Hitler.

She went on to speak of her other plans and all at once Nils realized what she wanted him for. He realized, too, that he personally meant nothing to this woman, that their affair was a trick and that she merely wanted to use him.

"You're a member of the Refugee Committee," she said. "It is you who decides whether or not a man is to be recognized as a refugee. You have helped a great many of these unfortunate, homeless people. And all of them want work and are against the Nazis." She went on to expound her diabolical plan.

All the refugees needed money, that was clear. The Peace Society would give it to them. In return, all the refugees had to do was to write down reports of people they knew in Germany who were anti-Nazi, people who were members of the German underground. Then anti-war literature would be smuggled into Germany to these people, and they would distribute it all over the country. The distributors in Germany would, in turn, report everything they knew about German preparations for war, German rearmament and German fortifications, and the Peace Society would publish the information. In that way it could strike great blows at German militarism.

The plan was clever. It sounded almost convincing. If Greta were a British spy, the idea would make sense. But if she were a Nazi agent—and Nils was quite certain that she was not working for the British—it was deadly. It could be a brilliant way for Admiral Canaris to catch the whole underground movement in its own snares. But it was still not entirely clear. We would have to learn more. For a time I had the wild idea that Greta was capable of working for both sides.

I advised Nils on the next step. He was to promise to help

her, but he was to say that he must first get the consent of the other members of the committee. She made him promise that he would try hard to convince the others.

Greta did not know that from 1934 to the outbreak of the War Nils had been associated with me in the smuggling of propaganda literature into Germany. Or perhaps she did know and wanted to get the names of the courier and liaison men from Nils. She pretended love, of course, in order to have him trust her completely. And her game had nearly worked.

However, we were not entirely sure of what she was up to. Still, we had an idea. We went to see my friend—let us call him Stig Anderson—an agent of the British Secret Service. He was Swedish-born, but his mother was English, and I knew he was strongly sympathetic to the British. He would deny that he worked for the British Secret Service—he was duty-bound to deny it—but in any case I knew that he could help me and that ultimately London would find Greta an interesting problem.

Stig listened attentively to our tales. He took notes and warned us to be cautious. He promised to have information for us within a week or so; meanwhile I must not publish a word about the affair until he gave me permission. Nils and I agreed.

Greta was a busy woman. She told Nils she had to go to Helsinki to discuss financial affairs with her husband and perhaps initiate divorce proceedings. As she said this, she looked archly at Nils. Meanwhile he was to do his part on the Refugee Committee and they would be ready to begin work in two weeks. Nils offered to get a few articles and publicity releases about the new peace campaign into the newspapers. We were leading her on until we could get some real evidence against her. She regarded Nils as an established member and willing tool of the peace organization.

In the meantime I talked with the editor of my newspaper about the case and was given the assignment to investigate the activities of the mysterious Greta. Our private detective work, then, would have some backing. I was hoping for some startling developments. However, since Nils and I had promised Stig to publish nothing until the whole case was broken, all I could do for the present was gather information.

I flew to Helsinki and investigated the activities of Mr. and Mrs. Veino Kainen. The first thing I learned was that Mrs. Kainen was not in Helsinki at all. She had been lying. Then I found out that Mr. Kainen was the manager of a German-Finnish shipping line which was recommended in the highest terms by the German Travel Bureau.

This information convinced me that Greta was quite as dangerous as we suspected. I hurried back to Stockholm, feeling somehow that my presence there might avert some great disaster. In Stockholm I went directly to the chief of police. I told him all I knew and all that Greta planned—though I did not say a word about Nils or Stig, my Swedish-English friend.

Chief of Police Torsten Söderström promised to set men to work on the case and give me first publication rights, which was only fair.

Things began to move rapidly. The British Secret Service, the Swedish Alien Squad and, as I learned later, the Russian Secret Service, also, pursued beautiful Greta. And I, an ordinary newspaper man who had become involved in this plot, tried to lead the pursuit. From then on, Greta's every step was watched.

It seemed that Greta had spent two weeks in Berlin at the home of no less a host than Propaganda Minister Joseph Goebbels. She had gone several times to the office of Canaris. That was why she had not been found at Helsinki. But she must have had a confederate in Helsinki, since Nils had received some love letters of hers postmarked in Finland. Mr. Söderström, the Swedish chief of police, passed on the information that she had once been given an audience by Mussolini. Thus there was plenty of evidence against Greta. But so far she had done nothing that was against the law of democratic Sweden. She had as much right to remain in Sweden as any Bundist had to remain in America in pre-War days.

In February, 1940, she returned to Stockholm. Apparently she suspected nothing. Shortly after her return she set out on her lecture tour, to speak against militarism. She addressed some fifty meetings, delivered strong speeches against war and played the part of a sincere pacifist. But in the question period that followed each lecture, Nazi Germany somehow emerged as a shining light on the road to peace. She always cited Hitler's many assurances that all he wanted was peace.

The Peace Society purchased newspapers and printed pamphlets; Swedish parliamentary deputies who were members of the Society suddenly came out in defense of the cession of the Sudetenland and Danzig to Germany. They argued that Germany had a natural claim on Danzig and the Polish Corridor.

It was quite obvious that the Nazis were spending huge sums of money to organize peace demonstrations. And, of course, the peace organization was sabotaging the rearmament programs of the various Scandinavian governments. Yet no one suspected who was behind this consistent program of undermining the anti-Nazi forces in the Nordic countries. These "pacifists" joined with the sincere religious groups, with Socialists and Communists, with Prohibitionists and the liberal press, to preach that the small democratic nations must rally to the idea of peace.

Greta sent delegates to peace conferences in England, Switzerland, Holland and the United States. And everyone, friend and foe, respected her as a talented and energetic woman. We and a few others knew that she was skating on thin ice. Finally arrived the day when Nils and I could go ahead.

I arranged a meeting between Greta and a man who was willing to sell her for one thousand kronor the following information:

1. Reports on German secret rearmament.
2. Names of two underground workers in Germany.
3. Photographs of fortifications in Northern Norway.

Our accomplice was a refugee who posed as a newcomer from Germany who had gone to Norway, had not received a permit to stay there and now desperately needed money.

He played his part very well, telling her a long and convincing story about himself; how he had escaped from Germany, where he had worked with the underground and where he had friends in German war plants. He offered himself as just the man we needed in our fight for "peace."

He deliberately spoke an illiterate German with a heavy Berlin accent. The unsuspecting Greta was easily fooled.

Not dreaming that the information was worthless, she bought it. An hour later she was arrested by the Swedish police.

In prison she continued to act the lady, though no longer so gracious. She maintained that she was a sincere pacifist who believed that all Europe should surrender to Germany without war, since England and France were degenerate nations. She confessed that she knew Mussolini, Goebbels, Goering, Canaris and even Hitler personally. Nevertheless, she indignantly denied that she had been working for the Nazis on orders. Everything she had performed had been done out of her own feeling for what was right, she vehemently insisted.

To their dismay, the Swedish police could find no evidence that Greta had spied against Sweden. Since she was a Finnish citizen by marriage, all they could do was to deport her. A piquant note in the affair was the attempt of Countess Fanny von Willamowitz-Moellendorf, the sister-in-law of the former Marshal Hermann Goering, to intervene in behalf of the Finnish-German spy. That Goering's sister-in-law pleaded Greta's innocence certainly did not help Greta's case.

I got my front-page beat, but Nils was not elated about the whole affair. You can't be happy when you have to employ the kind of methods we had used. Besides, even though Nils had recovered from his infatuation, Greta remained for him an extraordinarily attractive woman.

I still believe that pacifism is a great and vital idea and that anti-militarism ought to be the major subject taught in the schools of Europe after the War. But I have found out, as have many others, that all movements must beware of the company they keep. Admiral Canaris had insinuated his men into the European peace movement and used it to prevent rearmament and to prolong the defenseless state of the democratic countries. The moving spirit behind Nazi-organized pacifism was Greta Kainen.

Later, when Finland began fighting Russia as an ally of Hitler, both the Kainens—whose marriage no longer seemed an unhappy one—became very active. They organized harbor espionage in various northern ports. Veino Kainen's camouflage as a shipowner was very helpful in this work.

It was, of course, Greta Kainen who shortwaved Berlin when

the courier plane with the Finnish-Russian armistice documents was leaving Stockholm's airport.

The Göteborgs Handels Tidning launched an attack against this kind of espionage; all the other Swedish newspapers asked for an investigation and finally the Swedish airports were protected and the fields closed to non-passengers and "tourists."

CHAPTER V

The Very Complicated Story of Friedrich Ege

THE Russians knew very well that Greta Kainen was one of the most important Nazi agents in Scandinavia. Greta Kainen, who tried to deceive Nils and so many others, was a convinced militarist, not a pacifist. She was an ardent Finnish nationalist who hated Russia above all things. Laurenti Beria knew this and early began watching her.

In October, 1941, a few months after Hitler invaded Russia, Greta Kainen gave a cocktail party in Helsinki. A strange assortment of guests filled her splendidly appointed Helsinki home. As was usual at her parties, a number of pacifists were present. In addition, there were some German officials in civilian dress, some well-known Finnish Nazis, some poets and newspaper men—and Professor Friedrich Wilhelm Borgmann, Chief of the German Travel Bureau in Finland. It was a very gay party; everyone danced, drank and retailed the gossip of Scandinavian society.

Among the newspaper men was a German named Friedrich Ege, a prominent member of the foreign correspondents corps in Finland and one of Greta's favorites. It was consistent with her queenly manner that Greta always had favorites, usually a good many at the same time.

I knew Ege and despised him because he was a Nazi. Unquestionably he was a German spy; official investigations had proved that beyond a peradventure.

I had often met him personally. Like myself, he was a member of the Foreign Press Association, for in Sweden both democratic and Fascist correspondents were members of this association. Even the Japanese came to the meetings. As for Ege, even before he made the acquaintance of Greta Kainen, I had disliked him.

It was in April, 1933, that this tall, blond German, who resembled many other tall, blond Germans, crossed the Swedish border. He appeared to be in his mid-thirties. He was accompanied by his wife, a dyed-in-the-wool Berliner who spoke German with a frightful Berlin accent. The couple carried a large amount of baggage. They explained to the Swedish authorities that they were German political refugees who had been forced to leave Germany, having been warned by friends that they would soon be arrested.

The Swedish police examined his case thoroughly, with Mr. Söderström conducting the hearings. Ege was given tentative permission to remain in Sweden.

The Eges had quite a bit of money and behaved like sincere anti-Nazis. Refugees who were worse off than they were welcomed in their home and often given money. Despite this generosity, Ege was not well liked. An exiled German university professor told me that Ege had invited him to dinner and had kept slapping him jovially on the back and saying, "Come on, eat your fill for a change, my friend." Unquestionably Ege was not a man of very delicate feelings. Still, there are worse failings, and one does not damn a man for lack of tact.

Ege did not work. He spent his time studying Swedish intensively, attending refugee meetings and organizing anti-Nazi propaganda. Like all other refugees he had been cast adrift; the only difference was that he had a bit of money. Presumably the money went fairly fast, for during his first seven months he earned only small sums from the sale of an occasional article to some newspaper. Certainly he could not have lived on the proceeds of these articles.

Then the refugee society in Sweden experienced a shock. Friedrich Ege got a job, and a well-paying job at that. He became general manager of a publishing house—not a Swedish but a German publishing house. Ege accepted the position of director of the Scandinavian branch of the world-famous Reklam publishing house of Leipzig.

All the people who knew Ege were outraged. Ege working for the Nazis—it was a first-class scandal! He was cut by all his acquaintances, denounced to the police and accused of a hundred crimes he could not possibly have committed. All who had associated with him roundly abused him in order to clear themselves of any suspicion. A good many persons were highly embarrassed.

Ege tried to explain to his former friends that it was purely a case of "business is business." He was not a Nazi agent, he protested; he had taken the job solely because he had to support his wife and himself. But the Chief of the Swedish Police, Torsten W. Söderström, would not accept this explanation. He called Ege and his wife to a hearing at which no punches were pulled. The Eges had a rather hard time of it. Söderström presented evidence that Frau Ege's father was a Gestapo officer in Berlin; was, in fact, one of the more important Nazi officials.

Ege continued to protest that he was not a Nazi. To this Söderström replied: "You may or may not be a Nazi. But you sought asylum in this country as a refugee and now you are working for a Nazi publisher. Refugees don't collaborate with the Nazis. Perhaps you are innocent, but the Swedish police intend to take no chances with you."

The chief of police did not arrest them. He ordered Ege to leave Sweden within a week, but gave him permission to go to some other country if he did not care to return to Germany.

The Eges moved. The furniture and trunks that they had brought from Berlin were packed and shipped. To the few friends who came to bid him good-by, Ege poured out bitter complaint and repeated again and again that he was not a Nazi. "The Nazis are murderous gangsters," he declared. A few believed him and were convinced that he was suffering a grave injustice. I sided with the majority who felt that an anti-Nazi simply did not accept a job with a Nazi firm. At the last meeting of the Foreign Press Association, when he bade me and his other colleagues good-by, my opinion was momentarily shaken. He assured us with such sincerity that some day we would all find out he was not a Nazi that I almost believed him. Within a week or two, however, my doubts disappeared.

They had to disappear. For the German press used Ege's expulsion from Sweden as a pretext for a political campaign against the Swedish government and against King Gustaf. Overnight Ege became a Nazi martyr who had sacrificed his career solely because he worked for the Nazis. And Ege went to Finland, where he gave up his disguise completely. All the newspapers in Germany hailed him as a hero, and shortly after his arrival in Finland he became editor in chief of the Nazi colony's newspaper, *The German in Finland.*

The entire Scandinavian press now recognized Ege as one of the Nazi fifth columnists in the Northland. He held a prominent place on every list of Nazi propagandists, and all Sweden felt satisfaction that the country was rid of so dangerous a man. In more than one article I quoted Swedish newspaper comments on Friedrich Ege, the Nazy spy. After his deportation investigators established that he also worked for the Nordic Society, the most prominent German espionage organization. This society, whose honorary chairman was Heinrich Himmler, had been established ostensibly "to maintain cultural relations with the Nordic peoples." The Nordic Society had branches in every German port and in all the important cities of Scandinavia. After the occupation of Denmark and Norway, officials of the Nordic Society were appointed "administrators" in those countries.

One day in 1941 a high Nazi official visited Ege in his apartment in Helsinki. He was a tall, blue-eyed Teuton named Vitalis Pantenburg. Pantenburg was one of the heads of the Nordic Society and was also one of the chiefs of the Scandinavian section of the German Secret Service. The full story of this agent was told in my book, *Duel for the Northland.* Pantenburg was the man who bribed Olaf Sundlo, the commander of the Norwegian fortress at Narvik, to furlough his troops and officers while the Germans made their invasion of Norway. (This episode is one of the sources in real life of John Steinbeck's *The Moon Is Down.*)

Pantenburg commissioned Ege to help him fight Russian counter-espionage in Scandinavia. For, alas, from the Nazi standpoint, the OGPU knew all about Nazi secret military concentrations in Finland, Nazi espionage in Carelia and German-manned fortifications on the Russo-Finnish border.

Thus Ege became Pantenburg's assistant. He was assigned a woman collaborator known as Number 25. Pantenburg informed Ege that Number 25 would report to him and that she would take care of transmitting his information to Germany.

Anyone who saw Greta Kainen, alias Number 25, with Friedrich Ege would inevitably have assumed a love affair between the two. Few knew that it was Greta who placed Ege's information into diplomatic pouches destined for Berlin. And Ege supplied excellent information. He prepared reports on construction in Murmansk, on Russian activities in the Kola Peninsula, on the Communist Parties in Scandinavia. His employers were so pleased with him that he received two successive raises in salary within a short time. The Nazi Secret Service obviously considered him one of its most important agents, and was convinced that his information was almost always accurate. Before long five sub-agents were working under Ege. He had woven a tight and highly efficient espionage network. Both the Finns and the Nazis were able to make important arrests as a result of his information. . . .

In 1942 there could no longer be any doubt about Ege. The Swedish press referred to him constantly as a "viper in the bosom of Scandinavia," as one of the most dangerous spies and *agents provocateurs* in the northern countries. But the Finns refused to deport him; he had given them too much valuable information about the Russians. Few knew so much about the activities of the Communist International as Friedrich Ege.

* * *

Meanwhile I had left Sweden and Norway, had come to America and had almost forgotten Ege's name and the nightmare of the Nazi agents in Scandinavia. One day, while I was reading *The New York Times* during the morning rush hour in a New York subway, my heart skipped a beat. With growing excitement and astonishment I read the following item in the *Times* of June 7, 1943:

HEAR GESTAPO KILLED JOURNALIST

Stockholm, Sweden, Monday, June 7 (U.P.)—Reliable advice from Helsinki said today that the German Gestapo has executed Friedrich Ege, German journalist who was arrested by Finnish authorities recently for espionage. These advices said Herr Ege was handed over to the Gestapo and taken to Estonia, where the execution occurred. Herr Ege, a prominent member of the foreign correspondents corps in Helsinki, had been accused of transmitting information to Russia.

So Ege had been right after all when he spoke those prophetic words at his leavetaking in Stockholm: "Some day you will find out that I am not a Nazi"! But now it was too late. How tragi-comical it is that hundreds of articles were printed accusing Ege of being a Nazi spy and characterizing him as loathsome scum!

How tragic, indeed, must such a life be! Undoubtedly Ege had done more for the United Nations than all his defamers. All who had hurt him would gladly now have made amends, but it was too late. What, I asked, had become of my journalistic instinct, my nose for news? There was no comfort in knowing that hundreds of other newspaper men had printed the same distorted reports about him that I had. Yet the deception was a necessary one; had we believed in his truthfulness, he would not have been able to do his work.

I began investigating the case again. I interviewed a Finnish diplomat in Washington who gave me to understand that this latest report might also be false. Possibly Ege was still alive, he hinted. But I could get nothing definite out of him. From Stockholm, however, I got more detailed information.

The Germans claimed that Ege had passed on to the Nazis reports prepared for him by the OGPU. He had been working for the Russians for years. He had helped to conceal Russian parachutists who landed in Finland, had supplied the Russians with figures on Nazi troop concentrations in the Baltic and on the German "Ostsee" fleet and above all had been able to tell the Russians exactly what facts the Nazis wanted to learn about Soviet Russia. Knowing what the Germans wanted to find out helped the Russians guess what the Germans were planning.

Ege also reported to the Russians on American arms shipments to Finland during the first Russo-Finnish War, and on the arms shipments that were organized by Axel Wenner-Gren, the Swedish cannon king, the self-same Wenner-Gren who later lived in Mexico and was placed on the American and British blacklists. . . .

Ege's arrest was due to one of those ironical turns of fortune so frequent in the history of our times. Apparently the contempt of all decent men became unbearable to him. One day he told a Swedish pacifist that he was really against the war and that, fundamentally, he hated the Nazis. The pacifist was convinced by the sincerity of his manner, and passed the story on, not dreaming that all the pacifist organizations of Europe were swarming with Nazi agents. Thus it came to the ears of the former executive of the Swedish Peace Society, Greta Kainen. Her suspicions were aroused, for there seemed no longer any reason for Ege to continue to protest that he was no Nazi. She sent a report to Friedrich Wilhelm Borgmann, head of the Nazi Travel Bureau, and from then on Ege was watched closely.

But the Nazi Secret Service in Finland, which Borgmann headed, could find nothing against him. Nevertheless, they kept Ege on the list of suspected agents. Again and again they searched his apartment, his car, his clothes, but found nothing. Then, one day, they saw him in the company of a well-known woman, a famous Finnish playwright. She, in turn, was kept under surveillance, and finally a Russian parachutist was caught in her house. There the Nazi agents also found parts of a radio transmitter which according to Nazi reports bore Ege's fingerprints.

Eventually they found the transmitter itself, which the playwright kept well concealed in her home. It was this transmitter which Ege might have used to send reports to Russia and to receive orders from the OGPU chief, Laurenti Beria. The Nazi reports are true. The fate of the playwright is now known. She was arrested and sentenced to death, but later the sentence was commuted to life imprisonment, and she was finally freed by the Russians in 1945.

According to the same Swedish sources, the German Secret Service had proof that a code radio message informed the OGPU that an ammunition train was en route from Norway to Finland. This train was later blown up by saboteurs, and according to the Nazis it was Ege who had got word to the Russians that the train, whose contents were labeled "food," was on its way.

The accusation, of course, is not conclusive proof of anything. But it indicates the sort of work Ege was engaged in. I had an attack of remorse and decided that Ege was one of the many unsung heroes of this war. He wore no uniform; he was awarded no symbolic sword or medal. Everyone treated him as a contemptible creature, even the Nazis who hired him, for no one likes informers. How terrible must his life have been! For no one, probably not even his wife, knew about the double role he was playing. Almost inevitably it became too much for the man to bear alone. The very spirit that made him fight against the Nazis led him to his ultimate downfall.

But there is an anti-climax to this tragedy. The life of Friedrich Ege, the Misunderstood Man, was not yet over. The Finnish diplomat who suggested that Ege might not have been executed was right. A few weeks later *The New York Times* published another little notice. Ege had not been executed. His sentence had been changed to the light one of four years' imprisonment. We can guess what happened. Ege chose, in the end, the easiest way. If you are in this kind of business, you sometimes have to work for both sides.

CHAPTER VI

Shots Are Fired at the Admiral

ONE can easily surmise that the liquidation of Canaris and the ripping apart of his spy network in the Baltic, Arctic and North Atlantic regions were harder than Laurenti Beria had reckoned. Admiral Canaris was resourceful. His sub-agents might be caught, but substitutes instantly took up their unfinished work.

After the great Stalingrad defeat, when the tide of war turned against the Nazis, the Russian Secret Service set up a new department solely to protect American and British supplies and Lend-Lease shipments. This division of the OGPU set up shop in Iran, as well as in Finland and Northern Norway, from which latter points it guarded the shipping bound for Murmansk.

In Iran Beria's agents did an excellent job. They rounded up the quislings and foreign agents and stamped out sabotage and fifth column work openly.

Nazi-occupied Norway and Finland were very different problems. The submarine bases around North Cape, the Varanger Fjord and Petsamo were deadly menaces to Allied shipping. At certain times almost fifty per cent of the shipping to Murmansk was torpedoed by Nazi submarines stationed at these bases in the north.

The Russians and British took measures. They bombed Petsamo in Finland and many points in northern Norway. Bombs rained down on the battleships *Bismarck, Scharnhorst* and *Tirpitz*. The *Tirpitz* was forced to hug the shelter of the fjords. Norwegian patriots and Russian agents kept careful watch on the movements of those battleships. The *Bismarck* and *Scharnhorst* were thus observed leaving Norway. The agents had private short wave sets, so that within a few minutes the Allied Intelligence Services were informed. Only seven hours after the British Naval Intelligence received the message from the Norwegian agents that the *Scharnhorst* was setting out to sea the great modern battleship was at the bottom of the Atlantic.

Still Beria was not satisfied. The great battleships were a menace, to be sure, but even without them the northern submarine bases presented a permanent threat to the convoys bound for Murmansk. Beria dispatched more agents who parachuted into Finland and northern Norway. But the German-trained Finnish police and counter-espionage were notoriously efficient. Several of Beria's latest agents were arrested. The office of Canaris brought great pressure to bear against their brothers-in-arms. The Finns were ordered to execute the Russian agents. The Finns, aware that these executions would not be forgiven them when their eventual surrender to the Russians took place, wanted to change the death sentence of the Russian spies to life imprisonment. But Canaris refused.

The defeats Canaris suffered in the North stung him deeply. He lost his three great battleships; by the help of Russian and Norwegian agents, Russian prisoners of war continually escaped from internment camps in Norway; in spite of all his efforts, supplies continued to get through the perilous passage to Murmansk.

However, it was not chagrin alone that made Canaris insist that the Russian agents had to die. He was also pursuing the well-known Nazi policy of involving as many people as possible in his crimes. The more the Finns had on their conscience, the less eager they would be to make a separate peace with Russia.

No Military Intelligence office forgets the death of even one of its men. Very often the execution of an agent is prelude to a wave of deaths of agents on both sides. A spirit of vendetta sets in. Police forces have a similar tradition. They do not forget the murder of a comrade, and do not rest until their friend's murder is avenged.

We may assume from what followed that Laurenti Beria vowed to take revenge for every Russian agent who died. The form of his revenge was typical of the man: he decided to strike at the head of the organization responsible for the murder of his comrades. He would make Admiral Canaris pay in person for their deaths.

We know that two of Beria's choicest killers were selected for the job. Probably we shall never know their names—we may as well call them "Ivan" and "Boris." Both men were smuggled into Nazi Germany, where other Russian agents established contact with them.

German counter-agents may have been definitely tipped off. Or it may be that Canaris was clever enough to anticipate Beria's next move. At any rate, rumors reached the world press that Canaris had run afoul of Hitler, and that another Secret Service chief had been appointed. But these rumors did not deceive Beria and his agents. They did not alter their plans.

"Ivan" was a towering, flaxen-haired Russian, who had taken part in the Bolshevik revolution. "Boris" got his experience as a Secret Service agent in the Spanish Civil War. Both were good matches for any Fascist. Neither was terribly intelligent. But they were good trigger men, pure and uncomplicated. Others had to prepare things in advance; then at the right moment they would step in.

The Communist International often instigated kidnapings and even killings. White Guard generals, associates of Trotsky and anti-Communists were generally the victims. The trigger men were never captured, but they were always European "Ivans" or "Borises" who did not require much special training because they were natural killers.

Beria's two men waited patiently for the time to act. They settled down in a hide-out contrived for them in a beautiful villa in Berlin's suburb of Grunewald. Ensconced here, they were forbidden even to step out of doors, and for a few weeks they were no better than prisoners. Here they had to sweat it out during the nightly air raids over the city, and here they killed time by card-playing.

Beria did not want valuable agents to be in any way implicated. After the assassination, the trigger men were to escape to the same villa and lie low there for several weeks. Then they could make their way to one of the many small fishing villages on the Baltic where a submarine would call for them. It had been done before and could be repeated.

Meanwhile, Beria's agents in Germany assembled facts on

the most trivial details of Canaris's habits. The plot hinged on these.

Canaris enjoyed gambling. He looked upon the stock market as a vast gaming-table, and gambled both seriously and for amusement.

A strange relationship existed between Canaris and a Rumanian diplomat. The relationship was not intimate, but could be characterized as chummy. The diplomat was a hundred per cent Fascist and was well liked by the Nazi Foreign Office. He often gave useful tips to Canaris and the Ribbentrop office about things in his part of the world. Let us call this man "Betany." There are reasons for concealing his name, for, as we shall see, "Betany" was on the Russian pay roll. His position was something like that of his colleague in Finland, Friedrich Ege.

"Betany" was a passionate gambler. Canaris happened to meet him at the roulette casino in Zoppot one summer, and this was the beginning of their peculiar friendship.

"Betany's" luck was uneven; sometimes he lost heavily. Thus he was caught in one of the vicious circles of espionage. Agents get involved with women or gambling and are pushed to further extremes of desperation. "Betany" once gambled away some funds entrusted to him by the Germans for delivery to the quisling party in his native land. He tried to retrieve the money, but luck was against him. He recognized that not even Fascist countries tolerate misappropriations of funds.

Thus "Betany" became easy prey for Beria's Secret Service. Beria exploited the situation with remarkable tact. "Betany" was given the sum he needed. He was told that he need not do anything at all for the next four months. He had only to sign a receipt stating that he had received a sum of money from the Russian government for his services. This receipt guaranteed that he would not double-cross the Russians.

Beria knew that "Betany" was singularly safe from suspicion. He had never been in contact with the Russians at all, nor was he for a four-month interval after being hired. When that time elapsed, Beria gave his Balkan agent a few tasks which involved, not Germany, but Hungary and Rumania. This again left the Balkan diplomat free from compromising taints.

Now, however, "Betany" could be very helpful. He was not

called upon to do dangerous espionage work. He had only to inform the Russians about Admiral Canaris's personal life, so far as he knew it.

Again, "Betany" was spared any risks. He had a monthly meeting with the contact man of the Russians. This man was a German officer, an anti-Nazi, who later participated in the attempted assassination of Hitler by the officer clique in the summer of 1944.

One day, in 1942, "Betany" reported that a party was soon going to be given at the home of Foreign Secretary Ribbentrop. The newspapers in Germany later mentioned it. "Betany" was invited, as were all of the foreign diplomatic corps in good standing with the Nazis. These periodic parties of the "Ribbensnobs," as they were called, were always grand affairs. Canaris and his wife were going to attend, although Canaris cared little for the social attractions or the champagne provided by the former champagne salesman. What drew Canaris was the gambling room and the great winnings to be had there.

The contact man listened with interest. In a few days, "Betany" was given some simple orders. His chore was to attend the Ribbentrop party and leave when Canaris did. He was to accompany the Admiral to his car and conduct himself a trifle boisterously. As Canaris left, he was to sing an old German beer-drinking song, *"Trink, Bruederlein, trink."*

Such a task was certainly a small one for the fifteen hundred marks the Russians paid him every month.

The Ribbentrop party was a brilliant one, with Nazi high society well represented. There were quislings from all European countries, high German officials, military big-shots and Nazi beauties. There was a fabulous array of food. War rationing did not stretch out its forbidding hand, since all the delicacies were imported by plane from neutral Spain. The great ballroom was thronged. American swing was played, an unusual concession for Nazi Germany. The game rooms were filled to capacity. Men played bridge and poker. The Austrian and Balkan guests indulged in heated sessions of their traditional game, Taroc. "Betany" had one drink too many, but he was in high spirits. He was winning at poker.

Canaris was irritated by his conduct. He frowned at him to quiet down. At a card table, Canaris's icy self-possession is reputed to be perfect. He is sphinx-like and his close-shaven, colorless face becomes, if possible, even more colorless. This evening Canaris was losing. Shortly after midnight he rose from the poker table.

His wife had been left to her own devices all evening and had fallen into conversation with other elderly ladies of the diplomatic corps. Canaris approached, clicked his heels and raised his arm in a "Heil Hitler," which indicated to his wife that her lord wished to go home.

They said good night to the Ribbentrops and left. Somehow "Betany" tagged along. His conduct was offensively gay and he could not be shaken off. "Betany" even followed Canaris to the car, where a corporal was waiting to drive the great Mercedes. "Betany" was apparently too drunk to observe the proper forms. He did not even give a "Heil Hitler," but swayed and giggled and began to sing, with his heavy Balkan accent, *"Trink, Bruederlein, trink."*

Admiral Canaris shook him off and his car disappeared into the darkness of the blackout. Many other cars were leaving the Ribbentrop estate and heading for the city.

An army car plastered with the swastika outdistanced the other automobiles. In the blackout such speed was dangerous. But the car went still faster and suddenly, in defiance of all blackout regulations, a bright light was flung at the car of Admiral Canaris. Four shots rang through the air. a scream pierced the darkness and the swastika-marked car disappeared into the blacked-out streets, not however before a fifth shot was aimed at one of the tires of Canaris's car.

"Boris" and "Ivan" had fulfilled orders to the letter. Half an hour later they were once again sheltered in Grunewald. Their excitement lasted all night. It did not die when, on receiving next day's papers, they saw no word about the incident.

Canaris was alive and unhurt, and he allowed no word to be published about the assault upon him. Secretly he issued orders to every port in the country. Every suspect was to be rounded up. He knew that this attempt was a professional job, done by an Intelligence Service and not by underground amateurs. Amateurs would have tried to kill men like Goebbels or Goering.

Canaris must have known that the trigger men who tried to kill him were Russians, because he organized a special investigation at the harbors of Rostock and Stettin and all surrounding small fishing villages. There some information must have come to his ears that the two Soviet agents had finally left Germany through one of the Baltic seaports. The ports were closed. Gestapo and Intelligence agents arrested hundreds of people. When the newspapers in the German Baltic cities printed special warnings that enemy agents might land by parachute or in small rubber boats to sabotage German industry, Laurenti Beria very likely guessed that Canaris was on guard against his "Borises" and "Ivans."

Two months later the two reappeared in Moscow. But the boys had a glum meeting with their boss; Beria told them that the expense and trouble had been in vain. The perfect crime had had one flaw, like so many "perfect" crimes. However, the trigger men were not to blame for it.

Beria had not known that Canaris used an armored car, whose windows, too, were bulletproof. The only damage the Canaris family sustained was one flat tire.

Deeply disappointed, Beria could only try to shrug it off. He merely had the name of Admiral Walter Wilhelm Canaris put down on the Russian list of war criminals who would be tried and punished once Nazi Germany was defeated.

CHAPTER VII

Battles for Weather Stations

IN AUGUST, 1942, the Coast Guard station in Boston was more excited than it had been since the war started. The Boston docks were a scene of great activity, with police cordons closing the piers to the public. A big convoy of army cars was drawn up, and squads of military and naval police made an impressive spectacle in their uniforms. FBI agents, Naval Intelligence and Army Intelligence officials were also there.

A few hours earlier, the Boston Coast Guard station had received word from one of their cutters that she had captured an enemy vessel off Greenland and was bringing several dozen prisoners to Boston.

Under escort of the Coast Guard cutter, a small Norwegian vessel named the *Busko* came into Boston harbor. As the boat entered the port, the Quisling flag of the Cross and Sun was hauled down. The men on board began wildly gesticulating. There were only a few Germans among them; the majority seemed to be Norwegian.

The men cried out passionately: "We aren't quislings. We aren't Nazis." They were ordered to be quiet. Interpreters informed them that they would soon get a fair hearing. The few Germans among the *Busko's* prisoners of war were mute, pale and grim.

High officers of the Army and Navy conducted a search of the *Busko* that lasted for hours. They found that the boat was certainly not an ordinary Norwegian trawler or fishing boat. Penetrating its camouflage as a fishing boat, they found a half-dozen short-wave sets, highly specialized meteorological instruments, excellent maps of northeast Greenland and marine maps of the waters between Iceland and Greenland, the world's largest island.

The exhausted prisoners were well treated by the Americans and provided with fresh clothes, clean underwear, GI food and what they most craved—coffee and cigarettes, which they had not enjoyed for many months. The next day hearings began before a panel made up of men from the various government agencies conducting the investigation.

The Germans admitted that they had planned a surprise landing at Greenland. They refused, however, to give further details. The Norwegians claimed that they had been forced by the Quisling government to navigate the *Busko* for the Nazis. They were all experienced whalers and knew the Arctic waters. They protested that they were in no way responsible for any attack or espionage activity in Greenland. The Americans listened to the story with some perplexity.

One of the Norwegians whose name cannot be disclosed at the date of writing commanded attention. Let's call him "Anders Andersen." Andersen insisted that he be put in direct touch with the Free Norwegian government, the Norwegian Consul in Boston and the Royal Norwegian Embassy in Washington. He said that he would talk to them and talk freely.

There was no reason why the American authorities should refuse this—after all, Norway was a member of the United Nations. Andersen's interview with the American and Norwegian authorities proved of the greatest value, for he supplied highly interesting facts about Nazi activities in Arctic waters and in Greenland.

Andersen revealed he was a trusted member of the Norwegian underground, whom the Norwegian government instantly recognized. He had entered the Quisling Party as counter-agent for the government of King Haakon and played his difficult role well, for he had maintained at the same time an excellent record in the Nazi Party. This, and his knowledge of shipping, stood him in such good stead that he was appointed to the Arctic Office in Oslo, a bureau that had formerly been a research department of the Norwegian government handling all scientific questions referring to the Arctic regions.

The Nazis had taken over this bureau and made it into a war agency, and it now provided the Nazi navy and air force with necessary data on the Arctic regions. The head of the office, whose title in Norwegian is *Ishavskontoret,* was one Adolf Hoel, a middle-aged quisling who had worked with the Nazis for a long time. Andersen had worked under Hoel. Most of the Norwegians on the *Busko,* he revealed, had previously been employed by the Arctic Office.

Andersen explained that Hoel's Norwegian Arctic Office was a subsidiary of the Axis Arctic Office whose seat was in Berlin. This bureau had begun as a branch of the foreign division of the SS, the Elite Guard. The Berlin head was SS Colonel Paul Burckhardt, a prominent scientist and meteorologist, who had traveled much in Greenland, northern Scandinavia and Denmark. In my book, *Duel for the Northland,* I had occasion to tell a great deal about Burckhardt.

One day in 1940 a meeting took place in Berlin between Adolf Hoel, Burckhardt and his right-hand man, Vitalis Pantenburg. Pantenburg had worked with Greta Kainen and Friedrich Ege in Finland. He was fairly notorious as one of the chief spies in the northern parts of Europe. Pantenburg, then about forty-five years old, was highly valued by Admiral Canaris. The Canaris office had ordered him to whip together a secret expedition against Greenland. Hence this conference.

The expedition's purpose was to secure control of certain bases, which could be used as airfields. In addition, they wanted weather stations set up which would provide the air force with invaluable information for European operations. Weather stations were essential to Germany's war effort. From Greenland and other Arctic spots, the weather for the whole continent of Europe can be determined. In particular, the weather over Germany can be predicted, which means the ability to predict the strong likelihood of RAF or American Flying Fortresses' seizing good weather to make air raids against Germany.

All this was carefully explained by the counter-agent Andersen in Boston. He made it clear why Admiral Canaris wanted a foothold in Greenland. Canaris's object was the seizure of *Wetterstationen,* that is, weather stations for the German War Department. So Canaris had projected an expedition of two fishing boats, of which the *Busko* was the first. The second boat sent out, the *Furenak,* had likewise been captured—by a Free Norwegian patrol boat.

Andersen had volunteered for the Greenland expedition in order to escape from Norway. He had been hoping that the *Busko* would be waylaid by British or American patrol boats.

Andersen and the rest of the crew pieced together, from their separate bits of knowledge, a fairly complete picture of Nazi espionage plans not only in Greenland, but in Iceland and regions around the North Pole.

The German prisoners aboard the *Busko* feared they would be shot as spies. In their desperation they had tried an abortive mutiny while the boat was being brought to Boston. The voyage all the way from the icy waters of Greenland had been a hard one; it had included a narrow escape from collision with an iceberg. Though the Germans were treated decently in Boston, their hostility remained. One of their lieutenants offered a high bribe to the American guards to give them a chance to escape. However, as one Coast Guard man said in a mixture of German and English: "Mac, du could us nicht briben. Wir are Americans."

Not long after the official hearings, where evidence had been willingly supplied by the Norwegians, and unwillingly by the Germans, the author of this book was called in by the FBI and the War Department. Without disclosing any secrets, it can now be told that I was questioned for several days concerning Nazi agents in the Arctic regions. The FBI and War Department knew of my articles on Iceland and Greenland. They knew that in the past I had investigated Nazi agents in the Scandinavian countries. My information, it was hoped, would supplement that obtained from the *Busko* and *Furenak* prisoners.

The Norwegian counter-agent Anders Andersen had mentioned three names besides that of Canaris: Dr. Paul Burckhardt, Adolf Hoel and Vitalis Pantenburg. Did I know anything about them? I certainly did, for anyone acquainted with Nazi espionage in Sweden, Finland and Denmark would rapidly discover that these three were the ones who pulled the strings. They were all on the blacklist of the Scandinavian police and had been paid agents long before the War started.

The cleverest was Dr. Paul Burckhardt, a genial man who had had no interest in politics before the Nazis came to power. He was an expert meteorologist and geologist, far more interested in the bare earth than in the nations living on it.

The Nazis were prompt to appreciate his work. They saw it as a contribution to the building of the Nordic Reich. They praised him, gave him the title of Colonel, set him up in a splendid office and subsidized his studies.

One day he was asked by none other than Admiral Canaris whether he would care to visit Iceland. He was put at the head of an archeological expedition, and Burckhardt and ten other Nazis set out for Iceland. That was in 1937 and the Icelanders welcomed the scientific expedition cordially. In fact, the scientists became guests of the most prominent Icelanders.

Burckhardt's group stayed in Iceland for about six months, but by no means limited themselves to the cementing of social relations. Burkhardt drew up a careful analysis of the sources of raw material and the industrial possibilities of the country. He mapped certain parts of Iceland, marking out locations for possible airfields and meteorological stations. He noted the depth of certain fjords and harbors. He compiled a great many weather charts, and made a general report on weather conditions in Iceland and their significance for German aviation.

When he turned his mind to it, the scientist made a first-rate spy. His scientific expedition included a young lady named Gudrun, a native Icelander. Her mission was to scout for young Icelanders who were promising espionage material. They would be invited to study in Germany where they would be entered in one of Canaris's spy classes and groomed to be prospective agents in the Arctic.

When the party returned to Germany, Burckhardt was made head of the Nazi Arctic Office in Berlin.

A few months later, Admiral Canaris sent another of his good men, Vitalis Pantenburg, to the Arctic areas. But Pantenburg was so unfortunate as to be arrested after only three weeks, when he was caught photographing details of the Fortress of Boden in Swedish Lappland, and for this he was later deported from Sweden. Pantenburg's next mission was to Finland. There he completely mapped all of Arctic Finland. His surveys were the groundwork which enabled the Nazis to establish several submarine bases between the North Cape and the Finnish harbor of Petsamo. From these bases attacks were launched against the Allied lifeline, the convoy route to Murmansk.

Admiral Canaris, however, had to moderate his ambitions. A German invasion of Iceland, on which he had so fondly counted, was out of the question, for the British got there first. Moreover, in the invasion of Norway the Nazis lost over one-third of their fleet, and lacked sufficient naval strength to risk a battle for Iceland. While they hesitated, the British troops came in force and took over.

Canaris therefore had to look farther north. There the Arctic islands were still more sparsely populated, and afforded openings for *Wetterstationen*. His choice fell upon Greenland.

* * *

Greenland's population is very small. It consists of some seventeen thousand native Eskimos and about five hundred officials of the Danish government. The island's size is 736,518 square miles, which is an area equal to that of the twenty-six states east of the Mississippi. It is covered by perpetual ice. As you pass farther north, the winter twilight grows darker and darker.

The *Busko* expedition was only a small incident in the fight for Greenland, but it was enough to make the United States Greenland-conscious. The situation was sufficiently urgent to impel the Danish Minister to Washington, Henrik de Kauff-mann, to request the United States to take on the job of pro-tecting Greenland. Thenceforward, the U.S. Navy, Army and Coast Guard assumed responsibility, as did G-2, the Mili-tary Intelligence Service and the FBI.

One of the neatest espionage tricks of the War can now be revealed. It took place in this obscurest of battle areas.

The Arctic Office of Admiral Canaris knew that the northern reaches of Greenland, lying under heavy snow, were patrolled by a very small group of Danish officials.

Now, it is an almost impossible task to patrol an area covering seven meridians, whose rough coast is indented by thousands of ragged fjords. The Danish patrol squad relied on dog-drawn sleds. Greenland took pride in her Arctic sled corps which traveled about with all the paraphernalia of a North Pole ex-pedition.

Canaris calculated that this small patrol force could not pos-sibly protect the entire coast of the world's largest island. He decided to build his weather stations in Greenland. He was audacious enough to consider establishing a few secret airfields, too, and a possible submarine base. If he could do this, the Battle of the Atlantic might still be won for the Nazis.

Making their rounds in 1943, far in the North near Macken-sie Bay, the Danish patrol squad found evidence of strangers on the icy coast. They saw prints in the snow, prints of men and dogs and sleds. The Danish administration had no knowledge of any inhabitants' being there, or of any expedition, and consequently immediately suspected that the Nazis had landed. The sled corps sent word to the authorities at Julianehaab, the capital of Greenland. The Danes informed the Danish Minister in Washington, the Greenland Mission in New York and the United States Intelligence Service.

The drama began. The U.S. State Department notified the Danish sled patrol, headed by the army captain Ib Poulsen, to try to get the exact location of the intruders. After three weeks of cautious reconnaissance, Poulsen radioed the American Intelligence Service that the Nazis had landed a formidable expedition near the fjord of Eskimonaes.

It happened that there was another group of Danes whose permanent outpost was very close to Eskimonaes. The Americans suggested that this outpost, which was threatened by the Nazis, be given warning.

Two Danes, Eli Knudsen and Marius Jensen, were sent out as messengers to warn the other outpost. But the Nazis had already attacked. The small garrison of Danes managed to flee south to one of the ice islands, Ellaoe. This flight through ice and snow took two weeks, but luckily they had sufficient provisions. It was only their familiarity with the ice islands and their intimate knowledge of local conditions that saved them from massacre.

The Nazis then destroyed everything at the Eskimonaes outpost, retaining only the weather station which they moved to a point farther north to use for their own weather reports. Thereafter weather reports were sent daily to Germany. It may be presumed that Admiral Canaris was well satisfied.

Soon, however, the Germans in Greenland reported that two Danes of the patrol group had fallen into their hands. These men were the messengers who had been sent to warn the Eskimonaes group. Canaris was not elated at this news. He could well fear that the disappearance of the Danes would bring unpleasant developments. The Americans might come in! Therefore he short-waved his Nazis to hold on to their prisoners, since they would be useful as hostages. He also told them to move on to Sabine Island, where they were to continue to send weather reports.

The weather spies established new headquarters at Sabine Island, lying off the northeast coast of Greenland. Here they built huts, set up tents, supply depots and a meteorological station. Canaris even sent an icebreaker, equipped with ack-ack guns, from Norway to assist them. The Nazis seemed firmly entrenched.

In the meantime American reconnaissance planes were sent out to Greenland to discover the Nazi positions. They were to get aerial photographs and other information necessary for an attack on the spies.

The Nazis saw the planes and realized that not even Sabine Island was safe. They radioed Berlin for new orders. Admiral Canaris replied: "Leave Sabine Island and mop up any Danish sled patrols which interfere with you. Go on sending weather reports."

Then something happened which was not on the Admiral's schedule. One of the two Danish prisoners made a break for freedom. He managed to take one of the dog sleds and provisions. It was a daring feat. By a miracle Eli Knudsen came through successfully.

After several weeks he reached the outpost of Ellaoe. He brought invaluable information. He was able to report on the Nazi strength at Sabine Island, on the icebreaker, on the Nazis' military equipment. He knew the name of the leader of the German expedition, a Lieutenant Hans Ritter, from the Arctic Office in Berlin.

Now the Americans were ready to back the Danes up. They directed them to come south to Scoresbysund via King Oscar's Fjord and Liverpool Island. Here some American Intelligence officers waited to question them about their experience with the enemy expedition.

In the meantime the Nazis were not idle. They had planned to launch a strong attack against Ellaoe, since they did not know that the Danes had recently cleared out. They forced their second hapless victim to be their guide. With a gun at his back Marius Jensen had to show the way. When they reached the Mygge Bay station, Jensen informed Lieutenant Ritter that the attack could best be brought off by taking a short cut through Moskusoksefjord. Then the Nazi commander decided to send out a detachment to attack the Danes at Ellaoe. He himself remained at the Mygge Bay station to guard the prisoner, Marius Jensen.

The rest reels off like a Hollywood thriller. Jensen overpowered the Nazi leader and wrested his gun from him. He escaped with a dog sled loaded with provisions. He hastened by a short cut to Ellaoe with the intention of warning his Danish friends. Here he found what the Nazis discovered a day later: the Danes had cleared out. Jensen did not continue south to join his comrades. He returned instead to the Mygge Bay station and picked up Lieutenant Ritter to hold him prisoner. Replenishing his provisions, he set out on a long strenuous trip to the Danish headquarters at Scoresbysund. He traveled over ice and snow for three weeks. When he reached his goal, he was completely exhausted, but successful in turning in his prisoner. Lieutenant Ritter was a prize catch, for he was Canaris's right-hand man. He refused to give any information.

The Allied headquarters received a summary of events. A few days later American bombers came and sank the icebreaker at Sabine Island. Thus they annihilated the Nazi spies and the weather station on Greenland.

* * *

It was not in the nature of Canaris to give up. True, Greenland offered no foothold for his pet project, but he could still try farther north, as far north as the North Pole if need be. Once more the Arctic Office dispatched an expedition from Northern Norway. Its object was the establishment of weather stations before the big Allied invasion of Europe should be attempted.

The target of this plan was the polar island of Spitzbergen. It belongs to Norway and the Norwegian name for it is *Svalbard;* it lies only five hundred miles south of the North Pole.

On the same day in 1943 that Italy and King Victor Emmanuel surrendered to the Allies, the Nazis broke their boastful news. Their Arctic expeditionary forces had won a victory;

they had taken the tiny Norwegian outpost of Spitzbergen. It was proclaimed over the radio and in all their newspapers.

Spitzbergen had no inhabitants, polar ice being most inhospitable. It was therefore not hard for the Germans to make a landing on Spitzbergen. The last people who had been there were Norwegian and Russian miners who had been sent to work the rich coal deposits. They had departed two years before, at the time of the Nazi attack upon Russia in 1941. Beria and the OGPU suspected that the Nazis would land in that region some day. After the coal miners had left, the Allies had sent a small group of men solely to demolish the mining equipment and anything else that might be of interest or use to Canaris's Arctic Office.

In 1942, long before the occupation of Spitzbergen was triumphantly announced, the Nazis landed. They exercised the greatest discretion. They built a large airfield on the ice and left behind a small but well-equipped garrison. The Allies however had an inkling that something was up, and suspected the existence of the secret Nazi airfield even though they had no proof. Therefore it was decided that the Free Norwegian forces should send an expeditionary force of eighty-two men in an icebreaker and a fishing vessel to Spitzbergen. The Norwegians were ideal for this task, for they were best acquainted with Arctic territory, wished to see Norwegian sovereignty respected and wanted to undertake meteorological work of their own.

The expedition arrived at Cape Linn at the mouth of Ice Fjord on May 13, 1942. They saw no signs of Nazi occupation, nor any sled tracks or ski prints. At this time of year Ice Fjord is icebound and it was obviously impossible to try to reach the former settlement and seat of the coal operations, Longyear City, where the Nazis might be hidden. The Norwegian commander decided to try going through Groenn Fjord to Bärentsburg, where the Russians had done some mining. This was not far from Ice Fjord.

The May nights in Spitzbergen are as light as the days; at midnight the sun is as bright on the horizon as at noon—differing only in having less warmth and intensity than at noon. During the "night" the Norwegian polar expedition was discovered by a Nazi reconnaissance plane. When the Norwegians realized they were discovered, they made all haste to get their icebreaker to Bärentsburg, only a few miles away. They hoped to get there before the inevitable Nazi attack.

The Nazi garrison had been ordered by the ruthless Canaris to kill anyone who approached. He knew that his last chance to establish a weather station in the Arctic had to be defended at any price.

Before the Norwegians were able to reach their goal, four four-motored bombing planes made straight for the ship. The Norwegians defended themselves with all they had, which was not much. Their anti-aircraft and machine guns scored some hits on the Nazi planes but not enough to put them out of action. The Nazis had no trouble bombing their targets, plainly visible on the ice. Within fifteen minutes one ship was sunk and the other set on fire. Twelve Norwegians were killed and many severely injured. All the men could do was to jump overboard onto the ice or into the icy water. Although it was May, the temperature was about twenty degrees below zero. They dropped on the ice and pretended to be dead. There was no cover and their only hope was to fool the Nazis. The Nazis, however, were not easily taken in. They machine-gunned the exposed men for about an hour—an hour that seemed a lifetime to the Norwegians. By a miracle, only two were killed. When the hour was over, the Nazis found themselves short of fuel and ammunition and flew off in a northerly direction. The Norwegians rose from the ice all but frozen and, carrying their wounded, headed on foot for Bärentsburg and the deserted houses formerly used by the Russian coal miners.

There they gave what aid they could to the wounded. Fortunately, some of their medical kits and blood plasma had been spared. In the deserted hut that had been the Russian hospital they found bandages and alcohol, and these were used in saving the lives of some of the Norwegians.

The next and very grave problem was food and clothing. Their clothes had been soaked and were frozen to their bodies. They had salvaged no food from their sunken boats. Their entire salvage comprised only a dozen pairs of shoes, some light ammunition, fifteen pairs of skis, two knapsacks, a map, a compass and a broken signal lamp.

With desperate hope they sent parties to search the deserted houses of the mining town. To some it might seem that the hand of Providence was active. Or had the Russians anticipated that some day a small group would be seeking refuge there? In a short time the search party found large quantities of clothes, tea and coffee, margarine, crackers and dehydrated vegetables. It was enough to live on for quite a while, even without any meat.

The Norwegian commander, it happened, knew Spitzbergen fairly well; he suddenly remembered that the Russian miners kept pigs, and reasoned that the pigs must have been slaughtered when orders came to evacuate the island. Since men can eat artificially frozen meat, they can certainly eat meat frozen by nature at the North Pole, where the temperature never rises above the freezing point and frozen meat keeps indefinitely. Search parties were sent out again. Sure enough, they found the site of the former pigsties. The snow was scraped away and a number of carcasses were revealed. The men burst into shouts of joy. The carcasses, more than a year old, were fresh and fit for eating.

The next day Nazi planes came over Bärentsburg. They had seen tracks on the ice and had followed them to the Russian mining town. Now they attacked the Norwegians for a period of four hours. But they did not know in which houses their enemy was, for the Norwegians had deliberately made ski tracks leading to every house. They kindled fires in some houses so that the smoke might deceive the Nazis. Then they crept into the cellars to hide. The deception was very successful. The Nazis used all their ammunition against the settlement, but no one was hit. Nevertheless, the situation continued critical. It was decided that a band of nineteen equipped with six pairs of skis should try to find its way to a certain safe spot on the island. For reasons of military security the place cannot be described.

The Nazis returned the next day and the day after that; on these occasions they had two-engined bombers. They dropped heavy bombs on the wooden houses and set them afire. The

Norwegians had to run for it and carry their wounded to the shelter of a cement warehouse at the water's edge.

The next day the Norwegian commander dispatched a highly trustworthy group to find out what was happening in Longyear City. He was sure it was the site of the Nazi airfield and garrison. Certainly everything looked very desperate. With their boats sunk, there was no way of escape. While they were insured against death by starvation, they were powerless before the Nazi air assault. Twelve more men were sent to look for a place of refuge. Their explorations would take days and were, moreover, extremely exhausting and dangerous.

And then the miracle befell. A Catalina of the British Coastal Command appeared over Bärentsburg on a long-range reconnaissance flight. The Norwegians succeeded in sending an SOS message with their signal lamp, which they had managed to repair and equip with Russian batteries left by the far-sighted miners.

But it was nine days before the British rescue party arrived. Each one of those nine long days the Nazis bombed and machine-gunned the Norwegians. The Norwegians stuck stubbornly to their warehouse. After the fourth day, the Catalina came back and dropped a letter asking them to state what they needed. They flashed light-signals giving all the necessary information. The Nazi strafing subsided gradually. But the Norwegians were afraid that the Nazis might make a land attack and capture them.

Finally the Norwegians were able to shake hands with their rescuer. The pilot of the Catalina made his landing. Seven wounded men were taken away by the plane. The rest were left provided with ammunition and anti-aircraft guns and assurances that help would come soon.

It took over three weeks before a British naval force arrived at Bärentsburg. They were welcomed wildly by a crowd of ragged and bearded Vikings. A Norwegian force shortly followed. There was now a military concentration sufficient to wipe out every Nazi in the Polar area.

The patrol group which had gone to reconnoiter Longyear City had come back and brought valuable information. They knew the exact position of the Nazis and had seen the newly constructed airfield. Of course, they had not enough weapons to attack the Nazi expedition, but they had taken care to make many ski tracks. The Nazi weather spies must have thought the little group greatly outnumbered them, for the Nazi garrison did not have more than thirty men.

Now the combined British-Norwegian forces attacked Longyear City, only to find that the Nazis had evacuated it. They must have suspected that reinforcements were coming.

This, then, was another defeat for Canaris's Arctic Office. Spitzbergen remained in Allied hands until Canaris made still another attempt, which we have already mentioned, in September, 1943. That final raid was at first very successful. The Germans fell upon the Norwegian garrison and killed or captured every Norwegian. They instantly started to rebuild their weather station. But the triumph lasted exactly three days. The British and American navies arrived to wipe out the Nazis. And this time the Allies took over Spitzbergen for good.

CHAPTER VIII

Espionage Rides the Air Waves

Admiral Canaris was now forced to quit the icy region of the North Pole and repair to warmer climes, and the scenery of our narrative changes from icebergs and frozen seas to wide desert sands swept by monsoons. Canaris moved to Africa, where he personally supervised combat espionage in Tunis and Libya.

The battle of El Alamein was still on, with the civilized world quaking lest the Nazi hopes of a march to the Suez come true. There was one man untroubled by that fear. This man knew that with the thousands of planes and tanks and guns from the

United States—coming belatedly, it was true, but not too late —he would be able to administer a stinging setback to the would-be conqueror, Marshal Rommel.

He was not a man who saw himself as a Caesar. He liked to be comfortable; he did not like to wear medals. He was fifty-seven years old. His battle uniform consisted of sweater and slacks and a slouchy beret. Fate had appointed him to be not only the liberator of Africa, but the avenger of Dunkerque and the nemesis of Admiral Canaris's African agents.

General Bernard Montgomery, the son of a clergyman, habitually reads two books before going to sleep. The books are always the same—the Bible and John Bunyan's *The Pilgrim's Progress*. He never takes more than five or six hours' sleep, but that sleep is not to be disturbed; stern orders are issued to protect it. Nevertheless, he was aroused one night in his tent outside El Alamein. British Intelligence officers insisted on speaking to Monty right away.

They declared that their business could not wait and that the General, when he knew why they had come, would forgive their rude interruption of his slumbers. They had two prisoners with them. Their car was loaded with technical equipment. Finally they were admitted to Monty's tent. The prisoners—two Arabs, it appeared—were brought along. One of the officers spoke a few words to the General, who instantly became alert.

He had been looking for these two prisoners for many months. He had not known that they were going to turn out to be Arabs. But he knew that they were Admiral Canaris's principal spies in the desert.

General Montgomery need not have bothered cross-examining the two Arabs; the job could well have been delegated to a minor officer. But his curiosity was aroused and he opened the investigation then and there. He heard an exciting story that night.

The two Arabs, who were seized from the very midst of a caravan crossing the desert, spoke Arabian, English and German. The white burnoose apparently looked as becoming on German nationals as on Arabs, for these swathed figures proved to be Germans. They had been dropped by parachute into

Egypt from Marshal Rommel's lines. For many months they had lived among the natives. They had cleverly attached themselves to the Arabs employed in transporting the last-minute Lend-Lease shipments from the Red Sea ports. In this way the Germans helped carry the stuff right into General Montgomery's lines.

They were equipped with low-powered radio sets. They diligently short-waved everything they could observe about the armament shipments and the Allied troop positions. Some Arab students, fanatically anti-British, were their accomplices.

The dispatches were sent to Marshal Rommel and to Canaris's new headquarters in Greece. Some time before, the British Intelligence Service had detected a few of these faint code messages, but the location of the short-wave transmitters baffled them completely. The cleverness of the espionage lay in the fact that the faint messages emanated from mobile units, such as a car, a small boat or a wandering native caravan.

Monty became much concerned about it. He hit on the plan of outfitting every available car with radio-detection units.

And now the signals had been traced. The British found it hardly credible that these signals should appear to come from a lumbering Arabian caravan. Nevertheless, the caravan was halted for questioning. On a camel's back, among bales of merchandise, was found radio equipment. And the British laid their hands on the two spies who had been trying to play Lawrence of Arabia on Germany's behalf.

Brought before Monty, the agents begged for mercy. In the hope of buying their lives, they volunteered the names of other contact men. But they were shot the next morning.

The British exploited the incident to its fullest extent. They took over the code the Germans had been using and sent misinformation to the Nazis in Greece. Best of all, the British learned precisely what Canaris knew and just what he didn't know.

* * *

Short-wave transmission of espionage has unlimited possibilities. It operated in Greenland and Spitzbergen; it operated in Africa. It brewed a lot of mischief in the United States.

It was 1942 when a state trooper riding on highway patrol near Los Angeles was puzzled by a radio message coming in on the short-wave dial, of which he could not make head or tail. He jotted down what it was with the intention of giving the communications officer a good bawling out. Why broadcast such nonsense, to the confusion of an honest cop? However, the Communications Department of the Los Angeles police decided that it was far from gibberish. It was Japanese, and it was in code. This incident led Lieutenant Charles W. Ellison of Los Angeles to send out patrol cars equipped with detecting antennae. The cars ran down Japanese radio spies who were trying Canaris's shrewd technique of transmitting information by low-powered mobile short-wave sets.

The Federal Communications Commission (FCC) became increasingly concerned. Espionage in World War II was no longer a matter of invisible ink and cryptic love letters. Spy messages were almost invariably transmitted by radio. The Boston radio monitor station began hearing strange messages. The Baltimore station had the same experience. Presently disquieting reports came in from stations all the way from Alaska to Hawaii. It can now be revealed that the FCC has tracked down no less than five hundred illegal stations. Three hundred more were in operation in Argentina and Martinique. Finally, in 1943, the U.S. State Department sent an ultimatum to the anti-democratic governments of the South American nation and the French island: they must put a ban on amateur radio broadcasting—or else.

Most of these German and Japanese illicit radio stations were mobile. They attempted to shift location before the authorities could catch up with them—the same trick, incidentally, that was employed by underground patriot movements in the occupied countries.

What could be more convenient than a broadcasting station small enough to fit into a suitcase? An instance is recorded of a mystery radio being operated from a motorboat. The transmitter was cased in a waterproof box. If lake police or Coast Guard patrols approached, the box was lowered into the water, thus hiding the damaging evidence.

An interesting case was that of John Howard. A city dweller, he was nevertheless a great hunting enthusiast. In November, it's open season for deer in Maine. Howard liked to drive up from Boston for a weekend in Maine and would return with a deer or two stowed away in the back of his car.

New Englanders are reputed to be quiet people and slow to make friends. But hunting parties are different; there conviviality reigns, and the men spend their evenings drinking and telling tall stories. Howard was well liked and was invited to join the hunting crowd in taverns, lodges or camps. One time he shared a cabin at a small tourist camp patronized by hunters. On Sunday morning, when the hunters were out in the woods, an FCC inspector drove up to the camp. Did the camp owner know whether any of his campers had a radio transmitter? The owner was dumbfounded. He was sure that none of them had. The inspector told him to keep his eyes and ears open.

The hunters returned, the only newcomer among them being John Howard. He mentioned that he was going to drive down to the village and buy some cards for their evening bridge game. The men did play bridge that evening. But the camp owner followed John Howard down the street. He heard him make two calls to New York. Later it was learned that the calls had been made to two German agents who were operating a "message box" in New York City. Howard was their accomplice and had brought his transmitter to the Maine woods. Howard did not go on any more hunting trips!

In like manner, the FBI cracked down on radio spies in Miami, Detroit, Havana. Some spy radio stations were traced to Brazil, Chile and Argentina, whose governments ordered their suppression.

* * *

Fantastic though it sounds, agents of the Japanese Embassy dared to use secret radios right in Washington, D. C. Super-confidential code messages, which could not be entrusted to lesser men, were conveyed from these stations. One of them was located on the top floor of a Washington hotel. The Coast Guard was responsible for exposing this spy station. Others were uncovered close to the waterfront, where they operated to send messages to German submarines lurking off our shores.

Intermittently outside of New York Harbor peculiar code messages were picked up. The mystery station was estimated to be some one hundred miles out at sea. The Naval Intelligence Service was convinced that it was a German submarine, concealed close to our shores and communicating with enemy agents. If so, the submarine was probably receiving reports on departing merchant ships.

On the day that a vast cargo of American planes left for England, the FCC, the FBI and Naval Intelligence all heard activity from the suspect station. Orders went out to the England-bound convoy to turn back, and the counter-espionage unit of the Coast Guard girded itself for battle. By means of detecting antennae, several Coast Guard cutters with FBI men on them were guided to the source of the messages. It was no submarine. They beheld a battered old fishing vessel, lying at anchor. It was deserted. Boarding it, they discovered a secret radio transmitter, powerful enough to contact Europe or Argentina. The authorities left as silently as they had come. Two weeks later the pincers closed on an entire spy ring.

As far as radio espionage is concerned, the sky's the limit. It can be flagrant beyond belief. In 1943 a famous heavyweight champion was interviewed on the air. It was on a national, coast-to-coast hook-up with an audience of millions. The broadcast, a big attraction to sport fans, was of the most innocent variety. Nevertheless, right over the heads of several million Americans, this message was spoken in cryptographic code:

"S 112. S.S. Elizabeth sails tonight with hundreds of airplanes for Halifax, N.S."

Fortunately, the *S.S. Elizabeth* did not sail that night. Even more fortunately, no enemy agent was speaking this message. It was the experiment of a famous radio commentator who wished to prove to skeptics in our Intelligence Services that such messages could be forwarded to the enemy, with no one among the radio audience being wiser.

The lesson was so forceful that new radio classes were established to teach methods of combatting the enemy's radio espionage.

* * *

Let me nominate these three as the greatest coups of radio espionage of the war. First was the battle of Sedan, where radio espionage brought about the routing of the French. This defeat spelled total surrender for France.

The second was Admiral Canaris's bold stroke of sinking the *Royal Oak*. The third case was that of Bill Sebold, to which we shall now pay some attention.

Bill Sebold was once Wilhelm Sebold. He came to the United States and determined to be loyal to his new *Vaterland*. Like so many German-Americans, he was a skilled mechanic. He worked at the Consolidated Aircraft Company.

Sebold retained many traits from his national origin. He liked beer and sauerkraut and pickled pigs' knuckles. He had many friends of his own nationality. It's not surprising that he was a member of an innocent German glee club.

His aged parents and relatives lived in Germany. Sebold saved money to make a trip back home, crossing in June, 1939, on the Hapag luxury liner *S.S. Deutschland*. On board he exchanged American dollars for the discounted Reisemarks, which worked out very advantageously. What with the excellent food, dancing and the movies, Sebold had a delightful voyage.

When he landed at Hamburg, the then-beautiful city on the Alster, he ran into trouble with the German customs officials. He expostulated to them; his suitcase, he swore, contained only clothes and some presents for his parents. But there was no remedy for it; he would have to go to headquarters.

Headquarters were quite a distance from the harbor. "A funny country," he thought with superiority, "to put the customs house miles away from the harbor!" Two customs officers drove him through the city. They pointed out the new constructions, the tremendous railway station, the famous Hotel Atlantik. Then they stopped before a gray, sombre building.

Wilhelm Sebold looked for some name carved on the façade. No name appeared. Inside were hundreds of rooms, and men hurrying about in brown, black and green uniforms. Sebold began to be frightened. He had heard about the new Germany. Possibly he had meditated a little on its strange rise to power. He had doubted the atrocity stories of the concentration camps. He knew his own people and knew that they were not cruel.

He wondered what would happen now. At any rate, the American Consulate would protect him. That was good to know.

From the absence of crates or any evidence of shipping, he gathered that this building was not the customs house. The men led Sebold to a tremendous office. At one end stood an imposing desk, reminding one of Mussolini's. From behind it a man in dark uniform arose and came to Wilhelm. He shook his hand, smiled and was as cordial as an old friend.

"Welcome to Germany," the man in the black uniform said. "Sit down," he invited Sebold. "We are glad to have you with us."

"Yes," said Wilhelm, "but I don't understand what this is about. My luggage, I assure you, is all right."

"Pray don't be disturbed about your little presents," the man said. "We are your friends. You will find us, the new Germany, very hospitable. Have a cigarette."

Revelation came bit by bit. The man revealed his name and his true aspect. The name of Paul Kraus is not unknown in the annals of modern espionage, for it is the name of the notorious head of the Hamburg Gestapo. This man is known to have tortured and imprisoned Jan Valtin, author of *Out of the Night*. Subsequently he forced Valtin to act as one of his agents, until Valtin made a break for safety.

From his desk Kraus produced a folder; it contained facts and figures relating to the Consolidated Aircraft Company. He asked Sebold to check over the information.

Wilhelm Sebold bluntly refused that kind of co-operation. He stated that he was an American citizen and owed his allegiance to that country.

Kraus laughed pleasantly at the avowals. "Once a German, always a German. We do not change our country as we change a shirt." Still very polite, he reminded Sebold that his parents lived in Mülheim, not in the United States. "If you refuse to co-operate with us—I shall be very frank—we cannot guarantee their safety."

Bill Sebold was allowed to go when he promised to think it over. Kraus agreed that such a step needed careful consideration, but he was sure Sebold would see it their way. This former German will never forget his vacation in Naziland. He will never forget the struggle between his loyalty to his parents and to his adopted country, America. He knew that he was trapped. He had not heard of Canaris, but the brief interview with Kraus had been very instructive.

Bill Sebold took the only way open to him. He consented to work for the Nazis. He was to live in Hamburg for several months and receive espionage training. He was paid well. Sebold explained that he would write his friends in America some excuse for prolonging his stay. Moreover, he would have to procure an extension of his passport. He visited the American Consul, where his visa was extended. On this visit he transacted another bit of business. . . . . A few weeks later, a copy of Bill Sebold's confession was at the State Department in Washington. It had been enclosed in a diplomatic pouch and flown by clipper.

Bill Sebold moved to a "Pensionat" in Hamburg. The other lodgers in the house were students for the Gestapo and spy services, and were training for their future profession. Sebold was given a course in espionage and radio transmission.

In September, 1939, when war broke out, Gestapo chief Kraus informed Sebold that soon there would be plenty of work for him. The American had satisfactorily completed his course, and the Nazis were pleased with their bright agent whose family was regarded as hostages for his loyalty to the Reich.

On January 30, 1940, the *S.S. Washington* sailed for New York with Bill Sebold as passenger. He experienced a sinking of heart. He had confessed what his position was to the American Consul. But had his statement reached the United States? And what if there were Nazi agents inside the FBI? What if they had exposed his dangerous double game? Sebold seemed to see spies everywhere. He gathered small assurance from the sight of the Statue of Liberty in New York Harbor. He was between two fires, he told himself miserably.

When the customs and immigration officials boarded the ship, three FBI agents were among them. They accosted Sebold in his stateroom. They congratulated him heartily and asked him to give them the dope. They wanted the information right then and there.

Sebold's spirits rose. His adopted country would protect him. He reasoned that the Gestapo could not have detected him; otherwise they would not have let him leave the country.

In time, he was introduced to FBI chief J. Edgar Hoover who became personally interested in the case. Through Bill Sebold, the FBI learned precisely what the Canaris office had designed against the United States, and what information Canaris was fishing for.

The Nazis had given Sebold five micro-films, each smaller than a postage stamp. These micro-films carried complete instructions for his future espionage work and included the names of some contact men who would assist him.

The text of these tiny films required fifteen minutes' reading time. Once enlarged and translated, they were enormously revealing. This is the sort of thing the Nazis wanted to know:

1. Had the United States developed any ray-guided bombs?

2. Had Professor Bullard of Hobart College succeeded in perfecting an army uniform impervious to mustard gas?

3. What new aircraft plants were being built in Canada?

4. What anti-fog devices were being used by the U.S. Army, Navy and Air Force?

5. Did the United States have a shell with an electric mechanism?

They requested employment statistics of aircraft plants and an infinite number of details on anti-aircraft models, poison gas and gas-mask production. They wanted general all-round espionage directed at these and many other war plants:

> Bell Company
> Curtiss-Wright
> North American Aircraft
> Glenn Martin
> Douglas
> Boeing
> United Aircraft
> Lockheed-Wright
> Pratt-Whitney

It was an arduous plan of comprehensive industrial espionage placed in Sebold's hands. In addition, he was entrusted with quite a bit of money. He was to purchase top-notch "amateur" short-wave transmitters for broadcasting information to Hamburg. He was to make contact over wave length AOR.

J. Edgar Hoover made a lightning decision. America's most modern radio equipment would be put at Bill's disposal.

The "German spy station" was established at Centerport, Long Island. It was a beautiful spot. There, under the most pleasant conditions, Bill Sebold settled down to run the secret station. Men of the FBI would drop around from time to time to enjoy the countryside—and check on the latest developments.

Sebold contacted Canaris's office very soon. He informed Hamburg where he could be reached. He instructed Hamburg to communicate by wave length CQDXVW-2. The Germans had not given Sebold any code for his secret radio, for apparently Admiral Canaris did not consider it prudent to risk a code on an inexperienced man whose co-operation had been secured by pressure. Hamburg now used the primitive device of reversing the letters of each word.

It was quite a day when the "spy" at Centerport decoded the first message from Germany:

"To all Friends of the New Order: Information is urgently required on the size, quantity, type and description of all U.S. war material, the destination and shipping dates of such material and all other pertinent information."

The FBI formed a "little brain trust" to invent "phony dope" for short-waving to Hamburg. Inevitably, some of the facts had to be true. But they were to be unimportant facts magnified to seem very significant. Airplanes which had been judged obsolete and so discontinued could be described accurately.

The information, both genuine and fake, had to seem very convincing. Bill Sebold and his FBI friends cudgelled their brains and they did a fine job. Hamburg was well pleased and Sebold's prestige rose. He was given addresses of Nazi agents he was to assist. He was told where to go to receive more money. Bill explained that he was using a mobile unit, which ran into a lot of expense. The money was handed over to the FBI as well as the names of the contact men from whom it had been received.

The game continued for sixteen months. In that time, the

FBI received some four hundred and fifty messages from the Canaris office in Hamburg. Many more items to other agents were intercepted, for the Germans had finally put enough confidence in Sebold to provide him with a code used by other agents in South America.

One of the messages made the grim FBI men rock with laughter. The Centerport station had been cautioned: "Be careful. You are under surveillance by FBI agents. Do not attempt to communicate for one week."

The FBI was delighted at the "brilliance" of the Nazi superspies, who after sixteen months had not even a dim suspicion that they were dealing with the enemy's Secret Service.

Finally, it was time to call a halt to the cat-and-mouse game. J. Edgar Hoover decreed the arrest of every single German spy. In one day thirty-three of Canaris's agents in the United States were seized. Some of their sub-agents in Brazil, Chile and Uruguay were clamped down on.

We do know now what an ordeal Sebold's parents in Mülheim had to go through. And we can be sure of our debt to quick-witted Bill Sebold. His work with radio counter-espionage made possible the arrest of eight saboteurs sent out by Admiral Canaris; not long after the dissolution of the fake radio station, the eight were landed by submarine on Long Island, not very far from Centerport.

CHAPTER IX

The Man Who Really Sank the *Royal Oak*

THE War had not been going on long. It was October, 1939, only the second month of the struggle which was to last so long and be so bloody. Admiral Canaris had not left his office at 14 Bendlerstrasse for more than a week. He was there both day and night, snatching only a few hours' rest from time to time on the couch in his office. It was too much work for one man, but the Admiral had never liked to have close assistants, now least of all.

The first few weeks were terrific ones for him, as the thousands of reports streamed into his office. Plans laid for many years back were now ripening. Many of the reports were trivial, but many were without price. They issued from points all over the world, and were sent by letter, wire, code and short wave. Each tip had to be studied, analyzed; it formed the basis for future action and assignments.

Past midnight on one day of this October, a code message finally came through—a message for which the Admiral had been sleeplessly waiting. It read: *"We did it. Prien."* The Admiral tingled with triumph. He phoned the news to Hitler and Admiral Doenitz. Then he called the Deutsches Nachrichten Bureau and narrated the exploit of Captain Guenther Prien, hero of the German navy, who had that night torpedoed the British battleship *Royal Oak* at its supposedly impregnable base of Scapa Flow.

Never before had an enemy submarine entered the Scapa Flow, and never had anyone imagined such a possibility. But England's Pearl Harbor had been successfully attacked. Scapa Flow, synonym for a safe harbor, had been raided by the Germans.

At half-hour intervals during the day, the German radio exulted over the great naval victory. If Scapa Flow had been thus successfully assaulted, the German navy stood a real chance to defeat the Allied fleets. Why not?

The success went to the Nazis' heads. Both professional and armchair strategists envisaged a sea siege of Norway, Denmark, Iceland, Greenland and even Great Britain. The Scapa Flow attack seemed to confirm the contention of the Nazi military experts that they could do without big ships. They could win the war on the seas with submarines.

A welcome unprecedented in glory was planned for the hero of Scapa Flow. Flowers would rain upon him and contingents of white-robed girls would form a procession behind him, while they intoned poems of tribute to a German hero. A few days

later the submarine B-06 came into Kiel.   The sea was high
and rough and the day blustery, but weather did not deter the
welcoming crowds.   According to plan, Captain Prien was
pelted with flowers.   He was publicly decorated with the navy
cross.   He was interviewed over all the major radio stations.
A rich banquet was set up in the officers' mess hall, which was
succeeded by a victory ball, celebrating the fact that the *Royal
Oak* had gone down, taking more than eight hundred English
sailors and officers to their deaths.

In the midst of the celebration, one man not in uniform
slipped away from the dock to which submarine B-06 was
moored.   Though the newspapers gave citations to everyone
of the crew by name, not a word was said about this civilian.

The man had not been invited to the banquet.   Tall, dark,
past his youth, with traces in his bearing of former military
training, he walked to the Hotel zum Goldenen Loewen, of
Kiel.   He was tired, terrifically tired.   The others might have
zest for going to victory balls.   There they would drink and
in their intoxication bellow the *Horst Wessel Lied* and *Deutschland ueber Alles*.   He could dispense with that sort of thing.
The strange civilian who had so quietly disembarked was
drained of all excitement.   He wished for nothing but sleep.

He slept far into the next morning.   On rising he took a
train to Hamburg and there changed to a plane bound for
Berlin.

He noticed that all the newspapers showed the same black
headlines:

Heldentat des Kapitäns Prien

which was to say: "The Heroic Exploit of Captain Prien."   The
unknown civilian shrugged contemptuously.   His real name
was Alfred Wehring, which was what he had written in the
hotel's registry.   After sixteen years he had written his real
name for the first time.

The cheering throngs of Kiel had never heard of him.   Well,
that was the way of the world.   They were wasting orchids and
all manner of fine speeches on Captain Prien, the pompous ass.
Future Nazi history books would hail Prien as the conqueror
of Scapa Flow.   He, Captain Alfred Wehring, did not begrudge

the other his glory. He had had his own taste of it in the First World War. Then he had taken part in the Battle of Jutland, in which the *Royal Oak,* now sunk, had fought. Wehring had been in the Kategatt, in the Mediterranean, in Spain. Yes, in Spain he had worked with the man who was now his master: Walter Wilhelm Canaris.

He was now to see Canaris and report personally for new duties. Let the world think what it would, Canaris at any rate knew who was the real hero of Scapa Flow. The *Royal Oak* had not been sunk by this spruce Nazi navy captain, but by Alfred Wehring.

Wehring was expected by the Admiral. The two men, whose common bond was their experience in Spain, had not seen each other during all the years; nevertheless, they had kept each other in view and were indirectly in contact.

The world will never know what these two had to say to each other. Undoubtedly Canaris congratulated Wehring on his brilliant job of espionage. Canaris probably added that it was meet for men in their profession to do things in the dark, while others took the glory. Young Prien certainly did not deserve the ovations, but since the German people asked for heroes, heroes had to be dished out to them.

He personally, the Admiral probably said, was above the vulgar craving for glory. But Wehring was not entirely above it. A bitter note intruded into the conversation. Wehring may have said that his sixteen years of exile and seclusion had not been jolly ones. The further course of their talk is not known, but the British Secret Service has reason to believe that Wehring was thoroughly dissatisfied, that he told Canaris as much and that he indulged in a burst of self-pity. Be that as it may, it took the British several months to trace the facts on the raid of Scapa Flow. The story establishes Wehring as a man of extraordinary patience. It is rather surprising that so capable an agent was given no other assignments.

We must return sixteen years to the time when Alfred Wehring, retired captain of the Imperial German Navy, left Germany. It was 1923, year of the Munich Beer Hall Putsch, year of the Nazi Free Corps, year of the Nazi Leo Schlageter's blowing up of French freight trains in the Ruhr—for which feat he was enrolled on the Nazi calendar of saints. At that time Canaris was a nobody, an obscure officer living on his small pension. In reality he was engrossed in the task of reorganizing marine espionage and military espionage for the "democratic" republic and its Prussian generals and admirals.

In 1923 Canaris on his own initiative sent out Germany's first naval spy since the Versailles Treaty had been signed. In those distant days nobody suspected what revolutions would be seen in Germany, how the Ruhr Valley, then under occupation by the French, would change hands or how soon Germany would launch her *guerre de revanche*.

But the German army and navy knew this one thing: that they would have their war in ten or fifteen years. Since this was the case, they would require an espionage system abroad, for the establishment of which 1923 was none too early.

Alfred Wehring was one of the youngest captains in Germany. He had proved himself an able officer of the battleship *Admiral Hipper*. He was retained on the pay roll, in spite of there being little work for him after 1919. Canaris had a high opinion of his abilities, and in 1923 chose Wehring for the important new appointment. Wehring was to become a salesman for a German watch firm. A respectable representative of a harmless firm, he would visit many countries of Europe, in all of which he was to keep alert to new naval constructions.

After three years of this, Wehring was sent to Switzerland, where he apprenticed himself to a Swiss watchmaking concern and made himself into a proficient watchmaker. In 1927 he emigrated to England. Nobody knew that he was a captain, or even that he was German. It was a mere matter of routine for Canaris to outfit him with a new passport and a new name. He used the typical Swiss name of Albert Ortel.

He settled in Kirkwall on the Orkney Islands, close to the Scapa Flow base. The quiet district of Kirkwall needed a good watchmaker. Ortel worked as a clerk in several small stores dealing in jewelry and giftware. As a sideline, he undertook the repair of watches. His work was skillful, his charge small and his fame began to spread. Ortel lived modestly, saving every farthing toward his dream of opening his own little watch store and gift shop in the heart of Kirkwall. There the sailors

would purchase presents and souvenirs. Eventually the dream
was realized. Ortel became the proprietor of a shop of gifts
and Swiss watches. It was much patronized.

The people of Kirkwall were not rich, but they were able
to afford cheap watches, pretty brooches and fountain pens. A
watch mended by Ortel ran perfectly for years afterward. The
people took to their new neighbor. He was honest and pleas-
ant-spoken. He was invited to their homes, on sailing and fishing jaunts and to bridge games. In 1932 he became a British
citizen, which completed the process of assimilation.

A native of land-bound Switzerland, Wehring had an insa-
tiable and passionate interest in the sea. He was happy in this
coastal town. He was so firmly settled in Kirkwall that he was
loath to leave it, even for the purpose of making a trip back to
Switzerland where all his friends and family resided. Therefore relatives and friends, all speaking in marked Swiss accents,
came to see him during the summer months. Several were
quite struck with Kirkwall, and decided that they, too, wanted
to stay in England. Ortel assisted them in every way possible,
and found them jobs in the district.

Albert received an abundance of mail from his relatives in
Switzerland; a faithful son, he himself wrote at least once a
month to his old father. It happened that the old father was
none other than Admiral Canaris, and the numerous relatives
were officers of the Nazi Secret Service. But Ortel was never
in the least suspected.

The children learned that Albert usually had some Swiss
chocolate about him. He was fond of children, and always gave
them a few pieces when they visited with him in the shop.

The life of Kirkwall was peaceful and provincial. Then the
War broke out. Albert Ortel was the first to hang the Union
Jack over his door. He bought war bonds more generously
than the other citizens. "I'm far from neutral," he asserted to
his neighbors. "I'm British now, not Swiss." He regretted that
his age barred him from serving in the army. But he participated in the war vicariously; his radio was constantly tuned to
war news.

Ortel was a consummate actor of his role. It will never be
known from what sources he pieced together the information

concerning the inadequate defenses of Scapa Flow. Was it the children, nibbling his chocolate and babbling secrets which they had heard at home? Was it the harbor workers? Was it a tipsy sailor?

But the facts are positive. A month after the outbreak of the War, Ortel learned that the traps and nets on the eastern approaches of Scapa Flow were not in place. They had been inspected and found to be unsound, weakened by water-rot and the gnawing of wood borers. They had been removed. Perhaps Ortel managed to see them being lifted.

Replacements were ordered from South England. They were on their way, but the confusion entailed by the new war situation, plus ordinary red tape, held up the shipment. Some of the requisition papers were not signed according to form. Perhaps the delay in the delivery was accidental. Perhaps not. In any case, Ortel knew that the nets and traps were not in place. He knew what the rest of the world did not know— that there were serious loopholes in the defenses of Scapa Flow.

On the October day when the watchmaker discovered this vital fact, he closed up shop a little earlier than usual. "It's raining, and we'll have no more customers," he explained to his shop-girl. He closed the iron shutters before the windows and went home.

Albert's home was cozy and thoroughly anglicized. On the hearth a bright fire burned, over which a kettle of water was suspended. Albert turned on the radio, as was his wont, to get the war news. Then he went to his closet. He produced a pair of earphones; the closet seemed to contain an old-fashioned radio set, with the awkward dials and knobs of bygone years. But it was a short-wave transmitter. Ortel spun a knob, adjusted a dial and murmured cautiously into the mouthpiece.

The message was sent to the German naval attaché in then-neutral Holland. From The Hague the message was speedily forwarded to Canaris, who learned the essential fact that invulnerable Scapa Flow was in actuality defenseless and wide open to any submarine attack. A few days would elapse before the defenses were replaced.

The very same hour Canaris acted. Code instructions were sent out to all Nazi submarines in the North Sea and the Channel. The German naval attaché in Holland, Captain Baron von Bülow, was instructed to contact Ortel—Wehring—in Kirkwall.

Captain Guenther Prien of the submarine B-06 was singled out to execute the plan. He was ordered to bring his vessel to the surface close to the easternmost tip of Pomona Island. It was a dark and rainy night, with fog so dense that one could hardly see a foot ahead.

The submarine commander appreciated the fact that a single clumsy maneuver would bring disaster upon him. The British coast guard cutters were dangerously near, and if they were even slightly alarmed, they would train their searchlights on the sea and discover the sub. As the submarine came nearer and nearer to the coast, its commander feared that it might run into some reefs. Prien gave orders that the motor of the submarine be shut off. He lifted his glasses and scanned the vague silhouette of the coastline. Through the fog, he caught sight of a light. Yes, it was the agreed signal—one long, two short, one long. It was the signal that Canaris had fixed.

Captain Guenther Prien ordered the collapsible rubber boat to be lowered and manned by one sailor. A "friend" was to be rescued from England. It was not long before Prien shook hands with watchmaker Ortel-Wehring, who was brought on board the submarine. Without an instant's delay, the submarine dived.

Ortel handed over his data. He had prepared naval maps, with a complete diagramming of every yard of Scapa Flow. He pointed out where the defenseless parts lay. Prien took the map, and, going to the commander's mouthpiece, he gave his orders. The submarine cut through the water and twisted and turned, dodging the known obstacles of Scapa Flow until it had breached the eastern entrance.

"Prepare torpedoes" was Prien's order—and the long, silver, deadly projectiles were inserted into their chambers. Every Nazi sailor stood at his post. They knew that one mistake would entrap the sub in the nets and bring them all to a watery grave. The periscope was searching for its prey. They had entered Scapa Flow, an experience no other German crew had ever had. Through the fog, the periscope showed the massive bodies of several light cruisers and destroyers. But Prien was looking for the big boat that lay farthest away. It was the tremendous battleship *Royal Oak*.

The engines stopped. The periscope was fixed to give a perfect image of the *Royal Oak*. Prien gave the signal, while Ortel, beside him, snatched a glance through the periscope. *"Fertig, Schiessen"* was the command, and the first torpedo made its fatal flight toward the *Royal Oak*. They heard a fearful detonation, while a second torpedo was launched. Now the periscope revealed the *Royal Oak* burning and sinking inside England's safest harbor.

The sight afforded pure pleasure to Prien. He looked interestedly through the periscope, to watch these British sailors floundering, struggling, drowning. But Wehring turned away. As for the crew, it went wild. As soon as the submarine was navigated beyond danger, Prien had liquor given out to them. They had a private celebration, before the staggering public celebration that awaited them at Kiel.

The 29,150-ton ship sank swiftly. Conqueror at the Battle of Jutland, she went down with twelve hundred men, only 396 of whom escaped death.

Whatever emotions Prien felt, they were not shared by Wehring, despite the long, faithful and humble service he had given to the Canaris espionage system. These drowning sailors had often been in Kirkwall; they had bought little gifts for their mothers and girls at his shop. And this was how he repaid the British for their friendliness!

It may well be that conscience-stricken Wehring blurted out all his feelings to his master Canaris. For he was given no other espionage work. On the other hand, Wehring's retirement may have been a device by which the Admiral was enabled to use this excellent man under a different name, in another country —or even in another war, the war of the Nazi underground, the Werewolves. Who can tell?

CHAPTER X

Beauty Treatment à la Japan

Two men in America predicted that German submarines would come to our very shores. They warned the government to be prepared. These men were Walter Winchell and Curt Riess. The latter described a probable landing in a sensational article which appeared in *The Saturday Evening Post* just a few weeks before the submarines landed eight saboteurs on Long Island and in Florida.

Walter Winchell, who can boast of having many more friends than enemies, gave warning after warning of Japan's imminent entrance into the War. His column dinned away about the army of enemy agents Canaris was using against us. Winchell even told where they were thickest. "Beware of enemy agents in Hawaii," he wrote. Agents in Hawaii were watched and arrested, but too tardily. The Pearl Harbor catastrophe had already happened.

This is the story of espionage in Pearl Harbor, a battle which the United States lost, and which Canaris and Japan won, but not to the extent they had planned.

Modern crazes had hit Hawaii. Juke boxes and swing music had long ago drowned out the native music sung by the beautiful Polynesian girls. But here was a brand-new sensation for Honolulu. Every woman on the islands heard about it, but it was most appreciated by the Navy wives, the American girls living far from metropolitan luxuries.

The islands could now boast of an ultra-modern beauty parlor. Ruth, the store's manager, was universally liked. She installed elegant chairs and brought in a staff that knew how to give excellent permanents and facials, work that compared favorably with treatments on Fifth Avenue. Hundreds of women spent the whole day relaxing in the suave atmosphere of Ruth's beauty parlor.

The place was highly fashionable and was the clearing house of all Hawaiian gossip. Women discussed who was in town,

who was leaving, furloughs, assignments, ships' arrivals and de-
partures. This was the stuff that made up the life of the islands
and naturally it came up in conversation.

The beauty parlor opened in 1939—before Germany had as
much as hinted at her campaign against Poland. Nobody on
the Hawaiian Islands thought of war, and few back in the
mother country thought about it. But espionage does not operate intermittently. It is a long-drawn-out business and it is
always planned during peacetime—many, many years in advance.

For once the plot did not originate in the German War Office,
and the ubiquitous hand of Admiral Walter Wilhelm Canaris
was not in it.

All the credit is due to Propaganda Minister Joseph Goebbels. He had held office for two years, when in the beginning
of 1935 he threw a party at the Ministry for all the personnel.
It was a gala affair, with everyone feeling happy and proud,
inspired by the new-born strength of Nazi Germany. Goebbels
was in his element. He had never denied that his interest in
the female of the species was greater than befitted a happily
married man. His affairs with women were complicated and
extensive, and this evening promised the beginning of a new
affair.

His private secretary, Leopold Kuehn, was here with his
young sister, Ruth. The girl was stunning. Goebbels, who
when it suited his purpose could be extremely charming and
sociable, danced with her the whole evening.

They got a little drunk together and had a wonderful time.
Any halfway-intelligent girl would realize that an affair with
the Propaganda Minister was a big thing.

The young people of Nazidom had a new morality. Marriage for them was no necessary preliminary to having children;
neither was love a necessary preliminary to having an affair.
Besides, the Nazi leaders were gods and got what they asked for.

The trend the affair took is not known. We do know its
denouement. The Propaganda Minister hastily decided that
Ruth had to leave Germany. Was it that Frau Goebbels inter-
fered, or that Ruth demanded too much, or that she threatened

to tell? These questions are interesting but not relevant to the main story.

Ruth Kuehn had to get out of Germany. Goebbels, who was not really on good terms with Army or Navy Intelligence—they knew too much about him—turned to another quarter. One of his closest satellites was Dr. Karl Haushofer, son of the famous general and geopolitician. Father and son were in charge of the Geopolitical Seminar at Berlin University. The students of geopolitics graduated into the foreign service, principally into the spy organization under Foreign Secretary Ribbentrop.

General Haushofer was the man who had first welded the bonds between Germany and Japan. He was obligated to Goebbels for the incomparable prestige enjoyed by himself and his school of thought. If Goebbels wanted anything in Haushofer's power to grant, there was no further question about it.

Yes, Haushofer could use the young lady Ruth Kuehn. The old general, who had visited Japan and seen the possibilities there as early as 1914, was in constant contact with that country. Very recently his Japanese colleagues had expressed a need for white men and women. This was a new kind of white slave traffic. Japan's government through their liaison officers, the two Haushofers, requested the services of members of the white race to help in the Japanese espionage service.

Japan, in fact, needed a good many people for Intelligence work, and for many jobs native Japanese simply could not be used. Haushofer informed Goebbels that he had openings not only for Ruth Kuehn, but for her brothers and parents, provided they were intelligent and careful, and had a smattering of basic training.

It is not only theatrical blood that runs through a family. A flair for espionage is also inherited. In this case the entire family was involved and all, plainly, had a talent for it. Their background was unquestionably helpful.

The father, Dr. Kuehn, was born in 1895 in Berlin. When he was eighteen he enlisted in the Germany navy and served as a midshipman aboard an imperial cruiser in World War I. In 1915, when his ship was sunk in an encounter with a British battleship, he was taken prisoner and brought to England, where he quickly acquired the language.

When the armistice came, he was a young man without any real civilian profession. He re-entered the naval service of the German republic as an *Oberleutnant*. Six months later the German fleet was destroyed and he was stranded. They put his name down on the naval reserve list and he had to adjust to a civilian life.

Kuehn decided to take up medicine. He became a member of several chauvinistic officer organizations. Very early he espoused the Nazi cause.

He had trouble making a respectable living, for he proved no good as a doctor and was dismissed from several hospital posts. At last he accepted a position in the Gestapo under Heinrich Himmler, who was his personal friend. Long afterward Dr. Kuehn complained that the Gestapo had been unfair to him. He had been frequently promised a good job as police chief in one of the German cities. Instead, through the fault of his daughter, he was exiled to Hawaii.

American athletes were preparing for the Olympic games; Japan was a good customer for oil and scrap iron; the world had just come through the great depression and peace organizations were flourishing. This was the world picture when a German family landed in the Hawaiian Islands on August 15, 1935. They were not the usual run of giddy tourists. The father was a scientist, a trim, gray-haired professor. They were well-bred and handsome people. Doktor Bernard Julius Otto Kuehn came with his entire family, except his son Leopold, who remained in Berlin as Goebbels' secretary. With him was Frau Professor Friedel Kuehn, his six-year-old son Hans Joachim and his daughter Ruth. Ruth and the absent Leopold were not really his children but the children of his wife by a former marriage.

It was a well-knit family whose domestic life was a joy to behold. They were here because the father was interested in learning the Japanese language. Dr. Kuehn was also very much interested in the ancient history of the Hawaiian Islands. He traveled around, visiting the old stone houses of the early settlers. Very soon he knew the topography of the Hawaiian

Islands as well as he knew his own coat. He loved the seashore and all water sports, as did the whole family. They used to go swimming frequently, or they would hire a sailing and motor launch.

Friedel, his wife, was a commonplace sort of matron, but really extremely helpful. She could listen and observe details of military significance when to all appearances she was simply a housewife completely bound up in the care of her family.

Ruth, lithe and tall, made great headway with her English. She was a wonderful dancer and attended every important social affair. A constant guest at the naval and yachting clubs, she attracted scores of men much more handsome than her club-footed lover, Dr. Goebbels.

A family with such interests is fortunate in the possession of a commonplace matron who is beyond suspicion. Such a woman was Friedel, who traveled twice as a courier to Japan during the period 1935–41.

On political questions Dr. Kuehn would remark that he, personally, did not like the Nazis. He was, nevertheless, first and foremost a German. He wrote a number of articles on the early German settlers in the islands, and these were published in Germany.

Neighbors and acquaintances had the impression that the Kuehn family was very well off. Kuehn had some excellent investments in Holland and Germany. During his first three years on the islands, he received about seventy thousand dollars transmitted through a Honolulu bank by the Rotterdam Bank Association. On one of her trips, Friedel returned from Japan with sixteen thousand dollars in cash.

The FBI and American Army and Navy Intelligence have ascertained that during this period the family received over one hundred thousand dollars. There was undoubtedly more than that which simply has not been traced.

Considering the great expenses involved, espionage is certainly not so well paid as is commonly assumed. At the outset Intelligence work is limited to the reporting of gossip, information gleaned from naval and merchant marine men. Later on the espionage is directed against the officer class, especially if, like Ruth, the agent is clever, glamorous and desirable. But, with war drawing near, more and more was demanded of the loyal espionage worker.

Dr. Kuehn was in the service of two countries. Though General Haushofer had lent him to the Japanese, Kuehn undoubtedly worked for Admiral Canaris. Canaris had discovered that Kuehn was a very valuable man, not to be lightly dispensed with.

Copies of all the reports to Japan also had to go to Canaris. In consideration of this, Kuehn thought it reasonable to ask for more money. Besides, his appetite for high society life had sharpened, as had Ruth's.

Early in 1939, Dr. Kuehn decided that he definitely needed a quiet place to get on with his study of the Japanese language. He moved his family from Honolulu to Pearl Harbor. Now the Japanese Secret Service plan, for which he had been sent to the islands, began rapidly to take shape. Ruth established herself as a popular favorite among the young people and the wives of the Navy men. Unusually attractive herself, she had let it be known that she had a flair for the art of personal grooming. When she announced that she was opening a beauty shop, the enterprise was greeted with enthusiasm and assurances of the patronage of all her women friends. Despite the long planning behind this step, even Ruth was not prepared for its instantaneous success. Friedel, too, began to spend much of her time at the new shop. Daily both reported to the head of the family what they had picked up. This information was relayed out of the Hawaiian Islands by diplomatic couriers of the German and Japanese Consulates.

Then one day the Japanese Vice-Consul at Honolulu, sly little Otojiro Okuda, sent for Dr. Kuehn. Okuda told Dr. Kuehn that now was the time to get hold of some real marine information—exact dates, exact facts and figures on the United States Navy in the Pacific. He complimented Dr. Kuehn on his past work, but this job, he emphasized, was of another order. The Japanese would be willing to pay quite a bit more for the stuff, and it would mean a deadly blow against the United States Navy.

Kuehn agreed to take on the job for forty thousand dollars. Ultimately he was given only fourteen thousand dollars as an advance; the rest, he was promised, would be forthcoming after the "success."

Shortly after this conversation with Okuda, Dr. Kuehn began to take daily walks along the fortified sections of Pearl Harbor, accompanied by his young son, Hans Joachim, now ten, dressed in a child's model of the naval uniform. The father explained the waterfront scene to the child who was "just crazy about" every aspect of the American Navy. After a while the American sailors invited the boy on board a battleship, and pointed out some things about this wonderful giant toy. Dr. Kuehn, an alien, would never have been permitted on board such a ship, and he was far too clever to assume that he might evade regulations. So he allowed the boy to go alone.

Following these visits, Dr. Kuehn called on the Japanese Consul Okuda and told him that he had worked out a signal system. It was designed to transmit information on the number and kinds of American ships in Pearl Harbor, and on ship movements in general. The Consul suggested simplifying the code but agreed that it was practicable for signaling to the Japanese fleet.

Dr. Kuehn owned a small house in Kalama, a community located in Kailua, Oahu, very close to Pearl Harbor. Mrs. Kuehn went out to purchase a pair of eighteen-power Bausch & Lomb binoculars; this might be considered an unusual purchase for a commonplace matron to make, since such glasses are far too high-powered for ordinary purposes. Moreover, the high magnification made them very sensitive to vibration and necessitated their being used with a tripod or some other kind of rest. But nobody thought it suspicious. Ruth accompanied her mother and chattered, while they made the purchase, about how nice the instrument would be for trips in the sailboat.

The light signals were to be flashed from the dormer window. Kuehn, Consul Okuda and the fourth secretary of the Japanese Consulate, Tadesi Morimura, worked out a most practical code of lights. On December 2, 1941, they tried out their new system for the first time. On the same day, Vice-Consul Okuda received a written tabulation of the number, types and exact location of American ships in Hawaiian waters. The next day

Japanese Consul General Nagoa Kita, Okuda's superior, transmitted the data via short wave to the Japanese Naval Intelligence office.

All was now in readiness for the treacherous attack on Pearl Harbor.

Dr. Kuehn's dormer window was put to use on December 7, 1941. In Washington, peace negotiations were still going on when the Japanese launched their blow against the American fleet. Dr. Kuehn himself gave the light signals. The Japanese bombers hovered overhead, spreading devastation as they received all the necessary detailed information. Everything proceeded exactly according to the plans laid by Kita, Okuda and Kuehn.

But their plans in one respect went slightly awry. The Japanese Consul had arranged to have a Japanese submarine come to pick up the Kuehn family and bring them to Tokio. The Kuehns had planned the escape soberly. Nothing would have to be packed. They would leave even their toothbrushes behind and would bother with nothing but money. Moreover, once in Japan, the balance of twenty-six thousand dollars was due them on the deal.

But in spite of the chaos and disaster at Pearl Harbor, United States Intelligence officers spotted the lights coming from the window of Herr Dr. Bernard Otto Kuehn's house. Before the Japanese submarine arrived, Kuehn and his family were picked up by the authorities. The professor maintained an attitude of arrogance and blank denial. But all the evidence was against him. An outline of the signal system was found, and entirely too much money, some of it in Japanese currency. The binoculars were discovered, and copies of reports written in German. Dr. Kuehn finally admitted everything. He did his best, though, to shield his wife and daughter, and insisted that he alone was responsible for everything—without success. His family was interned for the duration.

On February 21, 1942, a court sentenced Dr. Kuehn to be shot. Nazis, once in prison, cease to be supermen. Kuehn began to be frightened. For years he had been in the service of German and Japanese Intelligence and now he offered his services to the Americans. They told him that he couldn't buy his pardon that way; the American government wanted no Nazi spies in its employ. The death sentence was signed. Kuehn found his lonely cell a madhouse. He had always been able to find a way out—but not this time.

He begged for mercy and promised to tell them all he knew about Axis espionage activities. Naturally, they made him no promises. What he told remains unknown, but his death sentence was commuted, on October 26, 1942, to fifty years at hard labor.

His son, Leopold Kuehn, who had remained behind with Goebbels, shared the general downfall of his family in another manner—death on the Russian front. Friedel Kuehn tried to commit suicide but was prevented. Beautiful Ruth was not present when her beauty shop was auctioned off.

CHAPTER XI

The "King of Belize," a Submarine Tipster

Two years before the onslaught on Pearl Harbor, the U.S. Naval Intelligence Department discovered a very rare book. No more than four copies had ever entered the United States. It was a handbook on Japanese espionage, written for the key agents of the *Nikonjunkai Hei,* the Japanese Secret Service. The copies were brought in by certain Japanese naval officers, for personal delivery to their men on the West Coast. A Los Angeles editor who has devoted his life to the task of tracking down enemies of his country made this notable discovery. The man was Joseph Roos, of the News Research Service, who, with the assistance of some members of the Korean underground, secured a copy of this highly interesting spy manual.

The book laid down rules for the conduct of espionage, and sketched the course the Japanese-American War was to take. Its outbreak, by the way, was confidentially stated to be near at hand.

Before the Japanese set up Miss Ruth Kuehn in her shop on the Hawaiian Islands, their spy manual had this to say about Hawaii:

"The occupation of Hawaii necessitates co-operation between Japanese army and navy. The ground must be laid by a preliminary capture of the Midway Islands, which would provide us with a good foothold. From them it is only one hundred and ten miles to Hawaii, a very convenient distance for our surprise fleet. This surprise fleet comprises mine layers of the type X, model 21. . . .

"Hawaii has about a hundred and fifty thousand Japanese, one half of whom are 'Nisei' (Japanese descendants of foreign citizenship). When news of Japanese naval victories reaches Hawaii, these Japanese will instantly rise up and organize a volunteer army. Without doubt, Hawaii will fall into our hands."

Well, Hawaii never did fall into Japan's hands. Except for the calamitous coup at Pearl Harbor, all Japanese fifth-column activities were foiled by the American Intelligence offices. They were amply forewarned of Japanese stratagems and goals by the spy manual which the enemy had naïvely drawn up.

The handbook not only gave diagrams for the conquest of Hawaii, but a careful exposition of the importance of seizing the Panama Canal. As events turned out, the Japanese did not get very far with either plan. Therefore all concealment can be dropped. The fact was that the espionage book devoted a complete chapter to the closing of the Panama Canal. The strategic importance of such a step was summarized in this way:

"The salient question is: What will become of the Panama Canal? Panama is a little over six hundred knots from Hawaii and about eight thousand knots from Japan; so an attack is not an easy matter, and requires a considerable naval force. If at the outbreak of the War we should proceed to attack and close the Canal, we would succeed in cutting off the Atlantic from the Pacific."

The Japanese agents in the Western Hemisphere were instructed to do their utmost to spin over the Canal Zone an unbreakable spy network. The Japanese designs reached very, very far. The spy manual continued:

"Japanese possession of the Panama Canal has a great bearing on the future peace; therefore by all means Japan must take the Canal and keep it *even after the War.*"

No Secret Service in the world could be more explicit and frank. For the Nipponese this War was a gamble involving their future existence as a power. However, they were not very astute gamblers. They seemed to have envisaged their opponents as sound asleep.

Japan knew perfectly well that the Panama Canal was heavily fortified. Nevertheless, both Germany and Japan had the naïve conviction that the Canal and the strip of country which is the Republic of Panama could be obtained through treason. They counted on the co-operation of a Panama President,* on bribed police chiefs and on purchased fifth columnists. But this War has taught one great lesson to the enemy's Intelligence offices, namely, they grossly overestimated the value of quisling help. They misunderstood the ways of the Anglo-Saxon mentality. True, the Axis was able to procure traitors, but they were too few to be very useful. Britishers and Americans could not be bought, and that was the great stumblingblock for Tokyo as well as for 14 Bendlerstrasse.

Combined German and Japanese energies wove a stout spy web around the Panama Canal. For a short time it looked formidable, but in the end its cords were snapped. The Nazis did their part by sending submarines into the Caribbean to paralyze the shipping of war matériel between North and South America. And the Canaris office provided the white agents the Japanese needed.

In 1939 Canaris presented Japan with one of his best men for work in the Canal Zone. This man's record is public knowledge now. For a long time, however, his subtle treachery deceived everyone.

---

* Arias, in exile in Argentina at the date of writing.

His career began in the last days of the disintegrating German Weimar Republic. At that time in Berlin there appeared a very liberal and socially conscious weekly. It was called *Berlin am Montag* (Berlin at Monday), since its edition came out on Monday when the other newspapers, due to the holiday on Sunday night, did not appear. Its editor declared himself a champion of human rights and put up a strong fight against the rising Nazi movement. The Nazis had already listed him among their *November-Verbrecher* (Criminals of the November, 1918, Revolution). Dr. Hans Wesemann, the courageous newspaper man, knew that he was doomed once the Nazis came in. But he stuck to his post.

The Nazis took over Germany and shackled the press. Wesemann was thrown into a concentration camp, as were other liberals, socialists, communists and church leaders.

After a year Wesemann was released. Absolutely penniless, he emigrated to Switzerland. He had undergone great suffering but he was not broken. He was eager to take up his career of writing once again. In Switzerland he had wealthy friends, the former owners and backers of his newspaper. They proposed starting a newsletter which would be translated into various languages and distributed to the world press and the democratic governments. This newsletter would expose the secret rearmament and war preparations of Nazi Germany. Wesemann suggested that the German refugees scattered all over the world should be called on to help. Many had found asylum in countries bordering on Germany and maintained various underground connections. Wesemann wanted to unite all of them and pool their information.

Among these refugees was one who possessed amazingly exhaustive information on the German war machine. His name was Berthold Jacob, a small fellow who wore a beard like Monty Woolley's. He had had to leave Germany as far back as 1929, for he had then exposed the fact that the "democratic German government" was secretly building military airplanes. His revelations were authentic and the military preparations were in defiance of the Versailles Treaty. However, he was charged with high treason and had to flee the country.

This little man was an old friend of mine. I had known him

in his good days and in his bad days. At the time, he and his wife lived in a tiny flat in Paris. They were so poor that they could not offer a visitor coffee. One evening I was with them and in whispers they told me the story of their association with Dr. Hans Wesemann.

A year before, in 1937, they had received a letter from Wesemann. The Jacobs were living in London and, like many political refugees, were having a hard time. This letter of Wesemann's, written from Basel, Switzerland, was a godsend. It offered an opportunity for Jacob to earn a decent living. Wesemann invited his friend Jacob to write for his forthcoming newsletter.

At this Berthold's wife broke in with an animated description of their difficulties. "We owed two months' rent. And we were utterly lost in the big city of London. Wesemann's offer came like manna from heaven. He called Berthold 'the man who knew more about secret German rearmament than anyone in the world.' He asked him to be editor, at fifteen pounds a week. Berthold was to go to Basel, where they would discuss all the details. Wesemann would send money for fare and traveling expenses."

It was understandable why Berthold Jacob should be offered this post. He was really an expert on the subject. My friend had come about his prodigious knowledge by a peculiar method. He was a great reader of newspapers. He was a subscriber to all the German-language papers published at the French, Belgian, Dutch or Czech borders. They were small-town or village newspapers, and in them my friend read chiefly the advertisements. He noted where laborers were wanted, where property was being bought, where concrete was sold, where building was going on. He was able to deduce the spots where the Nazis were building border fortifications. From newspaper ads in German papers he could tell where new airfields and factories were being built. The system was uniquely his own. Often it was based on wild guesswork, which nevertheless had a way of hitting the mark. He simply had a flair for the subject and he had applied himself to it for many years.

Berthold Jacob continued his story:

"Well, the money arrived, but it wasn't enough for me to

take my wife along. With some difficulty, I got my visa and
went to Switzerland. I saw little of the famous scenery, for the
meeting took place in Basel, which is on the frontier of Switzerland, bordering on France and Germany.

"Wesemann was there to greet me at the railway station.
He certainly was hearty in his welcome. I hadn't seen him
since I left Germany. We went to his hotel and had lunch
together, during which he explained the whole set-up. I was
to become the military affairs editor, while he would be the
managing editor. The newsletter would be prosperous enough
to buy information. I would have a large expense account,
which would cover subscriptions to as many publications as I'd
need for the work. I could also hire an assistant to help with
the research."

I watched Berthold's wife while her husband went on with
the tale. She seemed much younger than he, but then Berthold
looked old for his age. She was very thin and nervous, though,
and, as the story continued, her whole body expressed her inner
tension.

"That same evening Wesemann took me to one of those nice
little restaurants on the Rhine. I was happy. For the first
time since my exile I had a chance to do the work I loved. It
seemed that the publishers, two brothers who were financing
the newsletter, had invited us both to dinner. It was early
spring and the trees were breaking into buds of tender green.
The two publishers arrived, tall heavy men. Wesemann had
told me what they were like. They weren't the literary sort,
but good honest businessmen, with their hearts in the right
place, and strongly anti-Nazi.

"We had an excellent meal, with Rhine wine. I may have
taken a glass too much. We discussed future plans, but I became so tired that I couldn't think straight."

Here his wife interrupted again. "The scoundrels had
drugged him. They put him in a car, speeded him over the
border and had him in Germany."

"Yes, my dearest, but don't get excited. It's all over now,"
Berthold calmed her. "The newspapers all over the world reported my kidnaping. I was just telling Kurt how it came
about. . . . When I woke up, it was very cold. I was in a daze,

but my head gradually cleared and I realized what had happened. I was handcuffed and sitting in the back of a car between the two 'publishers.' A strange man was driving. My friend Wesemann was missing.

"I spoke. 'What's the matter?' I asked stupidly.

" 'Shut your mouth,' one of them said sharply.

" 'Where am I?' I asked, with constricted throat and pounding heart. But I already knew.

" 'In Germany,' the reply came, together with a stinging slap in the face."

Berthold Jacob had been shanghaied. He was brought to the Gestapo headquarters in Berlin. Canaris's men wanted to force the secret from him, for they were positive he had a definite source for all his information on Germany's rearmament. He was beaten and tortured—I saw the scars which remained.

The Nazis kept him for six months. Mrs. Jacob used her last money to wire the Swiss police and make desperate inquiries about her husband. The Swiss took Wesemann into custody and kept him as hostage for the kidnaped Jacob. The Swiss government behaved very courageously and threatened to bring the case before the Hague Court and the League of Nations. Their firm action made the Nazis release Berthold Jacob, who was sent back to Switzerland.

"Of course, I had to sign statements that I hadn't been mistreated in any way. They also told me that Germany's arm could reach me in England; that I had better keep quiet and discontinue my anti-Nazi activities."

Dr. Hans Wesemann stood trial in Switzerland for kidnaping. Democratic countries punish mildly; Wesemann was given a prison term of only four years.

My friends, the Jacobs, were in France at the time of Marshal Pétain's surrender. They fled to Spain, where they went into hiding. Since then I have heard nothing from them.

* * *

What became of Wesemann, the other principal? In 1939, a Dr. Heinrich Müller, German scientist and distinguished traveler, landed in the little Republic of Nicaragua. He was none other than Dr. Hans Wesemann, who had served his sentence and was now at liberty. He had a new passport, a new birth certificate and a new assignment.

The hard labor of the Swiss prison had changed him. He had grown pale, and had lost weight. But now he was more than a cold-blooded traitor; he was out for revenge. He was clay in the potter's hand, a docile tool of Admiral Canaris.

Wesemann was appointed spy chief at the Panama Canal. He worked for Germany and Japan, and collected a double salary. His accomplice was a Dr. Christian Zinsser, a hanger-on in Germany's Consulate in Honduras. The Consul of that legation met with sudden death, his body being found in a wild spot on top of a mountain. Only a few weeks before, Zinsser, who had been playing bloodhound, had found out that the Consul had some anti-Nazi associates. The accident that had befallen the Consul aroused suspicion and Zinsser had had to leave Honduras. Dr. Hans Wesemann thereupon took over his beat, while Zinsser went to Argentina. Wesemann now covered Costa Rica, Venezuela, Colombia and Honduras. He was a sort of regional director of the far-flung espionage aimed at the Panama Canal.

The German sanctuary was in Buenos Aires. When the War broke out, all the German agents who were in danger hastened to Argentina. From there they were safely transported to Japan.

Dr. Wesemann did not depart without leaving a worthy successor. He left with the sanguine feeling that Germany's espionage in the Caribbean was in good hands. The Axis sword still hung over the Canal Zone.

It took the U.S. Army's Caribbean Defense Command several years to hunt down Wesemann's mysterious successor. In the meantime the Nazis wrought grim destruction against Allied shipping in the Caribbean. The rate of sinkings sometimes reached twelve boats sunk in thirteen days, and once five vessels were sunk in a single day.

U.S. Naval Intelligence decided that something must be done rapidly. It was obvious that German submarines were being tipped off on Allied shipping. The problem was laid before a young American Intelligence officer named Allen.

Allen took his own plane down to British Honduras. He liked flying and was experienced, having previously been in the Air Corps. His plan was to confer with his British colleagues in Belize, capital of Honduras, and find out what they knew about harbor espionage around the Canal Zone.

He stopped a few days at one of Belize's cosmopolitan hotels. Upon preparing for his flight back to the Canal, he had reason to be grateful for his thorough technical training. He discovered that the plane had been sabotaged—parts of the motor had been removed and defective parts substituted. It was perturbing. Obviously someone knew about his mission and had tried to prevent it.

He could not leave until his plane was repaired. Meanwhile he returned to his hotel, intending to go later to the British War Office to report the sabotage.

Entering his hotel room, Allen was confronted by a scene of disorder. His bags had been ransacked and the contents flung on the floor. The locked drawer of the hotel-room desk had been smashed.

Allen called the British Intelligence, asking them to send someone over. He thought it best to stand guard in the room in the meantime. A British Secret Service man turned up and beheld the disorder. Both standing together in the room felt hemmed in by invisible enemies. The Axis was openly working in British territory close to the Panama Canal.

In the hotel room Allen and his friend discussed the situation. Allen suggested they have a drink. "To think better," he said. He stooped and took an unopened bottle of Scotch from the confusion his luggage was in. He poured out two glasses. A minute later, the Englishman had let his glass fall and had dropped to the floor. Allen rushed into the corridor and called for a doctor. The doctor's diagnosis was grim; the British officer had been poisoned. Paralysis set in from the hips down and lasted an entire day. Fortunately, Allen had not yet sipped his glass.

Allen was thoroughly shaken. The story spread through the hotel. All the native attendants wore the same expression, a faint ambiguous smile. Allen wondered if they were not all involved in the conspiracy. It was the merest chance that it had not been worse. He had escaped, and the Englishman recovered, for he had drunk very little.

Had the poison been put into the bottle when he bought it at the International Bar, where at night the girls danced their provocative dances? Had it been done in the hotel by the pillagers of his luggage? There was no time to solve this question. He had to smash the spy ring. The poisoners were somehow bound up with the spies who were signaling the submarines. All the puzzle would have to be solved at once.

* * *

For a time Allen's investigations made little progress. He learned, however, that many of the native laborers had a lot of money to spend. He also discovered that British Honduras was importing many workmen from the Republic of Panama. This fact was not in itself suspicious, since the War had created a serious labor shortage. The labor exchange was handled by a small employment agency, which was managed by a partnership of two brothers, the Gough Brothers, it was called. Contractors would ask for a number of laborers. The agency recruited them and they were transported to British Honduras by the ten small schooners which constituted the only passenger line. The line was owned by another Gough brother, one Captain George Gough. This Captain Gough was referred to as the King of Belize; he was Belize's greatest entrepreneur.

The projects must have paid well, for the laborers could pay seventy-five cents for a drink in the bars of Belize and Colón. Allen visited these bars and learned that Captain Gough owned them. They were tawdry little places, with plenty of low entertainment, from burlesque to Hawaiian dances. Rumors reached Allen that Gough ran a few low-class brothels for the seamen.

Gough certainly seemed to be a big shot in Honduras. But Allen characterized him as a big fish in a small pond. His enterprises were provincial and rather low. Allen took an instinctive dislike to him. He was annoyed to hear that Gough's boats were taking oil drums along on their runs. The United States had a serious oil shortage, and Honduras had no business being lavish with it. He reported the fact to the authorities at Panama, as well as to Naval Intelligence in Washington.

When one of Gough's boats put into port at Colón, a contingent of Canal Zone customs officials and FBI representatives was there to greet it. That was in April, 1942, and the inspectors were eager to find some evidence. They searched the boat for hours, during which crew and passengers were kept on board. No evidence of oil drums was found, but something else was. The searchers discovered among the effects of one of the seamen a copy of the plans of the Coco Sola Naval Airfield.

The sailor was arrested, but indignantly protested innocence. He had found the papers, he said, but he did not know what they were.

Whether lying or telling the truth, the sailor was only small-fry. The attention of the FBI focussed on his boss.

Captain Gough was not a certified captain. He was investigated and called up for a hearing first in British Honduras and later in Colon. He had not much to say. He admitted to having been a rum-runner, but for a long time he had been going straight, so he claimed. His money came in from the ten schooners and the cabaret business.

Eight secret detectives took several months to accumulate a few more details. They visited Gough's brothels and cabarets. They had intimate talks with the girls, paid them well and promised them immunity. They learned that:

1. Gough used short-wave sets to communicate with German submarines.

2. Gough sold the Germans black market gas and oil for the refueling of submarines.

Gough had managed it as easily as if he were selling groceries. Fuel had been provided for the enemy right under the noses of the Allied Secret Services. Gough was cunning, powerful in his little pond, and feared by the simple-minded natives whom he employed. His vessels had brought fuel oil to the hidden harbors used three centuries before by Caribbean buccaneers.

Warrants arrived from Lieutenant General Frank M. Andrews for the arrest of Gough and nineteen aides, from longshoremen to cabaret dancers. All were apprehended except the ringleader. Captain Gough, bootlegger, racketeer, white-slaver and arch-spy, had inexplicably escaped. Like the pirate that he was, he and a small crew had fled in one of his own vessels.

British and U.S. Navy Departments sent orders to all Allied naval patrol planes to look sharp for the pirate boat. An American plane spotted Gough's ship on its way to Argentina. The boat was ordered to stop, but paid no attention to the order. The plane glided down to land on the water. Gough's men were armed and a shooting battle seemed imminent. However, the pilot warned Gough that he had already signaled his position to Honduras. In a few minutes more planes would arrive. Gough, always a shrewd bargainer, surrendered. He was taken to Panama for imprisonment. Soon afterward the Caribbean was cleared of German submarines.

CHAPTER XII

A Screen of Twittering Canaries

The King of Belize, that outrageous and audacious entrepreneur, had still other sidelines. Bit by bit, the full pattern of his mysterious activities was pieced together by British and American Intelligence Services.

The FBI and G-2—the Military Intelligence Office—for a long time harbored suspicions against a person living in Cuba. He had all the behavior traits of a German, and was indeed a refugee, but he traveled on a passport from Honduras. After the Belize incident, the very mention of Honduras invoked thoughts of Captain Gough. The American agents naturally wondered if there might be a connection. It was a pure hunch. In spite of little evidence to go on, only a few months sufficed to have the hunch confirmed, and to identify a very important agent in the Western Hemisphere.

The holder of the Honduras passport was one Enrique Luni, who posed as a Honduras-born Jew. Nevertheless, he had lived a good part of his life in Rotterdam. After the invasion of Holland, he made a quick flight back to his natal continent, where he represented himself as a refugee who had lost all he had.

He wandered through all of Central America, applying to numerous refugee-aid committees. He accepted their offers of temporary charity and declared that he would soon be on his feet again.

Luni was a stout, tall man, with an unpleasant, puffed face, a dot of a mustache, thick eyebrows and hair which straggled down his neck. He might possibly have been taken for a Spaniard, and indeed he spoke Spanish very well, though his long sojourn in Holland had given him a trace of a Dutch accent.

Possession of a Honduras passport made traveling very easy. At this point we must anticipate and reveal that the passport had been provided by Captain Gough's spy ring. It had not been issued to Luni directly. The passport was an item in the collection of Inspector Paul Kraus, of the Hamburg Gestapo, and Kraus had outfitted Luni with it.

Luni had been one of the espionage students of Paul Kraus, the man who, the reader will remember, had recruited Bill Sebold for a course in radio espionage. After graduation from Kraus's sinister academy, Heinrich August Lüning, alias Enrique Luni, came to the New World.

Lüning was a native of Bremen, where he had lived all his life, and had a wife and a seven-year-old child. He had been engaged in Germany's export-import trade. Eventually the German *Auslandsorganization* (Foreign Trade Bureau) decided that it needed men with Lüning's business experience for "work of national importance." So in 1936 the *Auslandsorganization* transferred Lüning to the Dominican Republic, to the United States, to Panama and the Caribbean for "study." When he finally returned to Germany, he was ordered to Hamburg to be trained for the coming War.

Then, on the beautiful morning of September 29, 1941, the liner *Villa de Madrid* dropped anchor in Havana, Cuba. The boat brought many refugees who had secured visas just in time to escape deportation to the ghettoes and gas-chambers of Poland. Their relatives in the New World had paid fantastic sums to Cuban officials to obtain these visas. One of the passengers, who had ostensibly escaped by the proverbial skin of his teeth, was Enrique Luni. In his case, the saving factor was that by birth he was a citizen of Honduras.

He presented himself before the authorities and the refugee committee, to whom he told graphic tales of the German terror. He neglected to mention that he had three thousand dollars of United States currency with him. He went to live in a drab little room in the Havana Y.M.C.A. He intimated that he was hoping to make a trip to Honduras to look up some relatives who might set him up in some business or provide him with work.

True to his hint, he did find an employer in Belize, though Captain Gough was no relative of his. Between them, they drew up plans for a highly effective program of harbor espionage. The result was a deadly succession of blows against Allied shipping plying between Cuba and Florida.

Enrique Luni traveled hither and yon for several months, meeting other agents of Gough and of the departed Dr. Wesemann. In due time he returned to Cuba. All smiles, he reported his progress to the refugee committee. He had found a relative, an old uncle, who was willing to help him. Enrique Luni was to open a branch of his uncle's business in Havana. It would be a fashionable women's apparel and specialty shop.

Luni moved to a comfortable furnished room at Havana's Teniente Rey. He was eager to enjoy life. At last, after his harrowing experiences in Hitler's Europe, he was again safe and prosperous. It was natural that he should wish to make the most of it.

He was seen in many bars, night clubs and dancing spots. His taste seemed to run to the cheaper places, those frequented by seamen. One night chance led him to the New York Bar.

A stolid, stout man, he sat in a corner and listened to hot rhumbas and frenzied swing and watched others dance. Then Rebecca, an entertainer, came over to his table. She was a tall, slender Cuban girl, a lithe dancer but a rather poor singer. She made extra money by drinking with the sailors and entertaining the few landlubber patrons. Her task was to encourage their drinking; her incentive was the fact that ten per cent of the customers' liquor bill was paid to her.

Enrique knew this, but it did not dampen his feelings. He spoke to her about his shop, and indicated that he had plenty of money. If she would stay with him all night, he would pay her royally.

Rebecca became his steady mistress and Luni was consoled for the absence of his Bremen family. For a character in a spy story, Rebecca was most extraordinary. She turned out to be the most candid and faithful person Enrique had ever known.

It is not known how much she abetted his espionage activities. It may even be that she never knew anything about them. Rebecca was a simple, natural girl, and, when interrogated by Luni, she may well have innocently spouted the information concerning ship movements which she picked up from the sailors. Perhaps she had no suspicion that Luni was passing her information on to nearby Nazi submarines or to Captain Gough in Honduras.

The spy school in Hamburg had given no specific lesson in romance. Its students had been taught how to construct low-powered radio transmitting sets. Luni now bought part after part and the radio set in his room grew toward completion.

Along with the radio parts, Luni made a rather odd purchase. He bought a bird cage, and some bird seed, and a number of yellow birds. Erle Stanley Gardner, one of America's outstanding detective story writers, wrote a book about a murder case involving some canaries, but he did not foresee that singing canaries would one day be utilized for streamlined espionage.

We do not know whether Admiral Canaris recommended that Luni adopt the idea. The singing canaries chirped loud enough to drown out the ticking of Luni's secret broadcasts. Furthermore, when the landlady wanted to come in to clean the room or, as is a landlady's way, just for a bit of conversation, Luni had a pretext for stalling her off. He would cry out behind the locked door that he could not open it immediately. He had let one of his beloved canaries free in the room, where it was flying about. Luni begged the visitor or landlady to wait a minute until he retrieved it.

He would utilize the next few minutes to stow his transmitting set into a suitcase. Then, somewhat dishevelled and panting, Don Enrique would open the door, still holding the long wand and the little net, and he would smile and puff happily at having caught the bird.

For a long time he worked quite by himself. He knew no one whom he could trust. He reported what he had gathered and what was told to him by Rebecca.

His shop, too, had to be looked after. He was, it seemed, a diligent businessman. Daily he wrote twenty letters or more to various import and export firms all over Latin America. He asked about different merchandise and the shipping possibilities. He ordered small lots of this and that, and inquired when he could expect to receive the lading. When would the goods, for which he was impatient, leave the port of origin, and by what boat would they go? He wrote to American firms as well. They were harmless business inquiries. Nevertheless, the U.S. postal censors carefully scrutinized his letters, as did the British. Some trivial details looked a little irregular.

The American postal censors learned some facts which the Cuban government had not learned. Every so often a well-known bank in Boston sent Luni fifteen hundred dollars in American currency; the money was supposed to be a dividend on a patent which Luni had once sold to an American firm.

FBI operatives were by now highly interested in the case of the Havana merchant from Honduras. They did some digging in the archives of the Patent Registration office in Washington. After many hours, they were able to report to J. Edgar Hoover that no inventor by the name of Enrique Luni was listed in the U.S. Patent Office.

Now that Luni had been caught in a lie, the FBI had a sound pretext for informing the Cuban government of its suspicions. The police in Havana was informed of these points:

1. No relative of Luni's had been found in Honduras.

2. Luni was possibly in contact with the Panama spy ring.

3. The FBI held letters of Luni's full of suspicious questions about ship movements.

4. Counter-espionage agents had detected low-powered radio communications issuing from Cuba to Nazi submarines.

The Cuban police, dressed in their dashing uniforms, made an early-morning call on the rooming house of the Teniente Rey. Summarily, Captain Foyet, of the Cuban Intelligence Service, asked for Luni's room. He pounded on the door. Luni asked in sleepy bewilderment who it was, for it was not yet seven in the morning. "Open the door" was Captain Foyet's harsh command.

Luni heard the voices and heavy footsteps; he knew that it was the police calling. It was too early to put on the escaped canary act. In his pajamas he came to the door.

The police officers did not pause to speak to him. They made a rapid search of the room, confiscating all papers and taking possession of every book. They searched the closets and the bed. They shook out the pockets of his suits. They found nothing amiss.

Luni pretended great irritation. "You'll have to account for this. I will inform my consul right away. This is outrageous. You haven't even a search warrant."

At this, they displayed their search warrant. They asked him to dress and accompany them to his specialty shop. That, too, was to be searched.

Luni's indignation knew no bounds. He announced that he was going to phone the Honduran Consul, but found that the legation was still closed.

There was nothing for it but to be driven in the police car to his store. He still continued to protest. "What are you accusing me of, Captain Foyet? You found nothing in my room and you'll find nothing in my store."

"We'll see about that," said the captain. "If everything is as it should be, you've got nothing to worry about."

They proceeded to search the store. The police took pains not to damage any of the goods. Yet, search as they might, they found nothing incriminating. Luni's character was cleared. The FBI accusation seemed to be an unfortunate mistake.

But, just before the police were about to leave, the captain suggested taking a look in the cellar. Luni, in a great flurry, assured them that there was nothing down there. They nevertheless descended and came upon some spare radio parts. Then they found the suitcase containing the transmitter.

The FBI had guessed right. Havana had been the seat of flagrant espionage.

* * *

The Cuban prison was a pretty uncomfortable place. Now, penned within its thick stone walls, Luni recovered his calm. He recognized that the game was up. He made a clear and comprehensive confession.

He commenced by giving his real German name. Heinrich August Lüning freely admitted his responsibility for the torpedoing of numerous boats going between Florida and Cuba. He acknowledged his connection with agents in Panama and Honduras. He told about the training he had undergone in Hamburg. His family in Germany had received a regular allowance from Admiral Canaris. His fifteen hundred dollar payments came from a fund deposited by Canaris in a Boston bank before the War. Lüning requested that the money remaining to him in Cuba be passed on to his wife and child, who knew nothing of his guilty work.

He made no other plea. Five judges of Cuba's Supreme Court sentenced him to die before a firing squad. Lüning behaved with exceptional dignity. He stated that he was a German patriot and a believer in Nazism, who felt that his death was but a small incident of the War, like the death of a soldier.

Lüning was led back to the two-hundred-year-old Spanish fortress, the Castillo Principe. He asked to see Rebecca before he died. This request was denied, as was his counsel's last-minute plea for mercy from President Fulgencio Batista.

But Rebecca guessed that he would want to see her. On the eve of the execution, she waited all night before the prison gates. But Lüning's last pathetic request to see her was once more turned down.

Early in the morning Lüning quietly asked for a glass of orange juice and a cigar. These he received. Two priests, an officer and eight men marched him to the place of execution. As they passed through the corridors of the ancient fortress, Lüning saw his coffin, waiting to receive the body. It was made of a plain gray wood.

Witnesses say that Lüning became very pale. His steps faltered and, turning to the officer, he asked: "In Cuba gray coffins are for women, aren't they? Aren't men buried in dark ones?"

The officer dropped his eyes and did not answer. The question had been asked loudly, for all to hear.

They arrived at the courtyard. Lüning was led to the wall. A corporal wanted to blindfold him, but he composedly said, "Never mind; I don't want it."

The soldiers raised their rifles, the priest gave Lüning the crucifix to kiss and the order broke upon the sunlit morning: "Fire!"

Lüning was dead. It was the first execution for espionage in the history of Cuba.

Outside the Castillo Principe, Rebecca waited, and followed the cart bearing the coffin to the Potter's Field. Next morning she left a cheap wreath on the spy's grave.

CHAPTER XIII

The Nazi Spy Web in Denmark

THERE was a star agent in Admiral Canaris's great cast of spies. Just as history may say that Canaris was unsurpassed in the organization of espionage, so it may say that Horst von Pflugk-Hartung was unsurpassed as an individual agent. Beside him, people like Captain Gough, Mademoiselle Docteur, Mata Hari and Dr. Kuehn shrink to insignificance.

He deserves a book rather than a chapter. No one, as a matter of fact, would enjoy such a book more than Pflugk-Hartung himself. He is egotist and ironist par excellence. Picture him as a distinguished man of about fifty-five. His dark hair is graying at the temples. He resembles a professor, a diplomat or a scientist—anything but a Secret Service man. His manners are impeccable. He is a great man with the ladies, and women swarm about him. They are for the most part his sub-agents.

In addition to German, English and French, he speaks the three Scandinavian languages. Canaris knew him from far, far back. They fraternized in Spain during the First World War, when Pflugk-Hartung worked with Canaris on his manifold projects. Pflugk-Hartung was also a navy man, discharged in 1918 with the rank of lieutenant commander. He came from a celebrated family, his father having been an outstanding Prussian historian, the official authority on the kings of Prussia. Yes, Pflugk-Hartung was the inheritor of the purest Prussian tradition, the Junker in fullest flower. War and militarism ran in his blood.

When his Kaiser was deposed in 1918, Pflugk-Hartung refused to transfer his allegiance to the Republic. Instead, he organized the intransigent Free Corps, which took the law into its own hands and murdered many revolutionaries. Pflugk-Hartung was personally responsible for the death meted out to Rosa Luxemburg, founder of Germany's Communist Party and friend of Lenin. He shot her, and with his men pitched the body into the Landwehr Canal which flowed just opposite Bendlerstrasse, where Canaris resided at the War Department.

Pflugk-Hartung was arrested, and stood trial for the murder; he was acquitted by the judge, a man who was to become Supreme Court Judge under Hitler. The Communists, however, did not easily forget the pitiless murder of their beloved leader. They swore to avenge her. And vengeance was attempted, but upon the wrong man. In 1921 a bomb was thrown at a car in Frankfurt am Main. But the body which was hurled into the air was not Horst von Pflugk-Hartung's but his brother's.

Branded as a murderer despite his acquittal, Pflugk-Hartung found the Weimar Republic a closed world to him. He emigrated, first to Holland, then to Sweden. But, German or emigré, he was always preoccupied with the same obsession—the *guerre de revanche* against the Allies and the Weimar Republic.

He remained in obscurity until 1930, when the Swedish police clapped hands on him at his fashionable estate near Saltsjö-baden in the Stockholm archipelago. The arrest was made by Commissioner Torsten Söderström, zealous anti-Nazi, who was to handle the case of the beautiful pacifist, Greta Kainen, a few years later. Pflugk-Hartung's crime was organizing the smuggling of ammunition from Germany.

The Swedish police had halted some boats near the harbor of Kalmar. By the bright moonlight the police boats were as usual intent on hunting bootlegging boats from Estonia and Finland. Sweden's modified prohibition makes bootlegging of liquor and spirits a profitable racket.

This time the Swedish water police had nabbed a ship which contained, instead of barrels of vodka and aquavit, a hold full of brand-new machine guns and revolvers—several tons of them.

The police had no difficulty in tracing the origin or the destination of the stuff. The German Nazis were sending the weapons to a kindred organization in Sweden, headed by a Colonel Munck. The man who got the commission for having arranged the sale was Lieutenant Commander Horst von Pflugk-Hartung.

The arms were intended for insurrection against Sweden's democratic government. His complicity proved, the Herr Kapitän-Leutnant was deported. Since the trial had exposed his Nazi connections, he could not very well return to democratic Germany.

He drifted farther north to Norway. The Norwegian police were acquainted with his character. Copies of his record were in their files and he was asked to leave the country as soon as possible. Pflugk-Hartung complied, but not before he had met two sympathetic spirits in Norway. One was Vidkun Quisling, whose name was to become synonymous with traitor in all the languages of the world. The other was to be Quisling's future director of police—Jonas, alias "Judas," Lie. Pflugk-Hartung passed their names on to Admiral Canaris as people he could count on.

Now Pflugk-Hartung repaired to Copenhagen, where his friends in the German War Department had arranged an easy berth for him. He was to be representative of the famous *Berliner Börsenzeitung* in Denmark. Murderer, spy and ammunition smuggler, he was now metamorphosed into a foreign cor-

respondent. Like all other journalists, he was admitted to the
Foreign Correspondents' Club, where I had the dubious pleasure of meeting him.

As soon as Hitler took power, Canaris was transferred to a
more resplendent office, and Horst von Pflugk-Hartung received
a notable, though secret, appointment. It was, of course, not
made public that he had been named chief of all espionage in
Scandinavia.

At first he had only a few aides. But to cover the long coastline of the northern countries he found he had to enroll more
and more agents in his sinister service. By 1940 he had mar-
shalled seven hundred and fifty assistants. They ranged from
harbor pilots to fishermen, from shipowners to lighthouse keep-
ers. No harbor or seaside village in Norway, Sweden or Denmark lacked its spy for Pflugk-Hartung. Pflugk-Hartung
installed powerful observation instruments in the German consulates and paid agents for photographs of the southern Swedish
fortifications. No boat went by the Gulf of Bothnia, or the
Skagerack or Kategatt, without its passage being known to
Pflugk-Hartung and his superior, the Admiral.

During this period many thousands of German political refugees escaped to Denmark. The head of the Danish Alien
Squad, Max Pelving, was wonderfully situated to handle those
refugees, and Pflugk-Hartung selected him as a sub-agent. Pelving received thousands of kroner from Pflugk-Hartung for his
co-operation. The refugees were called up for hearings, in
which Max Pelving questioned them closely about their relatives and political associates in Germany. Copies of the hearings were delivered to Pflugk-Hartung and forwarded to Berlin.

Later, in 1938, Admiral Canaris suggested that Pflugk-Hartung pay a call on a certain lawyer, whom the Admiral thought
was an excellent prospect. The man had desirable connections
with high society and the government. He was Eiler Pontoppidan, the celebrated, dynamic and hideously ugly lawyer.
Pflugk-Hartung and Pontoppidan understood each other instantly. The attorney was interested in big money. For the
right price, he could manipulate matters as no one else could.
Denmark's worst criminals had been saved from prison by the
lawyer's clever court orations. They were now at his beck and

call. If Pflugk-Hartung wanted daring jobs done, Pontoppidan knew the men to do them.

A few weeks after their talk, Pontoppidan applied for incorporation papers on behalf of a rich client of his. The Continental Radio Corporation was established and set up a modern office at the Vesterport in the heart of Copenhagen. Continental was going to deal in exclusive but profitable commodities. It would handle Dutch and American radio sets. The German *Telefunken* radio would not be handled; the firm held to the policy of boycotting German goods. The directors emphatically would not do business with Hitler, and they told their occasional customers that.

Of course, the real clientele knew better. For the real clientele were receiving *Telefunken* transmitters and receiver sets to be delivered to the harbor spies in all the Scandinavian countries. The sets were concealed inside innocuous-looking radio cabinets. Small boats brought them to Denmark from points near the island of Rügen and the Frisian Islands.

Pontoppidan recommended two excellent technicians named Kyrre and Rambov to Pflugk-Hartung's radio outfit. They were electronic engineers for whom the most difficult technical problems were child's play. The men were really very clever; they tapped the telephone cable leading to the office of the Russian Trade Delegation. For, by an odd chance, the latter had its office in the same building which the Radio Corporation had chosen.

For about six months the Nazi Secret Service listened in on every one of the telephone calls of the Russian Trade Delegation. Continental Radio enjoyed a small volume of business. It was an eminently respectable firm and its imported radio sets gave full satisfaction. The technicians were certainly competent men.

They were, as a matter of fact, so competent that they attached lead wires to the telephone of the Refugee Club in Copenhagen. The club had among its members some who were in regular contact with the German Communist underground, men who grapevined information into and out of Naziland and smuggled in illegal literature.

* * *

Pflugk-Hartung had many dangerous schemes, but he felt singularly safe, since Max Pelving was in the police force and would give due warning of impending trouble. Trouble came, as was inevitable.

Through his telephone espionage, he learned that the majority party of Denmark, the Social Democratic Labor Party, was in possession of evidence that might endanger him. It related to all the German agents in Scandinavia; the party had sent copies of the exposé to their sister parties in Sweden and Norway.

Pflugk-Hartung now brought all his resources into play. Pontoppidan was told to provide his men and proceeded to rally a number of his former gangsters who had drifted into the Danish Nazi Party, headed by Dr. Fritz Clausen.* The Danish Nazis were sent to rifle the Social Democrats' office at the Rosenörns Allé. Police Chief Pelving was told what was afoot. He saw to it that no police would be in the vicinity that night.

The thugs were ordinary criminals, not experienced spies. They could not distinguish which documents were the right ones. Therefore they carted off as many papers as they could carry.

Naturally they left the office in extreme confusion. The Social Democratic Party had a strong suspicion of the identity of the burglars and the precise papers they were looking for. Moreover, they suspected the correspondent of the *Börsenzeitung* on general principles. Still, he could not be expelled from the country without its being an affront to Denmark's powerful neighbor. The Danes therefore seasoned their indignation with discretion. It was better, they reasoned, to harbor a known spy than to exchange him for an unknown one. Pontoppidan went about in his suave social circle undetected. But Max Pelving and his superior, Police Chief Andreas Hansen, were now definitely suspect.

With the documents in his possession, Pflugk-Hartung once more felt perfectly safe. He seized the occasion for putting over

---

* Dismissed in 1944 by Hitler for the crime of assaulting a German nurse. Arrested in 1945 by the Danish Government.

one of his most audacious coups. He sent one of his agents to the Island of Bornholm, a famous summer resort, which attracted tourists from all over the world. It was, in addition, strategically important.

The War had already begun. But this was the period of the "Sitzkrieg" and life was still comparatively unaffected. The Island of Bornholm was the site of many summer estates belonging to high administrators and members of the government who had no inkling of the coming invasion.

One day an advertisement appeared in the local paper of Rönne, the island's largest town. A chauffeur was wanted by the wife of Danish Admiral Türck. Her former chauffeur had met with an accident.

Nothing could have seemed more natural than this accident. Nevertheless, there were elements of artifice. Pflugk-Hartung alone knew how the accident to the chauffeur had come about. He also knew just exactly who the new applicant for the position would be.

A sun-tanned, athletic young man in white flannels applied for the job. He was a student, he said, and his summer earnings must pay for his tuition. He came from Schleswig and his name was Ernst Grüber. The admiral's wife engaged the young fellow. She soon decided that he was too clever to be a chauffeur and asked him to be her private secretary. Soon after that, he was given the post of private secretary to Admiral Türck.

Of course, the admiral and his wife did not know that the engaging young man made duplicates of the admiral's reports. He jotted down notes on the strength of the Swedish and Danish fleet, and on Scandinavian aircraft production. He sketched the location of mine fields. Last but not least, he scanned reports of conferences between agents of the British and Danish Secret Services, who were concerned with smashing German naval espionage. All these papers were open to the eyes of Pflugk-Hartung's spy.

The shadow of the War lengthened, and Denmark began to fear invasion. Pflugk-Hartung's harbor espionage was unleashing torpedoes against tens of thousands of tons of shipping.

The King of Denmark, liberal and courageous Christian X, wished to purge the country of the spies.

At this point, the Russian Secret Service reared itself for a blow. Officially still allies of Nazi Germany, the Russians were actually engaged in a bitter struggle against them.

One of Laurenti Beria's ablest agents, bald, massive Ernst Friedrich Wollweber, had a sudden flash of enlightenment. Surprisingly enough, he too had quarters in the building which lodged both the Continental Radio Corporation and the Russian Trade Delegation. To all intents and purposes, Wollweber was an engineer of the engineering firm A. Selo and Co. Wollweber had overheard German words from behind the door of the Continental Radio Corporation. He had a hypersensitive ear for just such things. His clumsy thumb stroked his lower lip and he speculated on tapping the wires of the radio company. But his suspicions were more drastically confirmed. He caught sight of Pflugk-Hartung entering their office. He would have recognized Pflugk-Hartung anywhere.

Wollweber instantly ordered the wires of the radio company tapped. What a surprise! In their work his technicians uncovered the lead wires to the Russian Trade Delegation. Wollweber saw the humor of the situation. This triangular game was going to get still more amusing, but he himself would not be a victim. Wollweber always strictly avoided using a telephone.

The Russians soon had evidence enough to blast the German espionage ring in Denmark to the skies and they had strong personal motives for wishing to do so, for Nazi harbor espionage was spying against Russian shipping. But they were in a difficult diplomatic position. Their sham friendship with the Germans rendered impossible any overt act such as calling in the police. A courier went to Moscow to consult with Laurenti Beria.

Laurenti Beria made some bland suggestions. The Soviets must abide by their alliance with their new-found German friends. But a discreet double-cross would be possible.

The British Secret Service in Denmark was represented by one man, experienced, foxy, old, but still only one against seven hundred and fifty enemy agents. Wollweber put his information in the way of the British. *They* would go on from there.

With real dismay the British discovered the truth about the Radio Corporation. Not knowing that the clues had been furnished them by the Soviets and anxious to bend the Soviets their way, the British made a friendly gift of their information. Did the Russians by any chance know that their Nazi allies were spying against them? Beria and Wollweber must have suppressed laughter with difficulty. They appreciated the meaning of the gesture, if not the information given, and indeed it marked the beginning of real co-operation between the future allies.

The British now handed the Danes conclusive anti-Nazi evidence, which the bribed police chief had so singularly failed to find. A sudden coup trapped thirty of the seven hundred and fifty Nazi agents in Denmark. Pflugk-Hartung was among them.

Police experts commented that the wire-tapping had been so clever a job that under normal conditions it would never have been discovered. As for Max Pelving and Pontoppidan, there was enough evidence to damn them twice over. The police found a contract between Pflugk-Hartung and the lawyer agreeing to render mutual assistance in espionage. Certainly such a brazen pact is unique in the history of espionage.

Pelving turned state's evidence, but that did not save him. Sentences ranging from one to eight years were handed down. Pflugk-Hartung, as head of the ring, got the maximum sentence of eight years.

This trial took place early in 1940. In three months the Germans were to invade. Fear already enveloped the land. The Danes were so afraid of German reprisals that they offered amnesty to every one of the spies, provided they would leave the country.

Only one, Pflugk-Hartung, rejected the offer. He preferred to remain in prison. The eccentricity is now explained. In the same Copenhagen prison were confined some agents of the Russian Secret Service. Pflugk-Hartung could not sacrifice this golden opportunity. Behind prison bars, he could prepare his revenge against Wollweber. The love of espionage was the profoundest instinct of his being.

Moreover, he was confident that his prison term would have a speedy termination. And he was right. In three months the Nazi troops invaded Denmark and Norway.

April 9, 1940, was a day of sardonic satisfaction for Pflugk-Hartung. Three German army cars rode up to the prison of Copenhagen. Hangman Heinrich Himmler made a brisk entrance. He emerged with his friend Pflugk-Hartung, who was not only free, but had risen in the world. Himmler had brought him a new uniform, in which he was now dressed. He was an SS Colonel. They drove through the deserted boulevards of occupied Copenhagen. Pflugk-Hartung saw the fruition of his work.

The master agent was now needed in fresh fields. He was sent to Rumania for espionage against the Russians in the Ploesti oilfields. He stationed an invisible regiment of Nazi agents in Bessarabia, while he himself worked more or less publicly among the dissolute pro-Nazi high society of the country. Prominent on his new staff was a woman of sixty. She was the notorious Mademoiselle Docteur who had dominated this region in the First World War. This was officially reported by members of Scotland Yard.

Pflugk-Hartung became a Balkan expert; he organized counter-espionage against Russia on a broad scale.

When Rumania surrendered and accepted the Russian armistice terms, Pflugk-Hartung headed the Russian list of German war criminals in Rumania. But the fox had fled; a Fokke-Wulf plane brought him safely to Berlin where he was attached to Admiral Canaris's personal staff.

But Laurenti Beria had not forgotten him and the Russians were waiting . . . waiting.

CHAPTER XIV

The King of Saboteurs

WHO was Wollweber? What manner of man was this adroit spy who put Pflugk-Hartung behind bars and exposed the Nazi ring in Denmark without implicating himself or his government? He was a man of parts, was Ernst Friedrich Wollweber—so many parts, in fact, that many called him the mystery man of Europe. For ten years he was hunted by nearly every police force on the Continent, and for ten years he outwitted the police with an ease that made their best efforts seem clumsy and ridiculous.

He also outwitted Canaris, as the incident in Denmark indicates. Walter Wilhelm Canaris knew that Wollweber was a good German Communist who fancied himself the Robin Hood of our time. In fact, Canaris knew a great deal about Wollweber; he had volumes of reports dealing with the man—but still could not catch him. And Canaris tried hard.

Ernst Friedrich Wollweber's birthplace was Hamburg; he was a German who knew his fellow-countrymen well enough to outwit them. His early youth had been a hard one, typical of the German proletariat. He was one of many children; his father was a drunkard; and he knew only too well what near starvation was. Struggle and privation were the commonest of his experiences. While a mere boy he ran away to sea to escape the misery and dullness of his home life. Hungry for adventure, he shipped to South America. As a sailor, he soon became active in the labor movement. In World War I he served in the German navy. He became one of the militants in Rosa Luxemburg's *Spartakus Bund,* which organized the revolution.

Wollweber it was who dared to be the first man to hoist the red flag on an Imperial ship, after others had been shot in the attempt. For this deed he was lauded as the hero of the *Wasserkante,* the waterfront. He continued during the revolution to be among the most outstanding of the Communists. In consequence he was elected a Communist deputy to the Reichstag.

The part of legislator was not congenial to him. His nature craved direct action and it was not to his liking to sit dressed up in the chamber of the parliament and deliver speeches. Wollweber returned to the sea.

Once more he achieved notoriety by an odd escapade. He roused the crew of his boat to mutiny against their captain. The mutineers took charge of the boat and brought it from the North Sea to Murmansk. The young Communist rebels wished to offer the vessel as a present to the new Communist workers' and farmers' state.

The journey was quite a feat of seamanship, for they reached their goal without the help of charts. In recognition of his services, embarrassing though this last one was, Lenin appointed Wollweber chairman of the International Seaman's Union. This union had locals all over the world, and its seafaring members may be called the first couriers of the Soviet Secret Service.

Wollweber shipped to China and Japan, to France, Italy and the Americas. He knocked about all parts of the world and in the end nothing surprised him. He was repeatedly arrested for Communist activities and for his inquisitiveness about the big harbors of the world. Arrests, too, came to be all in the day's work. *"Lumpenhunde,"* he would say to his friends, "the dogs, they arrested me again." Promptly on being released he would return to his old ways.

By the time Hitler came to power Wollweber was the most logical person to take over espionage against hostile Germany. He headed the Western European division of the Russian counter-espionage organization. His formal title was "Secretary of the Western European Office of the Communist International."

He chose Copenhagen as his headquarters. We have already mentioned his role as an engineer of the bogus firm of A. Selo and Co. Jan Valtin, author of that startling best-seller, *Out of the Night,* worked in the same office and describes in his book how Wollweber operated in his secret headquarters in Copenhagen. Valtin gives a vivid picture of the office:

"They occupied a flight of seven rooms on the third floor. The atmosphere there was that of a prosperous engineering firm. A score of typists, guards and translators, in shifts remained continuously on duty. The guards—Scandinavians, Latvians and Poles—were armed with fountain pens filled with tear gas. A system of warning buzzers had been built into the walls. Conspicuous was only the complete absence of telephones. All messages were dispatched by courier. Aside from the front office, the home of the Westbureau was divided into six departments. . . . It was but one of nine offices which the Communist International and the OGPU maintained in Copenhagen."

The Copenhagen "engineer" was only one of Wollweber's motley disguises, and the number of his aliases was very great. Police files have him listed under a vast variety of names, from Anton to Spring, Summer, Winter, Schultz, Müller, Andersen and Mathieu. His ability to appear and disappear seemed almost occult.

All the time, his physical traits were unmistakable. He is no mighty figure of a man; in fact, he is barely five feet tall and weighs two hundred pounds. Jan Valtin called him "short and burly. His thin hair was combed to cover a bald spot on his head. He had chunky hands, a hard round forehead and a thick straight mouth. His chunky face was of an unhealthy color, and the expression on it was the most saturnine I had ever seen. It denoted power, patience, ruthlessness, distrust. But the really outstanding feature in this man were his eyes— unblinking, glistening slits without a trace of white. . . . When Wollweber spoke, each word seemed to come out in a slow sullen growl. He gave the impression of being a man who was never in a hurry, who was utterly without fear, whom nothing could surprise and who had stripped himself deliberately of all illusions."

He drinks at least ten bottles of beer a day, without getting at all drunk. He has never had a fixed residence or anything resembling a home, but women have always been available to him, as assistants and lovers. No one of his many women has ever betrayed him. He is prodigal with his romances, for he is a believer in free love. He cites Danton and Marat, the great leaders of the French Revolution, as precedents. "Revolutionaries need plenty of women," he explains.

Wollweber is proud to serve Stalin and is still prouder of

being a proletarian. He hates theories and the elaborate theoretical basis of Marxism makes him impatient. "If less books had been written about the revolution, it would have come all over the world by this time," he is wont to declare. But while he is temperamentally an anarchist or nihilist, he obeys Stalin and Laurenti Beria. He will obey no one else, and he is utterly unable to subordinate himself to others.

For years he worked as he pleased in Denmark. Then Pflugk-Hartung muscled in. Pflugk-Hartung thought it a brilliant stroke to pay Police Chief Max Pelving for copies of the private Danish police records. Wollweber went him one better by employing the charwoman of the police offices as his agent.

When Pflugk-Hartung spied against Russian shipping in the Baltic, Wollweber countered by direct action. German boats which left Denmark loaded with ammunition and food shipments for the Fascist side in the Spanish Civil War never reached the Iberian peninsula. Sticks of TNT were mixed into the ship's coal, and an explosion took place on the high seas. The mysterious cause of the explosion was never divined, for the boats had been carefully inspected before they left Copenhagen harbor.

After the invasion of Denmark the German troop ship *Marion* left Denmark bound for invaded Norway. Four thousand Nazi soldiers were on board; not one reached his destination. Once more the fuel had been adulterated with TNT. There was a gruesome sequel. For several days thereafter, fishermen's nets were laden with German corpses. The German Consul in Malmö, Sweden, paid 75 cents to Swedish fishermen for each body.

These explosions were always ascribed by the Germans to Wollweber. A year after the invasion of Denmark, the Germans in Copenhagen arraigned some aides of Wollweber. The trial was held in the *Landsretten* on July 7, 1941. To six of Wollweber's aides the sum total of fifty-nine years' imprisonment was meted out. But the ringleader and chief saboteur, Wollweber, was conspicuously absent. The court made it known that he was wanted on charges of blowing up sixteen German, three Italian and two Japanese ships. Thus the destruction of twenty-one Axis ships can be credited to this man.

The Nazis slavered for his blood. For years Canaris and the Gestapo office advertised high rewards for the capture of Wollweber, alive or dead. But Wollweber's whereabouts were hard to discover, and, once discovered, the bird was invariably found to have flown.

Paul Kraus, the Hamburg Gestapo chief who ensnared Bill Sebold and who trained Heinrich August Lüning, finally conceived a plan for kidnaping Wollweber. Kraus engaged a man who knew exactly where Wollweber was to be found. This man was languishing in a German concentration camp; his name was Robert Krebs, better known as Jan Valtin. Inspector Kraus had Valtin released from the camp. He then induced Valtin to join the Gestapo; Valtin himself has vividly described the means employed. Together, Valtin and Kraus * went to Copenhagen.

As a former trusted Communist agent Jan Valtin knew every hideout of Wollweber's men. The trap seemed perfect—even before it was sprung, the Nazis began to gloat. On a dark night, the Nazi kidnapers lay in ambush near the shore of Helsingör on the Baltic coast in Denmark. Wollweber was due to pass. His headquarters were close. He would be overpowered, put in a Gestapo car and spirited away to Germany. Pflugk-Hartung had arranged all details and there would be no police interference. The unforeseen quirk was that the new-made Gestapo member, Jan Valtin, had contrived to warn his old boss Wollweber. The German ambushers were given a severe beating on the deserted street by some of Wollweber's men. The next day, Ernst Friedrich Wollweber arrived by plane in Moscow, rather than in Hamburg. Jan Valtin, for his part, fled; after many adventures he finally reached the United States and later served in the U.S. Army.

* * *

After the fall of Norway and Denmark, the Wollweber League moved to the safer precincts of Sweden. Report has it that Wollweber lived in an apartment near the Stureplan of Stockholm. He never went out of doors except for a few hours

* Kraus was arrested on the streets of Oslo several days after the liberation of Norway.

in the depth of night. No one besides his closest collaborators ever clapped eyes on him.

Nevertheless, in summertime, he appeared to some specially selected young Communists who camped on one of the deserted islands of the Baltic Sea. There they met a man named "Anton" who spoke Swedish rather badly, with a strong intermingling of Danish and a heavy German accent. He gave the young people a course in the ABC of espionage, the basic principles of dynamiting ships, buildings, bridges and railroads. In the course of his lectures Anton let fall the remark that on a journey to China, he had learned some tricks from the Koreans. They had shown him how to stuff TNT into a cigarette, and how such cigarettes might be used to blow up a Japanese-held bridge. Anton saw to it that his pupils grasped the lessons. Then he disappeared as mysteriously as he had come.

A glimpse of him was caught in occupied Norway. But that was all. The Quisling police could not find a trace of him. But Swedish iron ore boats were waylaid on the Baltic by Russian submarines and sunk. The Nazis were fairly sure Wollweber was behind the sinkings.

A small interval of quiet passed. Then the foremen of the famous Kiruna iron ore mines in Lappland were struck with consternation to find that five hundred pounds of dynamite had been purloined, sack by sack, from the supply depots of the iron ore mines. The Wollweber hunt was renewed with greater ardor.

The police seized a man who had a cache of TNT stored in the cellar of his house in Stockholm. Somebody had denounced him. But the man was not Wollweber, and had no connection with him. He was a Briton named C. E. Rickman. He was, moreover, a British commercial representative who had written an authoritative technical study on the Swedish iron ore mines. He was accused and convicted of conspiring to blow up the iron ore shipping installations in Luleå and Oxelösund, and was sentenced to eight years' imprisonment. In prison his health broke down. After four years, the British interceded strongly on his behalf, and he was released.

Wollweber, the real quarry of the hunt, was still unfound. He was, in fact, walking the streets of Oslo, for he wore a Nazi

Party uniform and a swastika pin, which seemed to be sufficient protection. Thus disguised, he supervised the disposal of the stolen dynamite which had been brought into Norway by skiers. There portions of it were used for acts of arson at the Oslo railroad terminal and at powerhouses and naval installations in the north. Points along the railroad line from Oslo to Bergen were blown up some sixty-five times.

It is for exploits such as this that Ernst Friedrich Wollweber earned the appellation "The King of Saboteurs." Not that he himself did all the work. Rather, he utilized his magnificent talent for organization to build up a hard-bitten coterie of saboteurs and spies. In Sweden alone, for example, he had at least fifty aides, according to the estimate of the Swedish police. Now and then some of them were caught, but the entire group was never rounded up.

For material Wollweber relied largely upon former Communists. However, having little use for officials of his party, he relied on members of the rank-and-file. He would denounce officials scornfully as Grand Moguls who were utter incompetents when it came to espionage and sabotage.

Wollweber had no patience with dramatic acts that accomplished little. He railed against the Communist leaders for publishing underground newspapers and leaflets, instead of lying low and engaging in sabotage and espionage. He ordered all the Communists who were loyal to him—all those with "guts," as he phrased it—to join the Nazi Party and form a fifth column inside it.

Gradually, the members of the Communist underground came to appreciate the good sense of this tactic, and Wollweber rose high in their estimation. They began to call him "little Lenin"—a name that pleased Wollweber's candid egotism. But he was more pleased with the results, for the Communists in the Nazi movement became priceless agents for Laurenti Beria and his Russian Secret Service.

The casualties among these agents were, of course, high—for Canaris and the Gestapo had excellent counter-espionage cells within their own party. But Wollweber felt that the casualties were well worth the results these men were achieving. Of course, it was necessary for him to travel about the capitals of

Europe constantly recruiting saboteurs. Jan Valtin relates that on such journeys he often fell into a frenzy of rage at seeing Communist officials orating and theorizing instead of doing active work. Valtin met him one day in Paris in 1937 and found him in a wild fury. According to Valtin, Wollweber said:

"I've been looking around. This Paris is a treasure-chest. I've learned more here in one week, I tell you, than in three years in Nazi Germany. In Germany, our comrades either starve to death or are beaten to death. And here? The boulevard cafés are lousy with deserters. . . . I'm going to round them up—one and all. I'm going to send them back to Germany where they belong."

Since 1933 Wollweber had been a fugitive. With pursuers always at his heels, he continued his work tirelessly, never pausing, never taking a vacation.

It was something that could not go on forever. Somewhere along the line a slip was bound to occur. It is amazing to record that in the end it was not Wollweber himself but one of his helpers who finally slipped up and left the fatal footprints.

In the harbor city of Gothenburg Wollweber was forced by circumstances to employ men who were fairly well-known as Communists. The espionage and sabotage league had had to be greatly expanded, and more and more men were needed. The order had come from Laurenti Beria to let no ship through which carried iron ore or ball bearings from Sweden, Norway or Denmark to Nazi Germany.

For many months sabotage operations ran smoothly. A telegraph operator on the Swedish *Telegrafverket* was running a short-wave transmission set which informed Russian and Allied submarines of the departing ships. This man was located in Gothenburg. Unfortunately he had to depend on a whole host of assistants. One of them was the leader of the former Aid Committee for Republican Spain, Victor Rydstedt, who was in a perfectly secure situation but was suddenly overcome with panic On a sudden impulse he went to take a look at the TNT which was hidden in a warehouse in Gothenburg, near the harbor. It was a foolish act, for he had no reason to be worried about it and such inspection trips were strictly forbidden by the Wollweber League. The police, who had intermittently watched him, happened to follow him to the warehouse that day. They found two hundred and twenty pounds of TNT in sacks bearing the label of the Kiruna Iron Ore Mines.

Rydstedt and his collaborator, the telegraph operator, were seized, convicted of espionage and sentenced to three years in prison. The Swedish police made further investigations. The sacks of TNT revealed fingerprints. A week later five workers in the Lappland iron mines were suddenly arrested.

One of them, G. Ceder, turned state's witness. He produced some dynamite shells which he had been given as samples and exhibited the method of secreting a number of such shells on an iron ore boat, close to the ship's furnaces. The explosion would occur spontaneously.

Ceder was also able to tell of his next scheduled rendezvous with "Anton," the King of Saboteurs. He was set at liberty and met with his boss at the home of one of the iron workers, close to the mines. The police put in an appearance almost immediately. Anton, alias Wollweber, was arrested, and in the course of the next few days some twenty of his operatives were rounded up.

Wollweber was monumentally calm. He had been in such situations before. There was no TNT in the home of the iron worker. There was, he swiftly calculated, no evidence at all. The Swedish court would have to have evidence. Wollweber contented himself with one succinct remark to Torsten Söderström, the police chief: "I am a Soviet citizen."

The Swedes instantly recognized that the situation was not quite so simple as they had thought. A Soviet citizen was no stateless refugee; he had powerful protection at his back. Confirmation was sought from Madame Alexandra Kollontay, the Russian envoy in Stockholm. She attested to Wollweber's Russian citizenship. The Swedes decided it was best to proceed slowly, delicately. They had the greatest saboteur of our time, but were wholly without proof of his guilt. Boats had been blown up in Denmark; airfields and submarine installations had been damaged in Norway; shipments of iron ore from Sweden had met their fate on the high seas; but no crimes had been committed on Swedish soil and no real evidence of Wollweber's complicity existed.

Of course, the Nazi authorities in Denmark and Germany made rabid official demands for his extradition, as did Quisling and his police chief, "Judas" Lie,* in Norway. But the Swedes did not dare to throw a Soviet citizen into the lion's den.

Now Laurenti Beria bestirred himself. He rallied the entire Soviet Foreign Ministry to the rescue of Wollweber. Stalin personally intervened and asked for the release of Wollweber. He made it very clear that there were a few Swedish engineers working in Russia who might do as hostages, if things came to a really critical pass.

While waiting for the outcome, the Russian Legation in Stockholm showered the imprisoned Wollweber with food and money and visits. Finally the Swedes decided to strike an unhappy mean between offending the Russians and outraging the Nazis.

The Swedish Department of Justice came up with the charge that Wollweber had been living in Sweden on a faked passport and under an assumed name. His entrance into the country was illegal. This could not, after all, be forgiven. The Nazis were advised that Wollweber would be tried on these charges. He would have to serve the sentence imposed by the Swedish court before there could be any question of extraditing him to Germany. The Swedes did not even bother to reply to the demand of the Quisling puppet government in Oslo. Wollweber, whom the Axis countries would have hanged, received a sentence of eighteen months, to be served in a relatively comfortable prison of a democratic country.

Wollweber heartily shook hands with the visiting friends of the Soviet Legation. "I'll be out in time to meet our Soviet troops in Berlin," he said.

The Swedish court judged it best to declare that the proceedings of the trial were to be kept secret for fifty years.

Canaris had the minor satisfaction of knowing that for a while Wollweber was out of his way. Suddenly that illusion was broken.

---

* Lie committed suicide after the liberation of Norway.

Wollweber was in prison, an indubitable fact. But still—
something strange happened in the small town of Krylbo in
central Sweden. Krylbo boasts two thousand inhabitants, a
railroad station, a bus depot and an inn. Most of the natives
are farmers or foresters of the nearby Dalekarlia woods. A
quieter place could not be imagined.

However, the day came when Krylbo was rocked by a terrific
series of explosions in the center of the town. Fleeing to the
woods, the inhabitants looked back to see tremendous flames
shooting up two hundred feet high into the air. The entire
town became an ocean of flames. The railroad station had
been smashed to smithereens.

Rescue squads found that the source of the explosion and
the fire was three railroad cars. They were now stalled on the
tracks and were enveloped in flames. The fire licked at them
for hours. Nothing was able to quench it. Many of the inhabitants of the town had suffered injury and severe burns, and
the railroad employees were disabled.

At the moment no cause could be assigned to the accident.
The Swedish government explained it by the fact that the bearings of one of the cars had become heated by friction. But two
days later the facts of the matter became too obvious to be
concealed. Clearly, it had not been an ordinary train accident.
It was a cunning piece of espionage and sabotage, and had
political implications.

The burning cars were freight cars bound for Finland from
occupied Norway. The town of Krylbo was the midpoint between the two Axis-dominated countries. Finland, at the time
an unhappy ally of Hitler's, was suffering starvation. The
Germans were allegedly sending food to their brothers in arms.

The Krylbo people searched the ruins and discovered bomb
fragments, and some bombs which had not yet exploded. They
bore the imprint of the German army. Among the ruins of
the Krylbo railroad station were the metal labels of the freight
cars, reading FOOD. Nevertheless the story did not hold water.
Food does not burn in quite that way; food does not explode
inside freight cars to the destruction of a whole town.

It was quite clear. Neutral Sweden could not have permitted
the transit of weapons and ammunition to Finland, for that

would have compromised her neutrality. However, there was no objection to the passage of food for Finnish civilians. But the agents of Laurenti Beria, the disciples of the imprisoned Wollweber, had been well aware that the freight cars contained no food. They had wrecked one among many ammunition trains going to Finland. Their act uncovered both perfidy and negligence. Either the Swedes had not bothered to inspect the munition train at the border, or they had deliberately closed their eyes.

Who were the saboteurs of Krylbo? The Germans accused Friedrich Ege in Finland, but he presented a perfect alibi. In their fury, they accused the master saboteur, Wollweber. Wollweber was called up for a hearing within the prison, and laughingly protested that he didn't know a thing about it—which was incontrovertible. How could he?

Nevertheless the stolen TNT had been put to use. And the young men he had instructed in their summer camp on the Swedish island had put their lessons into practice.

Wollweber was also obviously innocent of the greatest naval sabotage in the history of Sweden. It happened a few months after the Krylbo incident. Three Swedish destroyers of the most modern class, with crew and officers on board, exploded outside of Stockholm harbor. Wollweber, inside a Swedish prison, again had a perfect alibi. But it was he who had ordered every vessel escorting convoys to Finland or Germany to be sabotaged.

These disasters were not the last. Vengeance fell on other ships bearing contraband cargo; on the *Ada Gorthon,* the *Liljevalch,* the *Galeon,* the *Luleå* and many more, including the railroad ferry from Sweden to Germany.

In the fall of 1944, the Swedish insurance firms declared that they could no longer extend insurance to Swedish boats sailing to Axis-controlled countries. Shortly after, the Swedish government ordered that no Swedish boat undertake shipping to Axis countries for the duration of the War. And this was exactly what Wollweber and his friends wanted done.

In 1944 Wollweber completed his term—a little too early to see the Russian troops advance on Berlin. However, he was not extradited; by the time of his release Allied military successes had made it possible for the Swedes to adopt a much firmer attitude toward Germany. Sweden was no longer afraid to offend the Nazis. And so Wollweber was permitted to go to Moscow, where he was assigned to a new task—postwar Germany.

CHAPTER XV

A Spy in Every Port

THE battle for dominion over the Baltic was at its fiercest; the Russians had entered Estonia, Latvia and Lithuania. They were at the East Prussian border and even Finland's stubbornness broke at last; she sued for peace. Admiral Canaris, surveying the Baltic situation, saw that it was desperate. Whereas his other colleagues were evasive, he was frank and did not conceal his opinion from his master, Hitler. According to captured German army officers and prisoners of war, Canaris was the only man in the military staff who was allowed to tell Hitler the full truth, the only one to whom Hitler really listened. It is said that he insisted on getting the Admiral's opinion before he made his most far-reaching decisions. Canaris was one of the few men who were permitted to call the German dictator by his first name.

In the summer of 1944 Canaris had reams of bad news to report. Wollweber, at all events, was imprisoned in Sweden. But he had a successor who was, according to Canaris's reports, a certain Colonel Rudolf Haus. Haus, like Ernst Friedrich Wollweber, was a German Communist. He concentrated his own efforts on the small Baltic states, relying on Wollweber's disciples to cover Sweden and Denmark on the other side of the Baltic.

Rudolf Haus had been inspector of the Soviet Harbor Services for many years. His keen glance had fallen on every port in Europe, from London to Athens, from Odessa to Narvik.

Haus had never been a naval attaché, nor had he attended a naval academy. Without formal military instruction, he had nevertheless written an authoritative book on Friedrich Engels' strategy of revolution. He had written analyses of General Clausewitz' military principles and had served as a colonel in the Soviet army.

The author happens to have known Rudolf Haus. I knew him when he was still called Robert Hauschild. His father had been a poor weaver of Silesia. In 1917, Robert, a seventeen-year-old boy, created the first organization of "Young Communists" in Germany. After the German revolution he was put in charge of a counterfeit passport printing outfit in Berlin which provided the Communist International with thousands of faked passports for its various parties, affiliates and fellow-traveler organizations.

Around 1923 the early Nazis banded together in what was equivalent to the German Ku Klux Klan, a vigilante group which sentenced to death all those who menaced the rising Nazi movement. To oppose them, Hauschild was entrusted with the establishment of a "Red Cheka" inside Germany. It was a rival terrorist group which waged war against the early Nazi underground by fair means and foul.

For the short while that it existed, the Red Cheka was very effective. Hauschild developed into an excellent guerrilla leader, but his ambitions soared above that. The weaver's son started to read the classics of military theory. He became a lay exponent of military science, and lectured his Communist friends on the technique of sabotage, of barricade fighting and guerrilla warfare. In recognition of his specialty, he was named political advisor of the Red military groups inside Germany.

Of course, the young military prodigy became known to the Weimar Republic's police. Times were unsettled. In a savage fray between the police and armed Communists, Haus lost an eye and was unable to make good his escape. He was taken into custody, tried for illegal military activities and sentenced to eighteen months in jail.

The Weimar Republic had curious laws, laws whose typica.

Prussian morality would have puzzled other people. A man who killed for political motives was not considered a murderer in Germany; the rational motive palliated the offense. The sentence was not only short, but was served in an army fortress. The institution was called "Ehrenhaft" (Honorable Custody). Such a man was a military prisoner and not a criminal. It was to such a fortress that Hitler was sentenced after the failure of his Beer Hall Putsch in November, 1923.

On the whole, Haus enjoyed his stay at the fortress of Kuestrin. The life there was fairly comfortable and he was allowed time to study. His prisonmates were Prussian officers who had belonged to illegal Nazi chauvinist organizations. He made friends with them, and reciprocal teaching plans arose. Haus taught them the principles of Communism and the officers taught him military theory. A great many years later it was discovered that high German officers had worked for the Soviets during this War. Rudolf Haus had converted them as early as 1924. A whole group of officers believing in Prussian socialism turned to a new school of thought called National-Bolshevism. Lieutenant Scheringer was one of the founders of this movement which held that an alliance between Germany and the Soviet Union would give the Germans the chance to fight France, England and the United States and destroy the *"Schmach von Versailles"*—the "shame of Versailles."

* * *

An amnesty, frequently granted political prisoners, was granted to Rudolf Haus. Set at liberty, he married and then he and his wife Hilde went to Russia.

He was eager to enter the Red Military College. His studies, however, lasted only a few months. The OGPU put him to work. Even as Laurenti Beria was contemporaneously assigned to keep tabs on all Czarist officers in exile, Rudolf Haus followed up the cases of renegade Communist members and officials. Hundreds of people who had been Communists had experienced a revulsion against the party. They went to opposite extremes and served on Italian, French, German police investigatory groups, on the Dies Committee and on all manner of anti-Communist, anti-Russian organizations.

For his work, Haus did as Beria had done. He adopted the pose of a violent anti-Communist. He was feigning this role when I met him in Zurich, Switzerland, in 1930.

In that city lived an outstanding Communist named Hans Huerlimann. For a short while he had been one of the leaders of the Swiss Communist Party. But Huerlimann grew critical of party doctrines and tactics and ended by being expelled for his heresies against the general "line." After his expulsion Huerlimann started a new magazine, *Die Front,* dealing with economics, the social sciences and literature. It was a liberal magazine, and though critical of Stalinism it was sympathetic to the Soviet Union.

Rudolf Haus turned up in Switzerland, posing as a disillusioned radical. He applied for the post of assistant editor on the magazine. While I was not on the staff, I wrote book reviews for the magazine, and it was in this way that I met Haus.

He was a tall and handsome man with a splendid military carriage. He gave the impression of extreme uprightness and sincerity.

Of course, he got on the inside of the magazine for the purpose of spying on it for the Communist International. He became a familiar figure around the magazine offices. After a time, he paid a call at the home of Hans Huerlimann. He explained to the editor's wife that he had arranged to meet her husband here. He asked her to do him a favor and buy something in the store, while he continued waiting. Hans would be along any minute.

Huerlimann in his office knew nothing about the mock appointment. An hour later his wife phoned in great alarm. She had returned from the store to find Rudolf Haus gone. The apartment had been ransacked; the closets and desks were broken into. All addresses, mailing lists and documents which related to Huerlimann's co-workers and oppositional friends inside Europe's Communist Parties were gone.

* * *

A year before Hitler became German dictator, Rudolf Haus was in Germany again and the leader of the German BB. BB stands for the German words *Betriebs-Bespitzelung*—Commu-

nist factory espionage. Haus's task was to organize all firm
Communists and dependable industrial workers to spy on new
German patents, on armament models and steel formulas. The
findings were ingeniously forwarded to the Soviet Union. This
highly responsible job within Germany was very well paid by
the Soviet government. Haus's ostensible post for this task was
camouflaged as director of the German-Russian Gasoline Distributing Company.

Early in 1933 fate once more linked me with Rudolf Haus.
I was living in Berlin at the time. Haus obtained my address
from the telephone directory. He challenged me with one of
the wildest proposals I have ever heard. To this day I have
not succeeded in divining his motives. He came to my apartment and, with hardly any preface, declared his errand.

"Hitler is now in power. We have to oppose him with all
our might. I've gathered a group of five men, acquaintances
of mine. I myself have just sneaked into the country, from
Moscow, which is my permanent home now. These five men
have pledged themselves to fight Hitler with every possible
instrument, with fire, dynamite and sabotage. Will you make
a sixth? We meet tomorrow at seven o'clock in Friedenau."

He gave me an address. I confess that I was afraid to go.
It might be a newly organized sabotage group, but it might
also be a dummy group of the Gestapo. I remembered what
Haus had done to the Huerlimanns in Zurich. This might well
be a trap for "anti-Communists."

The next day he called me up and expressed his disappointment. He called me a "coward." He did not know that I was
editing an underground paper which was circulating throughout Germany. I could not take personal risks without endan-
gering the underground project and the lives of my friends
on it.

Years later I saw articles by Haus in the *Manchester Guard-
ian* and in various refugee papers. I wrote to him, in care of
these papers, just to discover where he was.

It was the period of the Moscow purges. I was living in
Sweden when a letter arrived from Haus. Its tone was most
friendly and he invited me to the Soviet Union. He promised
me a real haven there, and a job under his own supervision.

I guessed what the job was. This was the second time he had requested me to join his Intelligence bureau.

I declined the friendly offer, pleading my difficult personal situation. The Nazis had taken my wife as hostage. I could not abandon her and go to Russia; I had to remain in Sweden and press the Swedish and British governments to help me free her.

Haus and I corresponded for several months. Then, without any visible cause, he stopped answering. I wondered what had estranged him. I should have known. Reading the newspaper one morning in 1937, I saw an official communique stating that Rudolf Haus had been executed as a German spy in Moscow, as an accomplice in the Bukharin and Zinoviev conspiracies.

Well, this was a surprise. But it seemed to furnish the key to the mystery. I thought it confirmed my theory that the cleverest spies worked for both sides. You never knew where you had them. I was doubly relieved that I had refused collaboration with him.

The incident was completely forgotten. After a year, my wife was released by the Gestapo and joined me in Sweden.

Shortly before the outbreak of World War II, I was bitten by the desire to become foreign correspondent for my magazines and newspapers, and in this capacity to travel through all Europe. I wanted to see the Continent before the bombing, before the cruel destruction which I knew was inevitable. We set out, my wife Hilda and I.

London was unperturbed. No one would condescend to believe that there would be a war. British friends, members of Parliament, urged us to attend a session of the House of Commons. It was a lovely spring day, the last spring of peacetime. We strolled through the city. We were not more than a hundred steps away from the Parliament buildings, when a man who had just left the building recognized me and automatically raised his hand to greet us. Even as recognition flashed on our side, the man turned away. He disappeared.

The apparition in the London street was Rudolf Haus. He carried with him his inseparable briefcase. He was unmistakably the same Robert Hauschild who had been shot as a Nazi spy and Trotskyite in the Soviet Union.

Had I been alone, I would have doubted my senses. But my wife had also recognized him. Because of his one eye he could not see too well, and walked with a peculiar gait that was impossible to forget. He was as tall as ever, and carried himself with the same Prussian military erectness. However, he was much better dressed now. Evidently he was no longer playing the part of the proletarian leader, the man who preferred to go without a tie and with open shirt-collar.

There is no doubt in my mind that he recognized us also but remembered at the last moment that he was officially dead. He must have decided in a flash that it was safer not to speak to me, wiser to leave some lingering doubt in my mind, though I think he must have known I would keep his secret. And indeed it is only now, after six years, that I feel it is safe to reveal what we saw on the steps of the British House of Commons that March morning in 1939.

At the time it was a great shock to see a supposedly dead man alive again. Had he, who had deceived the espionage service of every country, deceived his own as well? Our brains reeled before the complexity of the plot.

Later on I was to learn from Baltic newspapers that Haus had been reborn with a new name. He and his wife traveled on Russian oil tankers to all the ports of Europe, reviewing the unseen army of harbor counter-espionage agents. Yes, Haus was alive and well. He worked prodigiously in 1943, 1944 and 1945, ridding the Baltic countries of every trace of German militarism, espionage and Gestapo.

* * *

It is no exaggeration to state that international harbor espionage has been the most fatal department of espionage in World War II, and has exacted more lives than can be told.

It was men like Rudolf Haus who discovered that German agents lay in ambush in waterfront branches of the Salvation Army. They loudly played the drum and fife and prayed for the salvation of erring sailors' souls. They fed the hungry and gave beds to the down-and-out, just to obtain information on ship movements. German agents joined the Seamen's Missions all over the world, with the same purpose.

Men like Wollweber and Haus went far afield. They waged war against the enemy on enemy soil and in strangers' countries. The FBI works largely within the confines of the United States, where the problem of liquidating foreign agents is fairly simple. But it sometimes took men like Wollweber and Haus, thoroughly familiar with the gamut of Nazi guile, to guide the FBI to the hiding place of Nazi harbor espionage in the Western Hemisphere.

There are Seamen's Missions in the United States, too. Hoboken, New Jersey, had one. It was a clean, well-lighted place which provided wholesome meals. In its rooms, the principal languages of the world were spoken, for the tribe of sailors is an international one. However, it was a German Seamen's Mission. To be sure, the pastor protested his horror of the Nazis. But Reverend Hermann Brückner's mission was distrusted by the authorities.

One of the evangelists would go to the taverns and exhort the sinners to repent. Richard Warnecke may have had other names, but under this name he approached Belgian, Dutch, Norwegian, French, Jugoslav and Greek sailors. He was interested in the souls of sailors exclusively from Nazi-occupied countries.

He put a very simple proposition before them. He asked them if they wanted to see their sweethearts, their parents or brothers. "Why not go home to Norway?" Warnecke asked. "Why not go back to Athens?" he asked another sailor. "Why are you risking your life at sea, when you can get a civilian job in your native country? True, it is occupied, but then the War is over for you. When the War is over for all, your country will be free again and you will be alive to enjoy it."

The proposal was both sensible and attractive. The evangelist even knew a way of shipping the men from Latin America to Spain or Portugal. Moreover, he would even pay for the tickets. "After all," he said, "we German missionaries wish you well. That is why we are going to pay your passage home."

Warnecke explained that it was strictly legal. Since the sailors were not American citizens, no one could force them to stay in the United States. If they dropped out of the merchant marine and tried to stay in America, they would only be drafted.

Warnecke was actually recruiting men to replenish the merchant marine of Nazi Europe. He offered every inducement. The sailors were paid three dollars a day until they were shipped home. They might sleep at Pastor Brückner's mission, and Warnecke was very pleased with his dupes.

Among the harbor riffraff were many deserters from Allied boats, too. Warnecke cast nets for their souls, as well. This much can be safely said: not one of these credulous sailors ever saw his native home. He was arrested in Spain or in Italy, and forced to work on German or Italian merchant boats and minesweepers. And the greater part of these ships were torpedoed by Allied submarines. The sailors were heartlessly used to fill in the Axis maritime manpower shortage.

Following Admiral Canaris's instructions to "stop as many seamen as possible from shipping to England," Warnecke started "neutrality" propaganda. He exploited the fact that the Communists were against the War; this was before Hitler attacked Russia, when the Reds were still defining the situation as an "imperialistic War." Warnecke's plan was quite simple. He sent his own men into the Communist-dominated seamen's union, the National Maritime Union of America. The meetings hammered home the lesson, "This is an imperialistic War." They taught that the British were no better than the Germans, that both countries were capitalistic. Seamen were exhorted not to take hires to either Germany or England.

Of course, no boats were going to Germany and the propaganda had pertinence only with reference to England. Neutrality meant anti-British action. The aim of the proselytizers was to sabotage shipping to Great Britain and in this they had partial success. The Nazi agents supported the Communist neutrality and anti-imperialistic policy with great cleverness. They spoke up at meetings, crying: "We want peace. Down with the War—we don't want to fight for Britain. Don't take hires to England." And the Communists, obeying the party line, applauded.

The National Maritime Union, then so much interested in

peace, cannot say it was victimized by a viper it had been nourishing for many years. The N.M.U. finally saw the day when some of its loudest and most active members were arrested as Nazi spies.

In January, 1942, the Federal Court House in Brooklyn saw the enactment of one of the outstanding spy cases in America. The entire Nazi harbor espionage system in the United States was involved. Among the principals were ten seamen, seven of whom were estimable figures in organized labor and members of the National Maritime Union. Indeed, they were the members who had consistently agitated for pacifism, for neutrality, for isolationism, for the slogans "Keep out of war" and "Don't sail to England."

There is no doubt that these spies had hoodwinked their union completely. Nevertheless, the blame must be laid at the door of the equivocal policy of the union. It advised its members to try for safe berths on ships bound for the Caribbean, rather than to England. This attitude of short-sighted self-interest played right into the hands of the Nazis.*

The following were spies who had infiltrated into the union:

Comradin Otto Dold: second steward on the export liner *Excalibur,* sentenced to 10 years;

Heinrich Clausing: cook on the *Argentina,* sentenced to 8 years;

Adolph H. Walichewsky: on the Moore-McCormack liner *Uruguay,* sentenced to 5 years;

Heinrich Carl Eilers: library steward on the *U.S.S. Manhattan,* sentenced to 5 years;

Franz Joseph Stigler: chief baker on the U.S. liner *America,* sentenced to 16 years;

Erwin W. Siegler: chief butcher on the U.S. liner *America,* sentenced to 10 years.

Admiral Canaris's harbor espionage network had functioned efficiently—that was clearly demonstrated by the testimony. The seamen-spies had informed the enemy about new war weapons and the destinations of cargoes. Complete freight and passenger lists were supplied to the Canaris office. The sailors

---

* The enthusiasm displayed by the National Maritime Union, once Russia became an ally, has been conspicuous.

in the N.M.U. were assisted by a huge network of spies in the port of New York who ranged from high school girls to old salts. It took the FBI more than a year to discover the spy ring, and enormous efforts were needed to round up the majority of the spies. Many sleepless nights, many hundreds of investigations were necessary. But finally the court had enough evidence against these harbor and marine spies to mete out the maximum sentence of eighteen years to some. The spy ring as a whole included ten seamen, twenty-three other men and two women. The court accused the seamen among other things of the theft of "plans of vital sections of the Norden bomb sight." All these radical union men, who won praise from the Communists for being "such good Leftists," were none other than Nazi couriers, plying between the U.S.A. and Spain, Portugal and the Latin American countries.

They worked on troop transport ships and on Lend-Lease vessels. They had applied for places on the ships carrying the Norden bomb sight to other countries. Their real master was higher than the agent-evangelist Warnecke, who had first thought of boring from within the Maritime Union. Their ultimate master was Admiral Canaris. And the captain of American harbor espionage was Friedrich Joubert Duquesne, who was well-known to the FBI. Duquesne was one of the secret collaborators recommended to Bill Sebold when Sebold played the game of radio operator for the Nazis.

The romantic story of Duquesne has been told in all its details in Alan Hynd's book, *Passport to Treason*. Hynd mentions Duquesne's connections with some employees of the Norden Company. Eyewitnesses at the trial report that Duquesne remained quiet and stoical throughout. He seemed quite resigned to his fate, but expressed a fierce desire to be free just once again, in order to "get" Bill Sebold, who had called the FBI's attention to him.

Duquesne was given the maximum sentence of eighteen years.

No doubt the case of the spying seamen would not have been broken until much later but for the gullibility of the Canaris office toward their agent, Sebold. With one stone the FBI that time killed many birds.

The German Seamen's Mission was closed down after Pearl Harbor, but Warnecke, master of wiliness, managed to escape to safety. However, the Admiral had lost his battle for the American harbors.

* * *

Canaris's employees wore many faces and many masks and used many methods. They were not always easy to identify. Sometimes his men were found on a small fishing boat off the California coast. Sometimes they were seamen off the Straits of Magellan in Chile. One was an editor of a fishery trade paper; one was a shipowner; one was a fire-tower guard. Some were stevedores or sentinels on duty at the *S.S. Lafayette,* the former luxury liner *Normandie.*

The *Normandie* was burning at its pier at 49th Street in Manhattan. The volume of smoke was so great that it wafted far downtown to the Battery. Every New Yorker leaped to the same conclusion—"This is sabotage." But the authorities, striving to calm the war psychosis, stated that it was a plain accident of mysterious origin.

Anyone who has met men like Wollweber, Gough, Pflugk-Hartung and Rudolf Haus knows that the chances of its being pure accident are very slim. Most ship fires, at least in war-time, can be traced to a mysterious hand dropping a dynamite-laden cigarette or pencil. Any stevedore had the chance to board a ship like the *Normandie.* A fifty-dollar union initiation fee creates a stevedore, and such a paltry sum would not exclude an agent like Warnecke or another of Canaris's hire-lings. Boats like the *Normandie* were guarded at that time, not by the Army, Navy or Coast Guard, but by private firms and private guards.

Congressional investigations revealed that one of these companies employed former Bundists and White Russians for guards. Congress collected evidence showing that the vice-president of such a firm was also former marine superintendent of the *Hapag,* the Hamburg-American line. This man had intervened in the arrest of Nazis and German agents by offering bail to the collective sum of one hundred and twenty-five thousand dollars for them. He certainly was not an anti-Nazi.

He was innocent of any connection with the *Normandie* fire. Nevertheless, the evidence was sufficient to provoke the Alien Property Custodian to further action. Some of this man's aides may have had chances not open to others.

It is enormously difficult to track down the source of a ship fire. No police force likes to admit that "it was sabotage, which we failed to prevent." Perhaps this is why the *Normandie* fire has been relegated to the sphere of the unsolved mysteries.

* * *

There was a plethora of ship fires during the War on both the eastern and western coasts of America. Many were not produced by simple accidents, and their mysteries were solved. New York suffered more ship fires than any other harbor city. Not far from Long Island the most terrific explosion known on the East Coast took place. All these casualties may well have been the work of Admiral Canaris's agents.

Agents have on the average a short life span, and Canaris has to employ them in droves. Not all of them are highly competent. A young member of the Hitler Youth, Heinrich Roedel, managed to jump a boat and make an illegal entrance into this country in 1936. For six years he operated with impunity. However, on July 28, 1942, before dawn, Roedel kindled a small fire in a pile of lumber at a shipyard. The conflagration spread through the Henry J. Kaiser Corporation's properties in Richmond, California.

Roedel escaped from the locality of his bonfire, but he had been noticed and was caught. His sentence was thirty years. At the trial he confessed that he was a member of the nautical division of the Nazi Party.

The same stern sentence was given to Ernest Frederick Lehmitz, of Staten Island. He was fifty-seven years old, and used out-dated methods. He fancied that his letters would pass the postal censors' infra-red rays, and used invisible ink to communicate to agents in Switzerland and Portugal such items as the following:

"Eleven ships leaving for Russia including steamer with airplane motors and 28 long-range guns. One steamer has deckload airplanes, below deck airplane motors. Boeing and Douglas airplane parts on steamer with Curtiss-Wright airplanes, motors and small munitions, searchlights and telegraphic material."

On the whole, he was less efficient than most German agents. He masqueraded not as a bar-owner like the King of Belize, not as a beautician like Ruth Kuehn of Pearl Harbor, not as a journalist like Pflugk-Hartung. He hit on a pose which he thought very ingenious. He was an air-raid warden of Staten Island, New York. In this capacity, Lehmitz watched the convoys leaving Staten Island and the Port of Embarkation. He took humble jobs like being a porter around the waterfront, and he was an habitué of waterfront taverns.

His wife made some extra money by letting rooms. Her favorite boarders were young sailors or merchant seamen, whom she mothered very nicely and from whom she learned the sailing dates of ships.

Harbor espionage always makes the same demands: "Inform us what boats are leaving and what cargoes they carry. How many men are the troop ships carrying?" The tip-off is transmitted to other agents, by airmail letter or coded commercial cables, or by a business telephone call to South America. But it was an infallible trick of Lehmitz to use some newly invented invisible ink, and write between the lines of a letter dealing with his victory garden.

Lehmitz employed an engineer of a war plant as his subagent. Neither man made very much out of his treacherous trade. Lehmitz worked for the paltry sum of fifty dollars a week. It is no wonder that his Hungarian-born wife cried bitterly when he was arrested. She did not weep because he had been a traitor and had received a thirty-year sentence. That, she said between sobs, was what he had coming to him. What distressed her was the scandal, which would frighten new boarders away!

* * *

Facing Staten Island and connected with it by ferry is Brooklyn and its Sheepshead Bay. This was the zone of operations for another of Admiral Canaris's agents. His mask was perhaps the simplest and the safest one to use. Twenty-seven years old, he was a proud member of the U.S. Navy.

He was a tall, good-looking fellow, five feet eleven and weigh-

ing one hundred and ninety pounds. So Bertrand Stuart Hoffman is described in the court records. He was born in Canada,
but lived most of his life in Detroit and Chicago. He worked
in one of the Ford plants in Detroit and made good money.
Nevertheless, Hoffman had a hankering for more money. One
day he was approached by a member of a Nazi spy ring in Detroit, the ring headed by glamorous Grace Bachanan-Dineen, a
Hungarian-born beauty. She was a graduate of Vassar College
and had received spy training at the famous school of Hamburg.

The Nazi spy ring had worked since 1942 with great success
in Detroit, and had obtained Ford models of war equipment.
Then the time came for Hoffman to leave the plant and be
drafted into the Navy. His role changed but he was still in the
game. From industrial espionage he was transferred to harbor
espionage. Soon the young man was reporting on the every-day
life of the Crosse Ile Naval Station.

His naval training completed, Hoffman was assigned to duty
in New York. He was stationed at Sheepshead Bay. In June,
1943, he began sending shipping information to his female boss,
the beautiful Grace of Detroit.

The FBI received anonymous warnings and commenced
watching the ring. The Ford Company admitted Secret Service
operatives into its plants to gather more evidence against the
gang. It was discovered that, besides paying big money for
blueprints of plane motors and tanks, the gang was busy fomenting discord in organized labor and between white and colored workers. Though there is no direct court evidence on the
matter, the Detroit ring obviously intended to create labor
trouble, stir up strikes and inspire racial hatred and open race
riots.

Time will show how the agents of Admiral Canaris worked
underground to organize anti-Negro and anti-Semitic riots.
Everything which would halt war production was grist for their
mill.

When finally arrested, Grace, the leader of the spy ring, knew
that she stood a fair chance of receiving the death sentence.
She therefore turned state's witness and confessed everything
she knew, with perhaps some fairy-tales for good measure. She
was Surprise No. 1 at court. But a still greater surprise was in
store.

Young Hoffman, arrested shortly after, appeared, still wearing his Navy uniform. He seemed quite unabashed, but rapidly displayed strange characteristics. He could not handle his own defense. He gave ridiculous answers to the cross-examining attorney, and seemed not to understand where he was.

There was much laughter in the court room. The suspicion was that Hoffman was just playing dumb. But he himself was quite serious. He admitted that he had told the spy ring in Detroit about ship movements. He had sent wires to them. Asked about the messages, he said he did not remember them. He had copied them out of newspapers. Asked what newspapers, he again could not remember.

Finally psychiatrists were consulted. After holding Hoffman for weeks of observation, they came to the conclusion that the defendant Hoffman was "mentally incompetent." In all probability his information had been of no value to the Detroit spy ring and Admiral Canaris.

The court was left gaping at the farcical outcome. A bystander remarked: "Now the Nazis have begun using imbeciles for spies. That is the latest trick." Perhaps it was. The case against Bertrand Stuart Hoffman was dismissed.

CHAPTER XVI

The Parachutist Who Spread Mischief in Ireland

THE homes of all the members of the Detroit spy ring had been thoroughly ransacked by the agents of the FBI. The agents found hundreds of pounds of disguised pro-Nazi literature, propaganda calculated to appeal directly to Midwestern isolationism. There was the *Broom,* an anti-Semitic hate sheet; there were pamphlets inspired by the Ku Klux Klan, an organization still very much alive and kicking. There were thousands of leaflets that purported to reprint letters from proud, anxious or indignant mothers. The leaflets were issued in the names of a dozen different imaginary organizations. All the propaganda sheets insisted that America must stay out of the War.

The FBI agents had encountered this sort of hate propaganda, with its spurious "pacifist" note, so often before that they were not in the least surprised. But they found some additional material in Detroit that was quite new to them. There were a number of letters and pamphlets about dear old Ireland. These were, inevitably, printed on green paper and were addressed primarily to the huge Irish-American population of the country. Ireland, they proclaimed, would stay out of the War; the Irish would never retract their good old slogan:

"Neither King nor Kaiser! Ireland alone."

And in praise of Irish neutrality these papers abused Great Britain without mercy and without shame.

It has by now been clearly demonstrated that the material was German-sponsored and often written by Germans. The Germans coaxed or hoaxed groups associated with the outlawed Irish Republican Army into distributing the literature. Not all members of the IRA, the Irish terrorist organization, were willing to co-operate with the Nazis; indeed, many of them were so sincerely devoted to the cause of freedom that they would never collaborate with Fascists. But there is no doubt that, out of hatred for Britain, some did become tools of the Nazis and even paid agents of Admiral Walter Wilhelm Canaris.

During World War II the United States State Department several times protested against Irish espionage, charging that Irish spies counted the American troops that landed in Northern Ireland and reported on American equipment and troop movements. The protests availed little, however.

Eire's leader, President Eamon de Valera, denied these charges because he refused to believe them. Such espionage, he felt, might happen anywhere else in the world, but not in Ireland; Irishmen could never be quislings. To the American protest he replied:

"The total number of persons . . . suspected of intentions to engage in espionage, and now held in Irish prisons, is ten foreign and two Irish nationals. These are facts, and it is doubtful if any other country can show such a record of care and successful vigilance."

This well-worded reply had the ring of sincerity. But informed people read it with amused smiles. According to the most conservative estimates of British and American Intelligence officers, there were in 1944 between three and four hundred enemy agents, at least, working in Ireland. The capture of twelve leaders did not impair the efficiency of the Nazi organization.

In Ireland Admiral Canaris had a firm foundation on which to build his espionage organization. Long before the War started he had conferred personally with his Irish agents in the course of his trip to Holland. Shortly afterward Canaris conferred with the former leader of the IRA (Irish Republican Army). This conference also took place in Holland.

It was on a bright day of spring in 1939, when the myriad flower gardens of the Netherlands were all abloom and war seemed very far away. A man with a long, narrow face, deep-set eyes and carroty red hair arrived at the Hotel Commerce in Rotterdam. His name was Sean Russel. He was accompanied by a blue-eyed man of German appearance whose name was Max Piel. Both registered under false names, giving their occupation as salesmen, their place of residence as Dublin.

Both men carried samples of textiles and of chemicals in their bags. But they were interested in a different type of goods. Sean Russel, the outlawed leader of the IRA, was to arrange for the smuggling of large quantities of explosives to Ireland, for the use of his terrorist army. It was not enough that an occasional bomb exploded in a railroad station, in a telephone booth or on some wharf in London. War was imminent, and the Nazis wanted to employ Sean Russel's undoubted energies on a grander scale.

Russel, with his storm trooper mentality, was a most willing tool. Violently anti-Semitic and almost insanely anti-British, he was ready to obey Nazi orders to the letter. The arrangements for the explosives were completed, and a few days later

Sean Russel returned to Ireland. He brought with him on his person that other prerequisite for espionage—money. Secret funds were deposited under Irish names in various banks. These funds constituted a war chest.

Max Piel had ordered Russel to stay away from the German Legation in Dublin. This was an elementary precaution, since Russel was outlawed and had to live underground permanently. But although he had no direct connection with the German Legation, Russel contrived to help every German spy that came to Ireland.

The Irish government, which officially insisted that only twelve spies had been detected during the entire War, was well aware that German spies were being dropped in Ireland by parachute. De Valera's government sent representations to the German Legation at 58 Northumberland Road, Dublin. The German Minister, His Excellency Herr Eduard Hempel, expressed incredulity. "What makes you think the parachutists are German?" he said. "In my opinion, they are British. We maintain the most amicable relations with Ireland, and would never commit such an act."

The Irish government was powerless. It was not long before British and American newspapers commented on these parachutists. The government of Eire was pointedly told that, even if it were unable to find the German spies, it might at least address a protest to the secretary of the German Legation, Major Henning Thompsen, who was Admiral Canaris's top man in Ireland. It was also suggested that the Irish lay hold of Sean Russel, the outlawed IRA leader; both Russel and Major Thompsen would know more about the parachute spies than the police.

Major Thompsen had organized an excellent courier system between British and American army camps in Ulster, Northern Ireland, and his own headquarters in Dublin. His agents smuggled money, propaganda leaflets and information, mostly on maritime affairs, back and forth across Eire's six-hundred-mile-long northern border. Ireland's police made diligent efforts to ferret out these couriers and spies, but the efforts did not get very far.

One day fishermen at Bantry Bay reported that they had

spied submarines off the wild Galway Coast. Their fishing nets had been callously ripped through by the undersea craft. Naturally, the fishermen did not dare to scold the crews of alien warships. But they watched carefully and saw the submarines draw in to shore. Packing cases were unloaded—large heavy crates. Instantly upon receipt of this report, the Irish police started a thorough investigation. They located the crates, which contained test models of German firearms: machine guns, German army revolvers, Mauser rifles, ammunition and TNT. These firearms, which Nazi submarines had transported to Ireland, were intended for the secret IRA. Some Mauser automatics and tear-gas bombs were found hidden in a Galway cave.

British undercover men tracing Nazi agents discovered that the agents had visited the home of a very distinguished family in Dublin, one of the most prominent families in the country. The police were informed. And one cool day in May four Irish detectives searched the home of one of the loveliest ladies of Dublin society, Iseult Gonne, wife of the well-known Irish novelist Francis Stuart.* She was the adopted daughter of Major McBride, who had been executed after the 1916 rebellion.

Here the Irish police found the first footprints of the parachute spy ring. The four detectives did not heed Madame Stuart-Gonne's coy protests. She demurred at their opening closets which held her personal belongings, but the detectives went about their work. Not a corner was overlooked; attic, cellar, bathroom and kitchen cupboards were searched with exemplary perseverance.

At last they found what they had come for. In a closet, behind fabulous frocks, lay a neatly folded German parachute. A tool chest held a small radio transmitter, and among a welter of books by Francis Stuart was one small black notebook that held nothing less than a code for radio transmission. Sub-agents had come to Madame Stuart-Gonne with information from Ulster concerning British and American ship movements and troop concentrations. This news she broadcast over her low-

---

* Author of *Julie* and *In Search of Love*. Both books were well received at the time of their publication in the United States.

power set to Nazi submarines that lurked along the shipping lanes, waiting to sink Allied troops and cargoes.

Mrs. Francis Stuart-Gonne was tried before a military tribunal and pronounced guilty of "jeopardizing the safety of the State." She admitted that she had received the short-wave transmitter from a Nazi parachutist who lived in her house for a few weeks, but she refused to give the parachutist's name or whereabouts. In the face of Iseult Gonne's confession, her husband nevertheless protested his wife's and his own innocence. But a few weeks after the trial Ireland heard the voice of a new Lord Haw Haw on the air. Berlin had given sanctuary to novelist Francis Stuart and had appointed him to conduct Nazi broadcasts to neutral Ireland.

Ireland and England continued to hunt for the Nazi agent whose parachute had been discovered. Likely spots near the harbor in Dublin and other cities were raided. Many professional informers were questioned. But all traces of the parachutists had been blotted out. Intelligence officers concluded that they must have left the island by submarine.

A few months later in 1942, however, new evidence cropped up indicating that the German agents must still be somewhere in the country. Canaris's men were in Ireland, wearing a new disguise from the master spy's well-stocked costume-shop. They were hidden in one of the neatly appointed restaurants of Dublin's O'Donnel Street. No one would have remotely imagined that this modest eating place was a hideout for Canaris and the IRA spies. This restaurant had for cashier a pretty young woman who had worked there for several years. Now, for the past few months, some new customers began patronizing the restaurant. They came there daily and sat reading newspapers while they ate. They did not linger after the meal, and the tips they left were small. Like all the other customers, they paid their checks up front at the cashier's counter. The cashier took the money, and with it a note was slipped into her hand. Sometimes, in handing change to these new patrons, a note was folded in among the coins.

Irene, the young woman at the cashier's desk, served as contact between the IRA and Major Thompsen's spy center at the German Legation. The IRA terrorists and saboteurs handed her coded information which the girl passed on to the Germans; and she delivered to the Irish agents what new instructions the Legation had issued.

The IRA always had its men in the Dublin police. They kept in touch with what was happening and learned when the pursuit waxed hot. So one day the pretty cashier at the O'Donnel Street restaurant got a telephone call wishing her "Congratulations on your birthday." Irene had no birthday that day. Immediately after receiving this warning, she left, together with one of the spies who was dining in the restaurant. Shortly afterward the police came to make their raid. The agents had fled; their leader, Major Henning Thompsen, was protected by diplomatic immunity.

The British were angry but not surprised. They had long ago come to realize that, though they might drive the spies out of British Ulster, they could not keep them out of neutral Ireland. After the spies had sprung the trap at the O'Donnel Street restaurant, they were expected to seek refuge in Ulster.

The ringleader and spy-master, Henry Luneberg, was a dining-car employee on the Dublin-Belfast express. His occupation made it a simple matter for him to carry information from Northern Ireland to Eire. But now he began to be apprehensive. The raid on the Dublin restaurant, unsuccessful though it was, presaged ill. When he left the train in Belfast, he felt somewhat nervous. Sure enough, the Ulster authorities were waiting for him. He was arrested and taken to the Belfast prison for questioning. Luneberg played the part of an innocent and dumbfounded law-abiding citizen. Yes, he admitted, he had sometimes dined at the little restaurant on O'Donnel Street, but so had hundreds of others.

He was asked whether messages had been slipped to him by the girl at the cashier's desk. His answer was an astounded "No." He added: "She may have given me a pack of cigarettes or matches which your detectives imagined were espionage notes. It's ridiculous."

Actually, the British authorities had no evidence. But, as was their custom, they searched his clothes and his bag. Hidden in the lining they discovered an order from the Nazi-IRA spy organization.

Henry Luneberg was a lost man. The damning document was a masterpiece of explicitness such as Secret Service agents rarely chance to capture. The original text read:

OGLAIG NA HAIRANN, GHQ

Dublin, Feb. 6, 1942

Dii, Intelligence, Northern Command

1. I wish to acknowledge receipt of your report of Jan. 30.
2. I am anxious for an immediate report on:
   (a) The number of American troops which arrived in Northern Ireland at the time of making your report.
   (b) The reaction of the nationalist element of the populace to their arrival. (I use the term *nationalist* in the broadest sense.)
   (c) What are the prospects for making friendly contacts with these troops?
3. I am preparing a comprehensive memo for your directions regarding the type of Intelligence most urgently required. In the meantime prepare a detailed report on the whole power system of Northern Ireland with detailed plans on the strength and disposition of protective forces. A list of factories engaged in war production should also be compiled.
4. Has the new Central Catholic Party made any progress? What is the element behind it?
5. Will you let me know as soon as you can the present strength of all British and American forces in the North? Give me approximate figures on: (a) British and colonial forces; (b) American troops; (c) auxiliary armed police forces; (d) the total armed enemy forces in the North.

SEAN C-5

The mysterious heading of the espionage instructions calls for explanation. Oglaig Na Hairann means "Warriors of Ireland," which is the IRA's title in Gaelic.

The IRA has always claimed to be sympathetic to America. This time, however, it tripped itself up by including United States troops in the category of "enemy forces."

The Green Hornet signature "Sean C-5" was, of course, one of the many code signatures of the IRA leader, Sean Russel.

Valuable as this document was to the British and American Intelligence Services, it said nothing about the location of the parachute spies, who were still at large. Nor was any light thrown on the whereabouts of Sean Russel, the political terrorist.

Russel has become a legendary figure in modern espionage. He comes and goes everywhere, almost at will. During the World's Fair he visited New York and was accused of being responsible for the explosion in the British Pavilion. He flitted through many American cities, raising funds for his movement and sprinkling his talks with anti-British, pro-German propaganda.

In Detroit Sean Russel was arrested for illegal fund raising. He was held in seven thousand dollars' bail. Some of the American isolationists, among them Representative Martin L. Sweeney of Ohio, called his arrest "outrageous detention of a distinguished scholar and soldier at the behest of the British."

After this Sean Russel, the spy chief, who was more of a distinguished murderer than a scholar or soldier, vanished. The remainder of his story is obscure. His friends say that the British finally tracked him down, removed him from an Italian vessel, brought him to Gibraltar and then killed him when he tried to escape. But the British have not admitted anything of the sort and hint that the story of his death is a fake. Rumor has it that Russel's "death" is no more real than Rudolf Haus's execution in Russia; that he engineered his own "death" in order to continue his espionage and sabotage work in safety. Whatever the truth, we shall probably not learn the whole story until years after the War.

Sean Russel's leadership of the IRA was then taken over by Stephen Hayes, an Irish patriot whose hatred of the British was as fierce as his predecessor's. But he differed in one important respect: though he was ready to fight the British to his last drop of blood, Hayes opposed any association with the Nazis. The German agents in the IRA were rather taken aback. They received orders from Canaris for a coup to remove Hayes and crush him as a potential political leader.

Hayes, new commander-in-chief of the IRA, was simply kidnaped by the Nazi spies. The kidnaping took place on a Dublin street, when an unknown person jolted against Hayes, flung pepper into his eyes and shoved him into a car. He was brought to a small room in one of the residential sections of

Dublin. Two guards stood over him. His hands were bound and a handkerchief was stuffed into his mouth. Thick curtains darkened the windows.

"Where am I?" he asked.

The two guards refused to reply.

"What are you going to do with me? Are you British?" His first thought, of course, was that the British were kidnaping him and intended to bring him to trial in Ulster or England. But he was soon to learn otherwise.

The Nazis and the IRA members in their employ had written out a confession for him to sign. It was written in the flamboyant style of the Reichstag Fire confession and was well calculated to ruin his career as an Irish leader. Hayes had to declare that he was an informer for the British Secret Service, that he sent copies of his reports to England and that he had been responsible for denouncing the men who organized the IRA bombings and explosions.

The document stated that Scotland Yard officers often visited Hayes, and that Hayes had abetted two Ministers of the Irish government in stamping out the IRA.

At this point the story of Hayes becomes a sordid one of betrayal and counter-betrayal. Persuaded by the gun at his back, he signed the confession. It was later printed and mailed to a number of outstanding Irish patriots. The Nazis knew well that, even if the facts of the document were doubted, Hayes would be condemned for having been so craven as to sign it.

The IRA leader thought he would be released as soon as he signed. But the Nazis held him for many days; they were unable to decide what to do with him. Alive, he would menace their whole organization; but if they murdered him, their difficulties with the police would certainly be increased.

Finally, however, they got Admiral Canaris's orders to kill him. Hayes learned of their intention from careless words spoken in front of Anne, the pretty red-haired girl from a nearby restaurant who had been bringing Hayes his food. Anne was a member of the IRA who conceived of the organization as a real movement for Irish freedom. Shocked by what she had heard from the guards, she warned Hayes that he was about to be killed. He resolved upon a desperate attempt to save his life. Choosing a moment when only his two guards were in the building, he suddenly flung his newspaper into a guard's face and seized the man's gun. In the gunfight that followed, Hayes shot both the men, but he himself was badly wounded. Covered with blood, he managed to reach the local police station at Rathmines in Dublin's better residential section.

It was a curiously ironic act, this flight of Stephen Hayes, wanted for his leadership of an outlawed organization, to the Dublin police. But pain and the threat of death had reduced Hayes to a pitiful state of terror. Just before he lost consciousness, he told the police the address of the house where he had been held captive.

A few minutes later a strong police squad arrived at the apartment. The two guards were still there. They were badly wounded but refused to surrender without a fight, and exchanged shots with the police. One police officer was killed, another wounded. Finally, after twenty minutes of resistance, the guards surrendered; they had lost too much blood to continue fighting.

In the apartment the police found many papers, code books, a radio transmitter and instructions in German to the ringleader. Who was he? Whoever he was, he had escaped once more.

He was no unknown figure in Ireland. Extensive records in the files of the Irish police dealt with this man. For he was the parachutist whose parachute had been left in Iseult Gonne's home.

Hermann Goetz was the mystery man who had descended from the sky. He had been at large for at least eighteen months, during which he had successfully eluded both Irish police and the British Secret Service. Arriving in Eire with the equivalent of two hundred thousand dollars in Irish currency, he had organized a harbor espionage system and financed the terrorist division of the IRA and its Fascist inner circle. And now he was still at liberty.

Had the British in 1939 suspected what would be Goetz's role in this War, they would never have released him. Just before the War, he had got into trouble in England for making sketches of RAF airdromes. He served six months in prison and was then deported to Germany. As we have seen, a few years later he turned up in Ireland.

Stephen Hayes, the thoroughly cowed IRA leader, begged the police to protect him. He talked to them freely, revealing for the first time the true situation in the IRA. The IRA was split from top to bottom, for Hermann Goetz had seized the leadership of the radical, pro-Nazi wing. Hayes amplified his revelations, and gave the names and addresses of IRA members involved in the Nazi spy ring. Warrants were issued for their arrest and some of them were later hanged in England as spies. What was most sensational—*Hermann Goetz was caught.*

Once captured, Goetz quickly broke down. He admitted working for Canaris and conspiring to kidnap and kill Hayes. He was the chief instigator of espionage in all Ireland. Had it not been for the co-operation of Stephen Hayes, the police would never have caught this arch-spy. But Hayes's testimony against his former associates did not save him from a prison term.

Hayes told Anne, the restaurant girl, and other friends who visited him that he was glad to be in prison for the duration. It was by far the safest place for him. But he added wistfully: "Even after the War there will be no peace for me. The Nazis and the IRA will never forget that I betrayed them. They will hunt me down."

CHAPTER XVII

Pelving's Mistress

IN THE Wagnerian halls of the former Reich Chancellery the distant echo of a bomb explosion still resounded like the thunder of *Götterdämmerung*. It was the bomb that had been meant to kill Adolf Hitler in the sum-

mer of 1944. For a time it indeed seemed twilight for Admiral
Canaris.

The Admiral was on an inspection tour of the Balkans when
the telegram arrived ordering him to report to the Wilhelmstrasse at once. It was a telegram he had come to expect of
late; he feared it but he knew it was inevitable. And now at
last it had come.

It was bound to happen. Hitler might forgive one blunder,
and even a succession of blunders in Africa, Italy or France.
But this was something that could not be overlooked.

As Canaris entered the Chancellery, where the pace of life
seemed quite normal despite the attempt on the Fuehrer's life,
he may well have told himself that this was the most important
meeting of his career. Should Hitler's wrath be unappeased,
Canaris might walk out again a condemned man. He braced
himself and went into the Fuehrer's study. At first glance it is
quite possible that he realized that his master, always a nervous
man, was at the last notch of tension.

Exactly what passed between these two men will never be
known with certainty. According to reports of neutral diplomats, Hitler said he was glad to see Canaris. He knew Canaris
could be trusted; he was no yes-man like the others, no syco-
phant afraid of the grim truth.

Hitler was aware of the truth in its full grimness: he knew
the War was lost. Only the most desperate measures could avail
now, and even these would only postpone the inevitable disaster.
He said he was sorry to discover that Canaris had failed him.
Perhaps it would be best to dismiss the Admiral from his post
of Chief of the Intelligence Division.

The Fuehrer had good reason to be tense. A group of German officers had just tried to kill him; the bomb had exploded
close enough to wound Hitler. And Canaris, his all-powerful
Chief of Intelligence, had known nothing about this festering
conspiracy!

Canaris's reply was a fight for his position and his life. By
his unfailing finesse in finding the right words, he regained Hitler's confidence, as he had done so often before. His explanation sounded very good. He knew he had been remiss; he knew

he should have better guarded his Fuehrer's safety. But he lacked the power to do so.

Hitler raised his eyebrows. Who had dared to hinder the Admiral? Canaris went on to explain. His domain embraced the military areas in the occupied countries but he had no power inside Germany. Heinrich Himmler, Gestapo head and new dictator of the home front, begrudged him any power within the Reich. It was Himmler and his Gestapo that had been at fault. The Admiral gave open expression to his resentment of Himmler.

According to the neutral diplomats, Canaris did a good job of passing the buck. Hitler relented and Canaris remained in power. As a matter of fact, Canaris's excuse was quite true. The responsibility had been the Gestapo's and not that of the Military and Naval Intelligence Service, which was fully occupied in supervising German interests from the North to the South Pole.

The wily Admiral pointed out to his master that this occasion might be turned to profitable use. An official statement dismissing him from office would be of value in deceiving the enemy and putting him off guard. This, Canaris hoped, would give him the opportunity to carry out a long-cherished plan.

The Allied landings in France, Holland and Belgium had demonstrated that the people of Europe were heart and soul for the Allies. At great risk they sheltered parachutists, Allied spies and underground saboteurs. Canaris wanted to insinuate his agents into the underground movements of those countries which were still under German "protection." He would blast the resistance movement before it had a chance to aid the liberating armies of the Allies.

Hitler acceded to this request, and the usual "neutral sources" carried reports of the disgrace and dismissal of Admiral Canaris. But Canaris was not successful in lulling the British, Russian and American Secret Services.

One need not look far to find Canaris's other motive for courting obscurity. He had hunted down countless Allied agents. He had decreed death to innocent civilians in many countries, and had often sacrificed his own agents. His activities had sent thousands of sailors to Davy Jones's locker. Now that times had changed, his intended victims might see a chance to hunt him down. And Canaris, that calm, brainy super-spy, trembled before the personal consequences of Germany's defeat. He saw that the game would soon be up. From a variety of motives, then, he had asked to be officially relieved of his office. He would like to hide away and be forgotten while the list of war criminals was being drawn up by the Allies. But it was too late for him to retire.

* * *

It became increasingly urgent for the Nazis to quell Europe's underground movements. The might of the underground had grown to fantastic proportions. It was taking only forty-eight hours for the French *Maquisards* to get a grounded British or American flier back to his base in England. In Jugoslavia a handful of guerilla fighters had liberated large parts of the country. Denmark had an efficient underground railroad that conducted escaped Allied war prisoners to neutral Sweden. From there Allied planes ferried the men to England, Iceland or wherever they pleased to go.

Admiral Canaris was determined to make the rebellious occupied countries feel his lash. How he did it can now be told in detail. Some of the actors in this story returned to describe the Admiral's tactics.

One of these was Flight Sergeant Andrew Pearcy, of Kansas. Pearcy was a first-rate tail gunner with thirty-one missions behind him. The thirty-second was "it." His plane, one of a fleet of a hundred bombers, had loosed its blockbusters upon the ball-bearing works at Erkner, a suburb of Berlin. En route they encountered a horde of fighters, and at Berlin the Germans put up a terrific flak barrage.

The plane was riddled, but Pearcy's pilot managed to fly it to the Danish North Sea. Here it became clear that their only chance was to attempt an emergency landing on one of the Danish islands. That would mean long imprisonment in a Nazi camp; but there was nothing else to do.

They landed safely in a small tilled field. About ten Danes clustered around the plane almost as soon as it stopped rolling. The American slang, the swearing and the asseverations that this was "one hell of a mess" identified the fliers for the Danes. At once they cried enthusiastically, "Welcome to Denmark!"

They spoke in Danish, which none of the crew understood. But it was easy to understand the friendliness of tone and gesture. Then one of the Danes who spoke a little English volunteered to help the Americans. The fliers were told to hide in a nearby house. Meanwhile the Danes set fire to the Flying Fortress, to make sure the plane would be useless to the Nazis.

Andrew Pearcy, the tail gunner, narrated to me how they were shuttled from farm to farm, from church to church. The Danish underground provided for all their needs. They were disguised as native fishermen, were given the best food available and were taught a smattering of Danish. Finally faked Danish birth certificates and identification papers were obtained for them. "The Germans are too dumb to know whether you boys are Danes or Americans," one of the underground fighters said to Pearcy. By easy stages they reached the vicinity of Copenhagen. Here they had to wait a while for the opportunity to escape the country. The process took months. Each flier fared for himself and followed an individual route. However, they were all to meet somewhere in neutral democratic Sweden.

The Nazis had a good idea why so many British and American fliers slipped through their fingers. Admiral Canaris set up a special Intelligence section to combat the Danish patriots who were aiding Allied airmen.

Allied counter-agents got wind of the new department of the Nazi Secret Service, and learned who its "deposed" master was. The queen of this special Nazi unit was a woman agent of great cleverness and competence. Andrew Pearcy was to become one of her many victims. Andrew had successfully drifted from Jutland to Copenhagen. There he was to wait for the boat that would smuggle him out of the country. All details had to be arranged with the utmost caution. To avoid risks, Pearcy slept in a different house every night. Even that did not altogether eliminate danger, for the Nazis frequently sprang a raid on a whole block, checking up on the identity cards of the inhabitants. For they were well aware that Denmark was a land of scientific saboteurs whose stubborn resistance called for the sternest measures.*

These Nazi raids complicated Andrew Pearcy's situation. Other fliers managed to get to Sweden after a few days or a week, but the tail gunner was stalled in Denmark. If he had been caught, he would have been shot. But the Danes were wonderful hosts, and, apart from the danger, Andrew enjoyed his underground existence. One of the most cordial protectors was a stunning, tall girl named Helvig Delbo, who reminded him of one of the girls he knew back home in Kansas. She was blonde, glamorous, intelligent and always vivacious and refreshing. Andrew saw her quite often, though the rules of the underground expressly forbade frequent contacts with any one person.

Helvig was the proprietor of a dressmaker's shop that specialized in alterations. It was a little place, but did tasteful work. And it had a good location in the center of Copenhagen—30 Sankelmarksgade. That made it more foolhardy than audacious for Pearcy to visit her there during daylight. But he imagined that his Danish was by now good enough to pass muster with the Nazis, who themselves knew little of the language. Evenings he would visit her in her pleasant, two-room apartment. Of course, this was another infraction of the rules.

Helvig was considerably older than Andrew—the flier was only twenty-four. But, lost in a foreign country and surrounded by perils, Andrew was eager to grasp at life. This is why he plunged into a romance with this woman of thirty-six.

Her charming apartment held all sorts of piquant secrets. Helvig Delbo kept pictures of President Roosevelt and Winston Churchill, of Marshal Stalin and General Eisenhower. Here, in an occupied country, she had hidden an American flag. When she archly showed it to him, Andrew felt close to tears. The pictures and the flag were dangerous indeed. Discovery of these trophies would have cost the girl at least ten years' imprisonment. And, as the final pitch of madness, the two of them listened in to the London and Moscow broadcasts, and to the American radio station in England.

---

* Denmark holds the world's record for sabotaging; an act of sabotage was committed every eight hours.

Helvig was a gallant Danish patriot, active in helping the saboteurs. She told him that by birth she was really Norwegian. She had escaped from Quisling Norway, and here the police believed her to be an ordinary Danish woman without the slightest interest in politics. Clearly the two of them, as fugitives, had a great deal in common.

Helvig asked Andrew many questions about America, and among other things she was curious about exactly how he had been rescued, who had helped him and who was arranging about the boat to Sweden. Flight Sergeant Pearcy did not know many names. As a foreigner he found the Danish names difficult to remember and pronounce. The only names he recalled were Larsen and Andersen—and numerous people in the country had such names. Helvig never pressed him; she always quickly changed the subject.

Finally the day came when all was ready for Andrew's departure. He spent his last night with Helvig. They were grateful for the time, short as it was, in which they had known each other, and they promised to meet again after the War. Then the hour struck for the heartbreaking farewell.

Andrew Pearcy, wearing ordinary civilian clothes, made his way to neutral Sweden. A few weeks later he was safely in England. There he told the Allied Intelligence Services all the details of his escape. Of course, he inquired about the other members of his crew.

But none of the others had been rescued. They had been taken prisoner, and it was a matter of great astonishment that Andrew had escaped. A Danish Nazi newspaper reported the arrest of the fugitives, and with them twelve members of the underground.

The Allied Intelligence Services began putting two and two together. What was behind Andrew's unique escape? Could he have been permitted to escape in order that his route might be traced? Was Helvig, his generous hostess, a bona fide member of the underground? No underground worker would risk his freedom to have at home pictures of Allied leaders; his life was too valuable to the movement. It was not worthy of a member to risk a stiff prison sentence for himself and to endanger the lives of his comrades, just for the pleasure of keeping a forbidden American flag.

The British and Americans decided to investigate the case of Helvig Delbo.

Intelligence officers visited Kingston House in London, headquarters of the Norwegian government-in-exile. One door in this building bears the legend: Department of Justice of the Norwegian Government. The British and American officers asked whether the Norwegians had any data on a Norwegian citizen named Helvig Delbo. Delbo? No, they had nothing on her, but the Norwegian officials promised to follow up the matter. "Underground boats" had been keeping up uninterrupted communication between England and Norway since April, 1940. By way of these boats an urgent inquiry was passed to the underground within Norway.

Underground Norway has its techniques for finding out what it wants to know. Not everyone in Quisling's Department of Justice or Quisling's police force was heart and soul for Major Vidkun Quisling. Norwegian Intelligence officers who wore the uniform of the *Hird*, Quisling's storm troopers, gathered some information. They had nothing definite, but they made an excellent start.

Their report named a certain Max Pelving as liaison officer between the Quisling police in Norway and the Nazi police in Denmark. Pelving is the same Danish police official who had been arrested in 1939 as an accomplice of the Pflugk-Hartung spy ring. He had recently been seen in Oslo at the Hotel Continental, where he had had conferences with the Norwegian Gestapo and the Quisling police.

With him was a tall woman in her mid-thirties. Her name was Greta Johannsen, but the description answered to that of Helvig Delbo.

Max Pelving, alias Petermann, who had done his treacherous work for Pflugk-Hartung and Canaris before the invasion of Denmark, was active again. It was a highly tenable premise that Pelving should be involved in constructing a trap for American fliers and their underground friends.

A Norwegian counter-agent had seen the two, Pelving and the woman, at the Theatre Café. The lead was worth checking. The Norwegian agent got further orders from London.

He was to proceed to Copenhagen and find out what more he could.

Ordinarily such a trip was impossible. But a member of the Quisling police and a wearer of the Nazi uniform has special prerogatives. As an employee of the Quislings, this counteragent was able to travel to Copenhagen. After a few weeks he reported to London that Greta Johannsen and Helvig Delbo were one and the same person.

This had more than one implication. First, it established that Helvig Delbo had worked for the Nazi Secret Service for years. She was a star member of Admiral Canaris's special Intelligence unit. But most important of all was the discovery that Max Pelving, arch-spy in the Pflugk-Hartung area, had resumed activity. He did not have, it seemed, enough deaths on his conscience. He was serving the now-entrenched Nazis as he had served them before the invasion of Scandinavia.

Helvig Delbo was something more than his girl friend. His first wife had tried to poison herself when her husband's arrest as a Nazi spy took place. She did not die, but was ill for many months. When she recovered, Pelving brutally deserted her, and chose Helvig as her successor. But the pair were never legally married.

Pelving's espionage trial in 1939 had resulted in a sentence of two and a half years. The District Attorney revealed that Pelving's father had been a German and that his real name was Petermann. Pelving had entered the Danish civil service by means of false statements. In 1918 he had fought in Finland's war against Russia and had been presented with several medals by Marshal Mannerheim. For a long time he had been a member of the illicit Danish Nazi Party.

These facts established, the underground was immediately warned. Parachutists brought news that Pelving and Delbo were working inside the underground. The arrest of American fliers and the death of many Danish patriots could be attributed to them.

The people of Denmark act straightforwardly. There is but one punishment for double-crossing and deadly guile. In December, 1943, Pelving felt his position so secure that he could be driven by his chauffeur through Copenhagen in a German *Dienst-Auto,* an official car. Beside him sat Denmark's Mata

Hari. Quite recently five Danish patriots she had exposed had been shot for aiding the Americans.

The Danish saboteurs were far from being murderers. However, punishment is sometimes necessary. Let us call them, rather, guerilla fighters in their secret war. Max and Helvig were driving down one of the boulevards of Copenhagen when, from another car alongside theirs, three shots were fired. Max Pelving was killed and the charming Helvig wounded.

The Nazis were furious and retaliated by taking hostages. But all Denmark rejoiced to learn that the lowest of the spies and traitors had met a fitting end.

Helvig Delbo was rushed to a Germany army hospital, since she was afraid to go to an ordinary civilian one. She recovered and in January, 1944, she fled to Norway, where she worked for the Norwegian Gestapo. She did some private work for no less a personage than Vidkun Quisling himself. In February, 1944, Quisling dispatched her to Sweden on a fake passport. There her task was to observe what the Norwegian refugees were up to, and to see what kind of goods the Norwegian government-in-exile was ordering and having stored in Sweden. She was also authorized to set up a working group of five trustworthy people.

The efficient Swedish police found out about it. They arrested the five who were working for her, but Helvig herself slipped through the net.

The undergrounds in Norway and Denmark were looking for her. The Allied Secret Services were on the alert. But she seemed to have vanished. A rumor came that she was in contact with Max Pelving's former chief, Pflugk-Hartung, then the head of Nazi espionage in Rumania.

Helvig had never done what she did out of principle. She performed her spy's duties because she was in love with Pelving, because she liked adventure and because it meant easy money. Her motives were quite commercial, and in the end it was her love of money that brought about her downfall.

She must have known that she was being hunted by everyone in Scandinavia. Nevertheless, she hated to leave for Germany or Rumania without making one little expedition to Copenhagen to get at Pelving's old safe deposit box. It had money and jewelry in it, the equivalent of the thirty pieces of silver that Judas received. The pair had not saved a fabulous sum out of the money they received for sending Danish patriots to the firing-squad or the gallows. The safe deposit box held some cheap jewelry and about twelve thousand kroner, or three thousand dollars.

It was guessed that she intended to stay only a few days in Copenhagen; perhaps no longer than a day. But Denmark is a country that knows how to destroy its deadly enemies. Five hours after Helvig entered Copenhagen, the underground knew where she was and the Allied Secret Services received the message by short wave.

Next morning every Danish newspaper carried a three-line notice to the effect that unknown attackers had shot down one Helvig Delbo, a Norwegian citizen. It happened near the Sankelmarksgade, where she had had her innocent little dressmaker's shop.

Now she was dead. Her life had had no beauty, no real romance. It is enough to say that two of the lowest criminals, two of the most dangerous spies of World War II, received their just deserts at the hands of soldiers of the Allied armies.

Her funeral, held on March 13, 1944, was attended by no one. But she was accorded one last courtesy. She was buried at the side of Max Petermann-Pelving.

CHAPTER XVIII

The Case of the Talking Dolls

WHOEVER prophesied that women agents would be little used during World War II prophesied recklessly. The First World War had demonstrated the superior talents of women for espionage, and experience with these talents had created in men an attitude of vigilance. No general any longer carried plans for his coming offensive in his pocket. No secret documents were left behind by enamored officers in hotel rooms, and soldiers were inclined to distrust automatically any woman who asked too many questions.

But the Japanese Secret Service did not see this mounting mistrust as a sufficient reason for discarding women agents. Where a man could be effective, they reasoned, a woman could do as well or better. The Japs, indeed, relied heavily on white women operators, wherever they could be obtained. The tribe of women agents was well represented by Greta Kainen in Finland, Helvig Delbo in Denmark, Ruth Kuehn in Pearl Harbor. In New York City, it was represented by an attractive fifty-year-old widow.

The scene opens in the fall of 1943, some thirteen hours' train journey from New York. In Springfield, Ohio, lived an eminent old family, the Wallaces. Miss Mary Wallace had never had a spy phobia. She was more interested in the enduring arts than in ephemeral politics. One morning she received a letter from Argentina. It was postmarked Buenos Aires. It was an air-mail letter, in a red-white-and-blue bordered envelope, and it was addressed, not to Mary Wallace, but to:

> Senora Inez Lopez de Molinali
> 2563 O'Higgins Street
> Buenos Aires
> Argentina

How on earth did this letter, addressed to some unknown in Argentina, get into Mary Wallace's post box? She puzzled over it a minute, and then, on turning the letter round in her hand, perceived that the back flap gave the return address as:

> Mary Wallace
> 1808 E. High Street
> Springfield, Ohio

The envelope was typewritten and bore, besides the Argentina postmark, a postmark from "Grand Central Station" in New York, dated a month back.

This was certainly a mystery. Miss Wallace had never sent this letter, nor had she any friend named de Molinali in Argentina. In fact, she knew nobody in Latin America.

She opened the envelope and read the mysterious letter. It was written in her name, but she could not make head nor tail of the contents. The signature read "Mary Wallace," and the stationary resembled her own, but was plainly an imposture.

How had this letter reverted to her? Again she examined the envelope, and noticed the Spanish stamp: "Moved. Left no forwarding address. Return to sender."

Evidently someone had written to Senora de Molinali in Argentina and had used the name of Mary Wallace. The Spanish lady had not been at the given address, and the letter had been returned to the alleged sender, who was Mary Wallace. She was really provoked. Who had dared to use her name and forge her signature? It was a fine piece of impertinence.

Besides, the letter was full of misspellings and was written in an English which Miss Wallace would have been ashamed of. She read the letter in great indignation. This was the strange text:

Dear Friend,

You probably wonder what has become of me as I havent written to you for so long. We have had a pretty bad month or so. My little nephew the one I adore so has a malignant tumour on the brain and isnt expected to live, so we're all crushed that we dont know what we are doing. They are giving him exray on the head and they hope to check it but give us absolutely no hope in a complete cure and maybe not even any relief. I am completely crushed.

You asked me to tell you about my collection a month ago. I had to give a talk to an Art Club so I talked about my dolls and figurines. The only new dolls I have are three lovely Irish dolls. One of these three dolls is an old Fisherman with a net over his back another is an old woman with wood on her back and the third is a little boy.

Everyone seemed to enjoy my talk I can only think of our sick boy these days.

You wrote me that you had sent a letter to Mr. Shaw he distroyed your letter, you know he has been ill. His car was damaged but is being repaired now. I saw a few of his family about. They all say Mr. Shaw will be back to work soon.

I do hope my letter is not too sad. There is not much I can to write you these days.

I came in this short trip for Mother on business before I make out her income tax report, that is also Why I am learning to type.

Everyone seems busy these days the streets are full of people.

Remember me to your family sorry I havent written to you for long.

Truly

Mary Wallace

PS Mother wanted to go to Louville but due to our worry the Louville plan put out our minds now.

Miss Wallace was perplexed, for there were startling features in the letter. It was true that her nephew had a serious brain ailment. It was also true that she had lectured to an art club in Springfield about her doll collection. But she had no Irish dolls. She had certainly not been in New York when the letter to Argentina was posted. Finally, she never used a typewriter, but wrote all her letters by hand.

She decided that someone was playing a poor joke on her and her habit of collecting dolls. Mary Wallace saw no other reason for informing the police, but from pique she turned the letter over to the postal authorities of Springfield to find out what was behind the senseless trick.

The Springfield postmaster forwarded the letter to the FBI.

In Washington the letter was carefully studied. It was too strange to be innocent. It was too pointless to be intended as a joke. Its contents had not disturbed the postal censor, who may have thought it merely illiterate and confused. In itself the letter might be interpreted as harmless, but the attendant circumstances, the false return address, made it more than that. One operative in Washington had a definite theory of the case. His theory might be all off, but it was decided that it was worth investigation.

Agent B's theory was that the "new dolls" were code words for warships newly operating in the Pacific. American aircraft carrier, he conjectured, was indicated by the Irish fisherman, for the carrier was draped in safety nets. The old woman with wood on her back might stand for a warship with wooden superstructure, and the little boy doll might stand for a new destroyer.

The Mr. Shaw who had destroyed the letter was interpreted as the *U.S.S. Shaw* which had almost been destroyed in the Pearl Harbor attack. This destroyer had just been repaired and given a new bow at Honolulu. It now made the run between the Hawaiian Islands and San Francisco.

As for the postscript, the agent made the wild guess that it referred to the *U.S.S. Louisville,* a cruiser which had been out to sea a long time, and whose whereabouts was a closely guarded secret. The postscript seemed to say that requested information could not be given.

It was a fantastic analysis. The postal censors refused to believe it. But, once the case had been opened, it was subjected to intensive analysis and all relevant material was laid on the FBI desks in Washington.

Mary Wallace was called upon for questioning. She told Agent B all about her doll collection. She had recently added to it, making a trip to New York for the purpose. She had bought several dolls at America's select doll shop on Madison Avenue near 62nd Street. She had chatted quite a while with the woman who ran the store, a kindred spirit.

"Did you speak about family matters to the store-owner?" asked Agent B.

"Well, yes, I did a little," confessed Mary Wallace. "Mrs. Dickinson was very nice. She gave me one doll at a bargain, and her collection is very beautiful and genuine."

"Did you mention anything about your nephew's brain ailment?"

"Yes, I happened to. You see, Mrs. Dickinson spoke with deep feeling of her husband's last months of life. It brought to my mind the condition of our nephew, who is seriously ill."

But still this was not enough evidence for an indictment of Mrs. Dickinson. Miss Wallace cited at least ten people who knew about her doll collection as well as about the illness of her nephew. The doll store was one of many clues. Agent B was interested in checking up on them all. He was more than ever convinced that the letter was sinister. He had worked long enough in the decoding department to be able to sense this. It was strange that the letterwriter was such a poor speller. Yet, in spite of the many errors, the letter seemed to be written by an American.

The dolls intrigued him. He reasoned that the allusions must be based on an intimate knowledge of the doll world. Therefore he decided to start his search among Mary Wallace's acquaintances in art clubs, hobby groups, doll dealers, et cetera.

Since he was already in Springfield, he started with an investigation of the art club where Mary Wallace had lectured. But he gathered nothing from it. The people appeared to be unconscious of any world outside of Springfield, Ohio. None of them had any connections in Argentina. It was going to be tough, Agent B saw; but he was a diligent worker. He had time. He knew in his bones that this letter was not an isolated incident. He ordered the postal censor to stop every letter which had the slightest allusion to the doll trade or to doll collections. Ordinary business letters of this description were held up and forwarded to Agent B for study. He wanted to get a clear picture of the doll import and export traffic.

Then the time came to have a look at the doll shop on New York's Madison Avenue.

The store was quite famous. Many movie stars were among its clientele. It was a luxury shop for wealthy doll fanciers and collectors of antiques. The blue letterheads of the shop's stationery read:

Velvalee Dickinson
Dolls—Antique—Foreign—Regional

The stock was rare and included no doll under fifty dollars. Antique dolls from the colonial period fetched five hundred dollars apiece. The store resembled a cross between an art museum and a marionette show. There were porcelain beauties dating from Paris of Victor Hugo. There were exquisite Marie Antoinette figurines. There were stolid dolls from the American frontier. There were bizarre carved wooden idols made by natives of Dutch New Guinea as playthings for their children. Round-faced, delicately tinted dolls from China sat on a shelf. The show window had a motley group of dolls, some toy horses and clay animal figures and tiny children's furniture, beautifully arranged.

The owner, Velvalee Dickinson, was a petite, attractive and chic widow. She was less than five feet tall, and had a pert little face. She did not look her age at all, though she wore glasses, for at fifty her eyesight had begun to decline.

FBI agents came to her store but made no inquiries. They posed as customers, and kept their eyes open. They lingered and looked, but bought nothing. They gathered a few general impressions. They remarked that the little lady was so slight that she must weigh no more than ninety-five pounds.

The operatives had been ordered to go slow. First, some preliminary investigations of Velvalee Dickinson had to be made. Her background might confirm or dispel suspicion. Washington's FBI collected some biographical data from the West Coast. She was better known there, for until 1937, when her husband died, she had been a native of California.

Her birthplace had been Sacramento, California. She had been a student at Stanford University. Her maiden name was Malvena Blücher, which might indicate kinship to the Prussian General Blücher who fought against Napoleon. She had no criminal record, but her name was found on the membership lists of the American-Japanese Society. She had belonged to it as late as 1937, when she left the West Coast. Her late husband had his offices in San Francisco in the same building as the German and Japanese Consulates. Still, this might be pure coincidence and reflected nothing against Mrs. Dickinson.

They learned that Velvalee had once worked as a bank clerk. She had also been employed by the California Fruit Growers Association, and both employers gave reports which were extremely favorable.

She and her husband used to live in the Imperial Valley, which was the heart of the Japanese colony. Mrs. Dickinson had a shrewd business head and for several years she had handled brokerage accounts for Japanese-Americans. Among her customers were some Japanese naval officers, but this was all before Pearl Harbor and could not be looked upon as necessarily suspicious.

During the last years of her husband's life she had need for a lot of money, for Mr. Dickinson was subject to heart attacks which brought in their train large doctor and hospital bills. But she seemed to have managed very well.

Widowed, Mrs. Dickinson moved to New York. During the Christmas season of 1937 she took a job in the doll department of Bloomingdale's Department Store. The next year she opened her own exclusive store on Madison Avenue.

There she made a lot of money. Customers flocked to the store, and Mrs. Dickinson's personality was engaging.

Sometimes she would mention her personal unhappiness. "Since my husband's death, life means nothing to me," she would say. It was very touching. She was such a frail little woman who tried hard to be gallant. Her clientele thought highly of her integrity. They knew that she would never try to sell any forgeries or junk.

She was in contact with doll collectors in all forty-eight states of the union. Velvalee often went on business trips, sometimes to the West Coast to see some of her customers in Hollywood.

The FBI watched impartially for several weeks. Then their suspicions were suddenly aroused. Tucked into the well-packed boxes of dolls which were mailed to distant collectors, among the excelsior and the tissue paper, were little notes. They referred to dolls, and used words in a sort of baby language, which might be the parlance of the doll trade and might be a code. Who could say?

In the meantime Velvalee had begun to feel uncomfortable. Strange customers were barging into her shop, whose questions revealed that they could not differentiate between a French and a German doll. Was she under police observation? Something was wrong. It was months since she had received orders from her chief. No letters from Argentina—what would happen if her friends in Argentina were arrested? What would happen if her letter to the Molinali woman fell into the wrong hands?

Velvalee fell prey to bad dreams. But she tried to recover her poise. Everything had been so neatly dovetailed that there could be no danger to herself.

If the Argentina letter failed to reach the South American agent, it would probably be destroyed in Argentina. Those

Latin American countries certainly would not bother with an unclaimed letter. And if the letter had been waylaid by the censor, why then they could arrest "that provincial woman" in Springfield, Ohio.

But Velvalee's troubled dreams could not be dispelled. She reasoned that if something had gone wrong, she would have been arrested long ago. Nevertheless, there were these queer men dropping into the shop. What were they after? Panic overcame her, which she once again tried to conquer.

These men must be spies from competitor shops. There was a New England dealer from whom she had snatched several Hollywood customers. It must be he. He was an unethical person, anyway, who accused her of forging some of her antique dolls and tampering with the costumes. He knew a thing or two, and he was right about what she did, but the collectors never knew the difference. She sold her dolls, both the authentic and the fake, at good prices. The trade was lucrative, but she was still far away from her $100,000 mark. She had to go on.

Nevertheless, she could not sleep. One night she left her bed in the middle of the night, put on housecoat and slippers and went to the kitchenette. A cup of coffee was what she needed. She read that night's evening paper and studied the stock market section. Her stocks were up again. That was a comfort. She drank her coffee and conceived a plan.

Alma, her sales assistant, could be left in charge of the shop. She herself would go to the West Coast. If anything happened in the interval, if the FBI made a raid on the store, she would be informed and she would not come back. She would give Alma a false destination, Florida or Canada. Time was all she needed. Time solves many problems. She had to see a former Japanese naval officer now operating in Portland, Oregon. He would help her. If anything went wrong, she could continue on to Mexico, and from there to places where Jap subs would pick her up. But all these dread eventualities were nothing but her imagination, she told herself. Nothing had happened so far, and nothing would happen.

She had to be cautious. Those men who had looked at the shop window that morning could not be plain-clothes men, for they were too suave and wore clothes which policemen could never afford. That was another ridiculous fancy. But she had to keep her departure a secret.

It was early morning when she finally fell asleep. She awoke in a sweat of fear from a horrible nightmare. As she dressed, she decided that she would not take any luggage with her on the trip—in case she was really being shadowed.

She took a taxi to the doll shop. Alma was already there. Mrs. Dickinson sent the girl to the bank to draw a check sufficient for running the shop for a few weeks. She said good-by and told the girl that her brother, Mr. Blücher, would look in from time to time, to help her if necessary. She posted a note to her brother and grabbed a taxi at Madison Avenue. Glancing around, she saw a car which followed her.

What was it? Was she discovered after all? But how? How? Once more she tried to laugh away her fears. There were hundreds of cars on Madison Avenue. But she would take no chances. She told the driver to take her to Saks at 34th Street. This department store has an overhead bridge which, without the necessity of going outdoors, led one to another large store, Gimbel's. In this maze of floors and exits, no one could follow her. She lost herself in the crowds, passed over into Gimbel's and descended into its basement, which connected with the subway tunnel. Through it she wended her way to the Pennsylvania Station. She thought she noticed a man who looked suspicious. Now all men looked suspicious and menacing. Her nerves were giving way. She did not stop to buy a ticket, but went through the gate to the next outgoing train.

It turned out that the train was bound for Philadelphia. She paid her fare to the conductor and planned to continue from that city to Chicago and then to Portland, Oregon.

She reached Portland and went immediately to the Chinese restaurant where her contact man worked. Her heart sank, for there in the window, between two pots of cactus plants, was the sign "Closed." Ruin stared her in the face. There was a very slim chance that she could meet some other contact man in California, but most of her Japanese friends had been relocated or interned. The long journey had been for nothing and had left her more exposed than before.

Several weeks later she was back in New York. She still clung to the hope that the FBI had not traced her misdeeds. Like a desperate incantation she told herself that if she had been discovered, it would all have been over long ago.

* * *

Of course, it proved nothing at all that she had so far been unmolested. Mrs. Dickinson could wait.

Of more pressing interest was the fact that the postal censors had stopped three more letters dealing with dolls, colonial and French ones seeming to be in question. The letters were not signed by Mrs. Dickinson or by Mary Wallace, but by three distinct names, which, when traced, proved to be the names of patrons of the Dickinson doll shop.

Now the FBI got busy tracing the source of the letter paper. It also found the typewriters on which these letters had been written. The typewriters proved to be the property of three hotels, one in Chicago, one in San Francisco, one in Los Angeles.

Mrs. Dickinson had thought that her excursion through the department stores had shaken the FBI off her track. But she was mistaken. The FBI had shadowed her pretty consistently from city to city. They obtained evidence that Mrs. Dickinson had stayed overnight at each one of these hotels from which the doll letters had been written. The letters to South America had the typographical mistakes of the Mary Wallace letter. The letters pulsed with nervous desperation, as the letterwriter asked for money and "answers." Velvalee was cut off from the rest of the gang, and she was screaming for help.

Agent B's hunch had been amazingly correct. The Irish dolls mentioned in the first letter referred to warships. The dealer in rare dolls was one of Nippon's most dangerous woman spies in the United States.

The FBI prolonged the term of waiting. They hoped to catch her accomplices and to warn the South American governments of the true contents of Velvalee's doll boxes.

Mrs. Dickinson was ultimately arrested when she visited a New York bank in which she had a safe deposit box, containing eighteen thousand dollars in cash. She had been keeping the cash on hand in case she needed it for a quick escape. The FBI agents followed her into the vault room. There they announced her arrest and prepared to confiscate the espionage funds. The wiry little widow struggled with the men. Scratching and squirming, she tried to make her way out of the vault room.

Mrs. Dickinson was arrested as a Japanese spy. More money and valuables were found, amounting to forty thousand dollars. This sum was roughly equivalent to what she owed the U.S. Treasury in unpaid taxes. Other accounts of hers were confiscated. Her earnings from espionage were estimated at about sixty thousand dollars.

In July, 1944, her trial came up. This was the first case of an American woman facing a possible death penalty for espionage.

Mrs. Dickinson wore the clothes she had on when arrested. She wore a trim brown tweed coat and a little blue hat. She was apathetic and pale, for the six months in the Women's House of Detention had not improved her appearance. Her attorney wanted to gain time. He hoped to secure a postponement of the trial until the end of the War. He claimed that the defendant had fallen ill during the period of detention. But the court ascertained that her heart condition was normal and that, as a matter of fact, she had gained twenty-five pounds during her imprisonment.

The District Attorney summed up his case. He revealed how the doll shop on Madison Avenue had functioned as an excellent front for espionage. The defendant had contact with Japanese naval officers. As evidence there were four code letters in her doll language. "The dolls talked," said the D.A., "and we finally learned to understand their language."

The woman spy tried to refuse to let her fingerprints be taken, shied away from photographers. In her high-pitched voice she explained, pleaded, minimized. Her eyes sparkled; her slender throat throbbed. In the face of the clear evidence, she knew it was hopeless to protest her innocence. But she tried to convince the court that the information had been of no great value. She admitted that she had circumvented the postal censorship regulations. But she avoided giving information which really would endanger the United States. What she had done was entirely for mercenary reasons.

"Yes," she admitted, "I was mercenary. All my savings had gone for my husband's ailment. And I was aging and I was all by myself. I was afraid of the future. I struggled to accumulate money to ease my old age.

"I was so sure that I would never be detected," she went on, as though that palliated the offense. She believed that the customers' names would be a safe camouflage. She believed that her clever code was beyond unravelling. As we have seen, she might well have put over her perfect crime. Then there would have been no ten-year sentence for her. But one detail had gone awry. The Japanese agent in Argentina had been removed.

The Japanese had been careless in keeping their part of the bargain. Mrs. Dickinson should have been informed. This one slip delivered Mrs. Dickinson into the hands of the FBI.

CHAPTER XIX

Hirohito in Harlem

ONLY sixty blocks from Mrs. Velvalee Dickinson's exquisite doll shop, which was to be auctioned off, lies Harlem. In a dingy little office in forgotten slum quarters two men met in the spring of 1940. Both were colored, one a Negro and the other a Filipino. Both were fanatics. They discussed the possibilities of pitting their united energies against the white race in general and the United States in particular.

They had been urged to meet by a little Japanese major named Naka Nakane. But the unification movement did not get very far. These two men could not unite. Each was a leader of his own group and each wished to remain leader.

Neither would give up an iota of his power or a dime of his money.

At last the Negro suggested to the Filipino that they compromise by marking out spheres of influence. The Filipino would work among the Negro church groups and the other among the Negro soldiery. This agreement fell far short of the scheme proposed by the Japanese, but it was a way out of the fierce rivalry between the two Fascist Negro organizations.

The two obstinate leaders were Robert Obadiah Jordan, Negro head of the Ethiopian Pacific Movement of Harlem, and Philippine-born Dr. A. Takis, alias Mimo de Guzman, alias Policartio Mannansala, alias M. Yamamato, alias Dr. Koo, who headed the Pacific Movement of the Eastern World.

Do not be incredulous at the string of aliases. All in all, Dr. Takis owned to nineteen names. He was a man who appropriated for his own use any name that tickled his fancy.

Dr. Takis was born in Zamboanga on July 6, 1900. He was a handsome man with deep-set eyes and a lofty forehead. His only defective feature was a thick upper lip. In 1918 he came to the United States and until 1930 served in the U.S. Navy and Coast Guard. Then he received a dishonorable discharge for some misconduct. It was at this point that he abandoned his real name of Mimo de Guzman and adopted that of Dr. Takis.

His political career started in 1930 when a Japanese naval officer invited him to a meeting of the Black Dragon Society, Japan's violently chauvinist organization abroad. Here he heard enunciated for the first time in his life the doctrine that "the dark-skinned races of the world must destroy the white-skinned races." An embittered, jobless Filipino, he found the idea strongly appealing.

It was still peacetime, but Japan was already tuning up her espionage machine against the white world. Dr. Takis was not asked to do spy work for the Japanese. He was named for a larger job, that of organizing the Negroes on a new basis, on the Hitlerite basis of racial chauvinism. This organized group would become a potent weapon for Japan as soon as the War started.

Nippon's gigantic plan was to muster millions of colored people in the United States who would work as a potential fifth column and would, when the order was given, stir up all sorts of unrest. They would be the blind puppets of their Negro leader. In *Mein Kampf* Hitler had stressed the possibilities of racial insurrection, claiming that he could arouse one, whenever he deemed it necessary, in a "melting pot" like the United States. The Japanese were going to apply this theory.

The organization had large funds at its command. Takis invited Negros to "emigrate" to Japan or to travel there. These "Guests of Nippon" would be trained as spies. Dr. Takis provided every prospective visitor or immigrant with sums ranging from one thousand to six thousand dollars. Volunteers were few and far between. Nevertheless, unremitting cajoling talks recruited several hundred.

The high-sounding title of the organization was the "Pacific Movement of the Eastern World"—Eastern being taken to mean the colored world. Branch offices were opened in New York, St. Louis, Indianapolis, Kansas City, Cincinnati, Pittsburgh, Philadelphia, Chicago and Detroit.

Large Negro mass meetings were announced. They were addressed by Dr. Takis, or by some other speaker from the St. Louis headquarters. Sometimes they were favored with a speech from a visiting Japanese. What the Negroes heard at these meetings was the purest high treason.

The meetings were well attended. The rooms were generally old ramshackle places, full of dirt, smoke and noise. Before the serious lectures, a musical program was put on, a medley of hymns and hot jazz. "The Star Spangled Banner" was never sung. Then the speaker would come forth and rant of hatred and destruction. A frenzied mass psychosis would overcome the room. Every one of the members listened intently and burst into wild applause when the speaker declared, "I have come here to promote international unity between the dark people of Japan and the dark people of America."

The speaker would evoke their most primitive feelings. He worked up hate against the whites and against America. Then he produced his slogans, shouting through the smoke-filled meeting hall: "Japan is making overtures to you. If she fails, you fail. This is the last chance for the dark races of America to overcome white supremacy and throw the white tyrants off your backs."

The audience clapped its approval. If any dissenters were present, they kept silent, subdued by mass emotion.

The chairman's closing words—when he was not the main speaker, Dr. Takis usually took the chair—would emphasize that the "Pacific Movement of the Eastern World" was already a powerful organization, with a membership of one hundred thousand.

When the War started, Dr. Takis began declaring, "This War is the Negro's chance for a free life." In a low, commanding tone he advised his people: "Leave the sinking ship. Leave the sinking ship of America before it is too late."

Dr. Takis became a roving preacher of race hatred, in which role he served his Japanese and German friends. He was accompanied on his lecture tours by a bodyguard and secretary and by another Filipino who was his closest associate, a former restaurant cook, named George A. Cruz.

Their dangerous propaganda emanated from a new division of Japan's espionage services. Japan considered this an experiment in morale sabotage, an experiment almost unprecedented in history. Its only parallel was the work of Franz von Rintelen, the "dark invader" who had organized strikes and rebellions within the American labor movement in World War I. Now this dubious colored organization, which never won the backing of any responsible colored leader, carried sabotage and race war one step farther.

The two Filipino agitators, Dr. Takis and George Cruz, toured the country from coast to coast. One of their trips took them to a little town near Blytheville, Arkansas. There was a Negro church in town and Dr. Takis, the distinguished visitor, offered to give a free lecture. His offer was gladly received, and the church was filled to the last seat. Some whites were in the audience; believers in racial understanding, they were interested in hearing what Dr. Takis had to say. He had announced a general controversial topic. Takis was discreet. He was careful to sound out his audience and temper his Japanese-inspired speech. But after him his companion Cruz rose to speak. Cruz was boorishly frank. He shouted at his audience:

"The world belongs to the colored races. Join with us, and hell will pop for the white man."

Uneasiness spread among the white people in the church. A few voices were raised in reproof of the speaker. The place was a church and it was hardly seemly to be speaking in that way. But it was too late. Violence broke out between Negroes and whites. The police were called. Before they came, shots were fired and the doors were barred against anyone leaving. Takis smashed one of the church windows and escaped, but Cruz stayed on until the police arrived and caught him. He was sentenced to six months for "anarcho-syndicalism."

The War saw the eruption of great race riots: the street battles of Detroit, the traffic tie-ups in Philadelphia where white union men protested the employment of colored men, sporadic riots in the South. We have blamed many things for them—housing conditions, employers, unions—and have tended to play down the fact that the Axis has spent millions of dollars to incite precisely such racial disturbances. It was part and parcel of the attempt to sabotage the War effort and disrupt morale. Men like Takis and the Harlem Nazi, Obadiah Jordan, were amply paid to blow on the sparks of national disunity.

Dr. Takis, fulfilling his part of the agreement with Jordan, set up a church of his own, "The Triumph Church of the New Age." Negro preachers who took a stand against the Takis movement were terrorized, beaten up and driven from their churches.

The character of the Takis movement was not lost upon the authorities. But they refrained from suppressive action, even when Takis, growing bolder as time passed and he remained unmolested, promised that after Japanese victory Japan would liberate the Negroes in America. Takis even said that Japan promised to give the movement its needed weapons. Until the arms came, the members had to get what they could from other sources. An armed Negro revolt, he intimated, was scheduled, to be bolstered by a Japanese invasion of American soil by way of the Panama Canal.

The members of the activist group lived in an atmosphere of civil war. They purchased and stole weapons and brought them to headquarters at the Argus Building, Market Street, in

St. Louis. From there the arms were apportioned to the many scattered groups throughout the country.

An interesting fact was that while Takis spoke flawless English, he simulated a heavy accent for his rabble-rousing lectures. He explained to his confidantes that he had to do so to substantiate his boast of having powerful friends in Japan.

Japan wanted this organization of one hundred thousand to be as disruptive as possible. Members were ordered to be quarrelsome at government ration boards, at their jobs, at employment offices, in every public situation. From small disturbances, major riots would grow. Bumping and pushing clubs were organized all over the country.

Finally, the FBI accumulated enough evidence to strike. Takis, he of the nineteen names, was arrested. He might have been charged with an impressive list of crimes, from rioting to grand larceny, for the Jap-Negro organization was a lucrative racket and its leader had not scrupled to use its funds for his own purposes. The specific crime was the forgery of money orders. The charge of espionage or treason was not brought up. There was not sufficient proof of espionage activities. True, the FBI had found pictures of airplanes, submarines, torpedoes and other military paraphernalia in his desk, but they were nothing out of the ordinary, being generally distributed news photos.

The arrest of the leader of the "Pacific Movement" abruptly terminated the life of this pro-Japanese Negro movement. In any case, the vast majority of the colored people of the United States had turned their backs on Takis.

* * *

America had asserted her authority and made short work of one of her enemies. But the evil forces working to undermine the morale of Negroes were not yet routed. The Japanese were vigorously supporting a second Fascist organization among the colored people, the Ethiopian Pacific Movement of Harlem. Takis had tried collaborating with this group, but, as we have already seen, the meeting between him and Robert Obadiah Jordan accomplished little. Now that his rival was out of the way, Jordan was eager to win control over the scattered and decimated following of Takis. Jordan had hitherto confined his work to the Negro service men in our armed forces. Almost foaming at the mouth, he would address hundreds of Negro soldiers on furlough in Harlem:

"We are just waiting to put MacArthur into the hole in the ground where he belongs. The Japanese under General Tojo will win the peace in the name of the peace."

Jordan's career as a rabid Harlem agitator had begun long before the War. When he was finally arrested, the District Attorney produced recordings of his numerous speeches. He played some, from which the following treasonable excerpts are taken:

"Japan is going to liberate the dark races . . .

"The little brown men from the East will in a very short time rule the world. The Axis powers are bound to win . . .

"Hirohito will give the Negroes all the benefits he has given the Chinese. Japan has brought to China a new culture, a new way of life and new opportunities."

Some elements in Harlem listened to the Fascist—a very small minority, to be sure. But the majority did not curb Jordan. At the end of his talks he would instruct the soldiers,

"When you soldier boys get over there, lower your guns, throw your arms around the yellow or brown man and then turn your guns the other way."

"Turn your guns the other way" was a Communist slogan in World War I. Lenin had recommended that the proletariat turn the imperialistic war into a class war. The Nazis and Jap agents utilized the same slogan, only they wished this War to be converted into a gigantic race war.

We remember that the Germans practiced enlightened self-interest in permitting Lenin and his revolutionary friends to travel through Germany in a sealed train in order to further the revolution in Russia. General Ludendorff had realized that the proletarian revolution in Russia would bring relief to warring Germany. Admiral Canaris and the Japanese tried to repeat the ruse. The discontent of the colored people would be used for organizing civil violence and revolts within the army.

Jordan would instruct his listeners,

"Now, go back to your outfits and start the whispering campaign." Should someone in the audience denounce him as a fifth columnist, he would boastfully retort:

"Yes, I am a fifth columnist. I fully expect to be put into a concentration camp. As for those who dare to put me there, I'm going to order their heads chopped off when the New Order is here to stay."

Vainglorious and threatening, Jordan followed the example of Goebbels and Hitler. FBI agents were always present in his Harlem audiences, listening in fury and impatience. They would have liked nothing better than to put a stop to the braggart. But they were not allowed to strike. In fact, the Negro Hitler was left immune even when he committed one of his grossest crimes; after his sermon on fraternizing with the Japanese, he dramatically pointed to the American flag draped at the back of the lecture stage.

"Here it is," he shrieked. "This is the flag we're supposed to protect."

A tension seized the audience. It was a dangerous act, for the soldiers, whatever hold Jordan had over them, were nevertheless fighting and dying under this flag; but the fanatic had lost all sense of caution.

"Tear it down! Tear it down!" he cried. There was a general movement to leave the meeting. Still, Jordan was not arrested. The silence of the forces of law led him on into ever greater daring.

Jordan was in close touch with Joe McWilliams' Christian Mobilizers. To them he explained why the Negroes would not fight the Germans and the Japanese. "Why should we?" he said. "Hitler has opened my eyes. I believe in his idea of racial purity, and we belong to the pure colored races. I am telling every Negro soldier if he is going to die for these United States, he ought to have these words put on his gravestone:

> Here lies a black man
> who fought a yellow man
> for the supremacy of the white man."

There was dead silence, then sudden applause. For the Negro and the white Fascists were after all meeting on common ground; both were working for Axis interests.

In the old days Jordan had given speeches before Father

Coughlin's Christian Front and at meetings of Italian Fascists in Queens. He was the spokesman for Fascism among the Negroes and preached the killing of Jews. The FBI gathered a sheaf of evidence against him.

Finally the Harlem agitator, with his entire ring of white agents, of Japanese spies and colored adherents, was arrested. It was found that Jordan was receiving definite orders from a high officer in the Japanese army, one Hikada. The Japanese Gestapo, the Ho-Kohu-Dan, financed his Ethiopian Pacific Movement.

The Negro Hitler had a remarkable career behind him. He was born in the British Indies, Jamaica, and hence was a British subject. In 1914 he left Jamaica and went to Liverpool. He worked several years as quartermaster on Japanese boats which belonged to the Japanese Mail Steamship Company. In this manner Jordan traveled all over the world. In 1940 he visited Costa Rica, where he may have met old acquaintances of ours, such as Dr. Wesemann and Captain Gough. That same year he visited France, Japan and, last but not least, Germany.

Though Hitler terms the Negroes "an inferior race," he did not disdain to use them for Nazi purposes. Berlin and Tokyo groomed Jordan for his task.

The trial of the Harlem Fascist had a surprise feature. Dr. Takis, Jordan's old rival, appeared on the witness stand. Takis testified for the government, asserting that in prison he had reconsidered his whole life. "I myself have made statements favoring Japan in this War. I am bitterly sorry that I ever thought so and I would never think so again." There was naturally some incredulity at this sudden change of heart. But Takis continued with the utmost earnestness: "I honestly believed that the Filipinos would be better off under a colored race like Japan. Now that my native Philippine Islands have been invaded, now that I have seen what Japanese rule means, I see that I was entirely wrong."

This was a new motif. Takis'. apostasy was a bad blow to Jordan's case. It was Takis who supplied the missing evidence concerning Jordan's armament traffic and his connection with the Japanese agents. Takis also supplied damning details on Jordan's soldier organizations.

The Harlem leader was sentenced to ten years' imprisonment.

He was, however, not sent up for espionage, since his treason had not been directed against military installations, but only against the morale of the armed forces and the dignity of the American flag.   Had he gone farther, the death sentence might well have been his share.

Many Negroes were present at the trial.   When it was over, one colored minister remarked: "Thank God he was convicted. Men like him tear down what we have worked years to build."

The loyalty of Negro America to the United States has again been proved in World War II, when Negroes have died as gallantly and selflessly as they have done in all our country's previous wars.   After the conviction of Harlem's Hitler, a new prayer was introduced to the congregations of Negro churches in Harlem, a prayer that is a promise of loyalty and understanding and an omen of hope for all mankind:

> Father of every race,
> Giver of every grace,
> Hear us, we pray.
>
> Let every land be free,
> May all men brothers be,
> All mankind honor thee
> Now and for aye.

CHAPTER XX

The Hand of Canaris in the Arab World

And the Lord spake unto Moses, saying, Send thou men, that they may search the land of Canaan. . . .

"And Moses sent them to spy out the land of Canaan, and said unto them, . . . Go up into the mountain: and see the land,

what it is; and the people that dwelleth therein, whether they
be strong or weak, few or many; and what the land is that they
dwell in, whether it be good or bad; and what cities they be
that they dwell in, whether in tents, or in strong holds; and
what the land is, whether it be fat or lean, whether there be
wood therein, or not. And be ye of good courage, and bring
of the fruit of the land. Now the time was the time of the first
ripe grapes. . . .

"And they returned from searching of the land after forty
days."

* * *

Many thousands of years later the order was repeated. The
man who gave it was no Moses. He was a zealot of a new and
curious religion. Officially still a practicing Catholic, he had
accepted the pagan religion of Nazism, and acknowledged as his
god the founder of the Reich which was to endure for a thousand years. He was, in a manner of speaking, an apostle of this
new religion and set up his headquarters in the desert near the
ancient shrines. Moses had sent spies into the land of Canaan.
So likewise did this man, whose purpose was to organize the
Arabs into a crusade against the British, the Americans and
the Palestine Jews in the Near East.

A poor sort of prophet he was, without any grandeur.
Though washed and well groomed, the man somehow always
looked dirty. He lacked the studied manner which gave dignity to Hitler and Goering, though he himself was once a
Reichskanzler and a deputy chancellor to Hitler's own cabinet.

He was the notorious Franz von Papen. Master spy and saboteur in the United States during the First World War, a proclaimed practitioner of espionage, he nevertheless rose to the
position of German Chancellor. He later acted as ambassador
to Austria, which country he helped to betray. Finally he was
foisted on the Turkish government as a Minister of the Reich.
Though every diplomat in the world knew his record, the Turkish government had no choice but to accept him; it would have
infinitely preferred to arrest the cold-blooded enemy agent.

Papen was Canaris's missionary to the Mohammedan world.
His net stretched from Istanbul to Cairo, from Alleppo, Damas-

cus and Teheran to Afghanistan and India. Palestine, Egypt, Iraq, Iran, Saudi Arabia, Syria and Turkey were his territory. And Papen was a recognized master of this trade of espionage. Now he turned his hand to the fomenting of racial war. He would raise the banner of the Prophet; he would incite the Mohammedans against the British. Why not? It would serve the cause of the Axis in the Near East.

Papen was well equipped. He worked with a budget of three million dollars a year for espionage alone. An equivalent sum was set aside for diplomatic and political bribery.

Franz von Papen ensconced himself in the palatial quarters of the German Embassy at the Agas Pasha Caddesi, opposite Istanbul's fashionable Park Hotel. From its windows the view is of the Byzantine splendor of the ancient city, the Blue Mosques of Pera, and far in the distance the sapphire waters of the Straits of Bosporus, strategic in many wars.

Herr von Papen had a formidable task entrusted to him. He came to Turkey in 1940. The Admiral required reports on the airfields of the Middle East, with data on the arrival of Allied planes, and copies of their passenger lists. Papen was to organize harbor espionage around the docks of half a dozen countries. Before sending him forth, the Admiral himself had given Papen a tip which might be useful in this new area. The Arabs were not interested in the Reichsmark, nor in the various Oriental currencies. They did not even want the American dollar. Papen would do best to operate with gold, and gold alone.

Gold was imported inside German diplomatic pouches. And the gold was munificently handed out to the Arabs and to Turkish officials; it was handed out to Arab leaders in Syria and Iraq, Iran and Palestine. But Laurenti Beria's Soviet agents, too, brought gold into Persia. The British equipped its Secret Service with gold by the bushel. And the Arabs put out their hands and received gold from both sides. It was a gift which, as far as they were concerned, committed them to nothing.

The Allied agents watched with an amusement exceeded only by that of the Arabs the egregious briberies of von Papen. They knew that they could overbid him. For Papen was watched. He was more carefully watched than any other man in Turkey. He never left his embassy without agents tripping at his heels. Either on a train or on a plane, he was not alone. He kept one man as a personal bodyguard, but he was trailed by a much greater entourage comprising men from the Turkish Security Police and agents of British, American and Russian Intelligence.

Everyone knew that von Papen had been the organizer of the "Black Tom" disaster in World War I. Germany's greatest saboteur and spy, he could not conceal by an urbane exterior the unsavory business which was his lifelong profession. He kept other men to do the dirty work, organize his murders, drug the victims and throw their corpses into the Bosporus. But he was never able to throw off the aura of criminality that surrounded his person.

His first case in Turkey was espionage against the Soviet Union. Germany had occupied the Crimea and was rushing through the Ukraine; Odessa and Kiev were in Nazi hands. The seizure of the Dardanelles was an imperative necessity. It would force Turkey to enter the War on the side of Germany, as she had done in the last war. Papen invited to the German Embassy people who might be useful in his hands. They were shown into the Ambassador's study, a room equipped with a trapdoor. An electric button governed the trapdoor, which served either as an emergency exit or to dispose of a threatening character. Papen's biographer, and many visiting reporters, have seen this camouflaged trapdoor.

Von Papen invited Russian Mohammedans and Tartars to be his sub-agents. Emigrés who had fled the Russian Revolution, refugees who cordially detested the Soviet system, volunteered for espionage on the Russo-Turkish border and in the Ukraine.

These emigré Russian Mohammedans were under close surveillance by Laurenti Beria's OGPU. A few hours after their hire, the Russians knew of the von Papen plan.

Laurenti Beria knew that the most elementary method for combating border espionage was to liquidate the spies. But he determined to overlook these spies in occupied Russian territory; instead he would bring his battle directly to the spy headquarters in Istanbul.

Since Turkey was neutral, Russians could travel between Moscow and Istanbul without undue difficulty. Turkey never forgot that the Soviets had been her only friend for many years after the First World War. For the last twenty-five years Russo-Turkish relations had been excellent. That factor would help. Two enterprising Russians flew to Istanbul. They were met at the airfield by consular officials, who assured them that everything was in readiness.

The two earnest young men took lodgings in a cheap hotel near the Bosporus waterfront. Lovers of fresh air, they took prodigiously long walks. Day and night they walked, sometimes together, but mostly each walked by himself.

They wore dark unobtrusive clothes which blended well with the night and did not attract attention by day. Though they had never been in Turkey before, they were quick observers. They soon could have drawn a map of the crooked tangle of streets which Franz von Papen occasionally followed. They followed Papen to the Turkish Foreign Office or to his nocturnal meetings with secret Turkish Fascist groups. The two dark-clad men were George Pavlo and Leonid Kormiloff, triggermen of Beria's OGPU.

One morning Papen, his wife, his bodyguard and an Arab friend went for a walk on the Boulevard Attaturk. It was one of the few times Papen was not using a car. The sun made the ripples of the Bosporus dance and the gilded minarets gleam. The lush Oriental glory made a sharp contrast with austere modern architecture. Suddenly the sound of a terrific explosion burst on the air. Papen fell. His wife fainted away. A second explosion was heard. Glass splintered from nearby windows. Passers-by rushed to the scene, cars stopped and all was screaming and confusion. On the street corpses lay in pools of blood. But Herr von Papen and his wife and retinue were unharmed. The bomb had struck seventeen yards away. Only the innocent had been killed. But those guilty of the explosion were apprehended.

It was a sensational trial. Diplomats of all nations were present. To many in the court the defendants were heroes.

"Who hired you to kill Ambassador von Papen?" queried the Turkish prosecutor.

"No one," they both maintained.

"Where did you get the bombs?"

"We made them ourselves."

Privately, the Turkish court was sympathetic to the Russian defendants; but they had to shun international complications. Turkey's neutrality might be at stake.

The two Russians refused categorically to say anything more. They would submit to the decision of the court. Since von Papen had not been hurt, they would be spared the death sentence. More leniency than this they did not expect.

They never admitted that they had orders from Laurenti Beria; they made no admissions concerning the Soviet Union. Each was sentenced to sixteen years and eight months' imprisonment. But two years and five months after the trial Turkey broke off relations with the Nazis. Unhampered by artificial restraints, the Turks ousted the master spy Papen and released the two Russians. Nevertheless, a good bit of espionage work would have gone undone if the bomb had killed the gentlemanly scoundrel, von Papen, who later was captured in Germany by American troops.

But we are running ahead of events. Admiral Canaris's orders were to consolidate the German position at the Dardanelles. Kaiser Wilhelm had dreamed of the Berlin-to-Bagdad railroad; the same imperialistic dream fascinated his successor, Hitler. He demanded that steps be taken to weaken the countries of the Near and Middle East, and to gain a foothold in the lands from Turkey to Palestine, from the Transjordan to Afghanistan and Burma.

The Nazis came as friends. Von Papen assured the native Arab leaders that he was the protector of Islam. It is an established fact that Papen's sub-agents informed the people of Iraq that the Germans were fellow Mohammedans. And it took the natives years to discover the lie. Many were not enlightened until they had occasion to witness the burial of the son of the German War Minister, Hans Blomberg. The Minister's son had been assassinated by unidentified agents and he was accorded a Christian burial. It was at this point that the Mohammedanism of the Germans began to be doubted.

Papen promised all manner of concessions to the chauvinist Turkish groups. Palestine would be given to them. The Nazis would elevate the country of Attaturk to the position of a

Rome in a Pan-Islamic world. True, he made identical promises to the other Mohammedan nationalities. But Papen gave
some tokens of his sincerity. He saw to the establishment of
secret societies such as the "Turanians." They were provided
with money, smuggled weapons and radio sets. Turkish Fascists were engaged as spies against the Turkish government,
as well as the Soviet Union.

Papen organized the Turkish quislings according to a time-
honored principle which he had already applied to Austria.
His puppets received everything they asked for, from money to
T.N.T. Their newspapers were financed. Papen, purchaser
of their souls, was generous. He paid well for value received.
The native Fascists were given weapons in return for information on shipping in the Black Sea and the Bosporus. They
were paid in gold for passenger lists of the airlines. They were
satisfied with the terms of the bargain. Then Admiral Canaris
thought that the time had come. His secret Fascist societies,
"The Grey Wolf" and the "Turanians," had been well paid,
well armed. Police chiefs and generals had been recruited into
the fold. It was the moment for overthrowing the Turkish
government. The new government would be assisted by German airplanes and troops, as Franco had been in Spain. Canaris thought it would be the opening wedge for the conquest
of the Middle and Near East. The oil of Iraq would fall into
German hands.

But even while Canaris was thinking, the Allied Secret Services acted. Warning went out to the Turkish government; evidence was exhibited. The entire ring was suddenly blown to
pieces. The Turkish Fascists, glutted with gold and armaments, were led off to prison. In the picturesque and motley
gang which included generals, terrorists, assassins and journalists, there was one absent—and that was Franz von Papen.

It was a new defeat for the German Intelligence Service.
Not the least of it was that Turkey's eyes were opened to Hitler's true intentions. Turkey reacted by inclining more and
more to the Allies. Papen's underground work ended in mul-
tiple disaster. Papen was ordered back to Berlin.

He spent some hectic days at the Foreign Office. Newspapers
reported that Papen was arrested. But that was an exaggera-

tion. His career was far from terminated. Kept for three hours at 14 Bendlerstrasse, Papen emphasized that "Berlin had no idea of the difficulties of the Moslem problem." He did his best to extenuate his failure. Had he not furnished adequate information about shipping on the Black Sea and the Bosporus? His agents were still operating successfully in Palestine, Iraq, Syria and Iran. If he were dismissed now, the whole system would disintegrate. There were, after all, other concerns besides neutral Turkey.

The roles had been reversed. In the First World War, Papen had been Canaris's boss. Now Papen stood sheepishly before Canaris, who treated him with no especial respect. Nevertheless, Papen was not yet outworn. Admiral Canaris decided to give him another chance. He was to return to the Near East, to Palestine. His was still the historic mission of bringing venom and confusion into the Mohammedan world.

They made their plans in other than general terms. Blueprints of conquest and sedition were ready. Names of the men Papen was to enroll in his service were on file. The leader of the Pan-Arabic movement was already nominated. He was to become the quisling of Arabia and to shepherd the Arabs into Canaris's Secret Service.

* * *

In Palestine was a man who had worked years for the Germans, and upon him the choice had fallen. He would be the figurehead for Germany's rule in the Orient.

Protected by a retinue of two hundred Arabs, Hai Amin al Hussein lived in seclusion in the holy mosque of Omar, which is the Saint Peter's for two hundred million Moslems. Built on the site of King Solomon's temple, it overlooks the Wailing Wall of Jerusalem, where through the centuries the Jews have come daily to pray for their unhappy people.

Hai Amin was the "Grand Mufti" of Jerusalem. As an official, he received from the British the yearly salary of six hundred pounds. In addition, he controlled six hundred thousand pounds a year of Moslem religious contributions. Lastly, Hai Amin al Hussein received a yearly salary from the Germans and the Italians.

Only a little over forty, he had risen almost to omnipotence as an Arab leader. Every Arab conspiracy, every bomb explosion, every insurrection and every smuggling of armament was inspired by him. But the underlying plan was a product of the Canaris office. In the memory of man, no figure in the Arab world had exerted such a hold over his people, or unleashed so much hatred and destruction against the Allies.

It is a curious reflection that this Arab despot owed his freedom to a member of the race he persecuted—to a Jew. In 1920 Hai Amin worked as officer of the British Intelligence Service, spying against Turkey. For this he was arrested and put on trial by the Turkish government, but the case against him was dismissed. Then the young Hai Amin, still a student, made a sudden reversal and whipped up the first Arab hostilities against the Jews and British in Palestine. For this he was not excused, but sentenced to ten years' imprisonment. The fiery, slight Arab leader, costumed in the flowing robe of his people, proclaimed himself a martyr. He made a hasty dash to Transjordan, where he remained in hiding.

Viscount Herbert Samuel came to preside over British government in Palestine. The Jewish statesman believed that it was in accordance with Britain's tradition of liberalism to pardon the hostile Arab leaders. Gentle treatment would reconcile them to the regime and dispel some of the bad feeling the Arabs directed against the Jews.

The sentenced outlaw, Hai Amin, the Viscount discovered, was a member of the most powerful Arab family in Palestine, and was to boot the younger brother of the then-reigning Mufti of Jerusalem, head of the Arab religious community.

In consideration of these factors, it was one of Viscount Samuel's first acts of state to pardon the fugitive. Hai Amin accepted the amnesty and returned to Palestine. He continued to wear the halo of martyrdom, and he gave no thanks to the British.

Fortune smiled on the returned exile. He had scarcely returned when his brother, the Mufti, died. The principal Arab families contested bitterly for the office. Viscount Samuel, consistently upholding the principle of reconciliation, ruled that an election be held for the office.

Hai Amin became a candidate, but the election returns put him in fourth place, despite his prestige as a martyr. But, to the astonishment of all, the British Viscount would not approve the candidates who preceded Hai Amin. The coveted post of the Mufti of Jerusalem was awarded to the former fugitive. Viscount Samuel was sure that this favor received at the hands of the British would make a friend of the Mufti. But here British colonial policy erred.

Not for one moment did the Mufti devote himself to purely religious duties. He was a dangerous and shrewd politician, whose ambition was to be the political as well as the spiritual head of all the Arabs. He secured personal control of the funds of the WAQF, the Moslem religious body whose wealth derived from tithes, church-owned property, legacies and other sources. Its revenues came to six hundred thousand pounds yearly, which Hai Amin put to use for his political aggrandizement.

As religious leader and comptroller of the Moslem funds, he had supreme authority over all the mosques and their religious officials and teachers. All were subservient to him, and he dictated their wages, their doctrines and their political affiliations.

Admiral Canaris quickly realized what the Grand Mufti was worth. The fanatic Arab nationalists looked upon the British and the Jews with a hatred that surpassed even Germany's. It would be a rare stroke to draw Palestine into the Axis. The Grand Mufti had some experience with secret organizations. His training within the British Secret Service during World War I would stand in good stead. Canaris saw in him the perfect collaborator. Hai Amin would rouse the entire Arab world to arms against the Allies. There would be a revival of the crusades, with the Mufti, von Papen and Canaris as generals of Islam.

The plan was wonderfully in tune with the Mufti's private ambitions. He envisaged Jerusalem as the Rome of Islam, and himself as both Caliph and Moslem Pope. He had no rivals. Turkey had abolished the caliphate in its domain. In India, King Hussein of the Hedjaz had been barred from the post by reason of the Indian Moslems' objection to him. King Ibn Saud of Saudi Arabia was busy with material affairs revolving around oil exploitation and had no hankerings for ecclesiastical power. Besides, he was a Moslem "nonconformist" and hence ineligible.

There was only one appropriate ruler for Greater Arabia, and that was Hai Amin. The Grand Mufti therefore announced a Pan-Islamic conference at Jerusalem and had himself elected Supreme Dictator and President of the Executive Board.

The delegates to this Pan-Islamic conference were a strangely unrepresentative lot. Mussolini sent "Arabs" from Libya. The Fascist Turkish groups sent delegates. Von Papen dispatched some of his agents from Iraq, Iran and Syria. At the conference the Mufti made a frank declaration of principles: his main objective was the stirring up of revolt in Palestine, Iraq and all of Arabia. He had behind him the support of Admiral Canaris, the German Foreign Office and the still-existent Colonial Office of Mussolini. They were outfitting him with weapons, ammunition, military advisers, spies and unlimited funds.

Their business concluded, the delegates departed. Then a wave of unrest swept Palestine: kidnaping, arson, burglary, pogroms and robbery on the highways became widespread. The anarchy was by no means spontaneous. Its organizer was the Grand Mufti.

At the same time the harbors and Red Sea ports came under the watchful eyes of the Mufti's agents, whose reports were copied and forwarded to Berlin and Rome. For several years the Mufti's reign of terror continued unchecked. Finally the British had no choice but to arrest him.

Hai Amin did not wait to be caught. He disguised himself as a Bedouin and escaped the British police. A motorboat carried him to French Syria. He settled in Lebanon and did not abate a jot of his anti-British activities.

The French did not dare to extradite him to Palestine, for fear of protest revolts from their own Arab population. But when the War broke out, the Mufti of his own accord left Syria and went to Iraq.

Britain issued a formal protest against the immunity accorded to the criminal. Iraq responded with assurances that Hai Amin would be restrained from political activity. The futility of

such assurances soon became evident: Iraq was rocked by a revolt. Its object was the capture of the oil route from Haifa to
Bagdad. Iraq's oil fields had long been coveted by the Nazis,
and the country swarmed with Canaris agents. The Mufti
supervised their activities.

High officers of the Iraq army were pressed with dinner in-
vitations to the Nazi legation. Five pound notes were artfully
slipped into the folds of their dinner napkins. For a while
Bagdad's hotels and embassies were among the busiest of the
world's spy centers. The Mufti met often with Franz von
Papen and other of Canaris's personal couriers. "The Green
Flag of the Prophet" was erected as banner for the forthcoming
Arab revolt.

The Germans were impatient to seize the oil of Iraq. They
wanted to precipitate the revolt and set up a quisling government without delay. On the other hand, the Mufti insisted
that he needed time. He needed more weapons and gold.

In the meantime, white-robed Arabs were everywhere. The
conspirators had taken over the city. The Arabs filled the cosmopolitan hotels, and it was impossible to know who was trustworthy or who was one of the revolutionaries. Information
was openly peddled in the hotel bars against a background of
pulsating Arabian music played by a native orchestra.

In this state of emergency, both the pro-British and the pro-
Axis Arabs worked as hard as they could. Fakhri Bey Nashibi,
a leading Arab who supported England in this War and had a
considerable following, was a counterfoil to the Mufti. Fakhri
Bey learned that the Mufti was secretly in Bagdad. The fact
had been carefully concealed, for the Mufti intended to emerge
at the right moment and lead the uprising. Fakhri Bey was to
rue this bit of knowledge. One morning on the street he was
stabbed in the back. The killers merged into the crowd of
thousands of white-draped Arabs. Who was to recognize them?
The Mufti somewhere in the mountains was glad to hear of the
end of a powerful and well-informed opponent.

After six months, Hai Amin had gathered an army of twenty-
five thousand headed by a few Iraq officers. He gave the signal
for the *coup d'état*. Eighteen thousand Arabs pillaged Bagdad,

killing Jews and foreigners, burning shops and seizing government buildings. The quisling premier, who was chosen by the Mufti and Canaris, was one Rashid Ali. He forced the old regent, Abdul Ilah, at pistol-point to resign. The regent donned disguise and fled to the Persian Gulf and on to Palestine.

The British came in the nick of time. They were able to quell the revolt before it got out of hand and to rescue the oil sources from the Nazis. Iraq was in a state of chaos. Bagdad was crawling with spies. The chief rebel, the Grand Mufti of Jerusalem, was hidden away in the mountains again.

The British offered a reward of two thousand pounds for the Mufti's capture, but he had again disappeared. He had dyed his ruddy beard and hair black, and outdistanced his pursuers. The hunting cry went up for this descendant of the Prophet. For the Mufti seriously claimed to be a direct descendant of Mohammed, and heir to the throne of all Islam.

Once more in the disguise of a Bedouin, the Mufti fled to Persia, whose modern name is Iran. His purpose was still sedition. Admiral Canaris had ordered, "Overthrow the government." But the Mufti had barely a chance to begin work. The Allies had taken the lesson of Iraq to heart. Without delay Russian and British troops went into the country and mopped up the Nazi spy network.

The chief malefactor could not be found, though the price on his head was raised to ten thousand pounds. He enjoyed the sanctuary of the Japanese Legation, until his rescue was arranged by his friend, Franz von Papen. Then he was spirited away to Turkey, where he suddenly turned up on the streets of Istanbul.

There was not much that he could do in Turkey. But he accounted his stay there not wasted. He incited many Arabs against the British before he flitted on to Saudi Arabia. He tried to win King Ibn Saud to his cause, but the King, who had an oil deal with the Allies in his pocket, repulsed the Mufti's proposals.

Mecca was packed with Moslem pilgrims at the season that the Mufti appeared there. A murderous incident took place— an attempted assassination of the King, for which Ibn Saud's police arrested a drunk and unbalanced individual, who was the culprit. Mecca regarded it as a local affair and saw no connection between the assassination and the presence of the Mufti in the city. But in London the *Daily Express* made an astute analysis of the incident when it wrote: "The conspiracy to murder King Ibn Saud was hatched, not in the sultry courtyards of Mecca, but in the chill, tiled-floored galleries of the Wilhelmstrasse."

In confirmation of this fact, it is well to note that the Mufti left the country at the earliest opportunity. The ground was becoming too hot. The unfortunate drunkard who had been caught was jailed for life, while the man with the red beard returned to Syria.

France had been conquered and the Germans had appropriated Syria, a French protectorate. They seized three airfields, to which were attached some five hundred planes. After the failure of the uprising in Iran, Syria made a convenient home base for the fleeing conspirators. Syria, since she was already in German hands, provided no occupation for the Mufti. He went to Albania, and in 1941 proceeded westward to be guest of Mussolini. Not long after the Italian visit the papers showed pictures of the bearded and turbaned Hai Amin standing beside Adolf Hitler in the Reichchancellory. He had a holiday complete with guards of honor and royal suites in Berlin's swank hotels. But the glory was of short duration. The bearded Mufti could not idle away the time. The Prophet's banner had to be raised in every British-controlled Moslem city. Hai Amin made some brisk journeys between Berlin and Rome to discuss plans.

Canaris decided to give the Mufti powerful radio stations in Germany, Italy and occupied Greece from which Hai Amin was to broadcast to the Arab world, urging them to revolt against the Allies. He was to cover all of Palestine, Iraq, Syria, Iran, down to the frontiers of Burma and India.

Other Arab refugees and political exiles clustered around the Mufti's staff in Berlin. He himself lived in a very comfortable house in the suburbs, a house confiscated from a Jew. And every day upon the wide waves of the air, the Mufti cast his words. He addressed the Arabs as "my people" and exhorted them to fight to the death against the Allies. One of his speeches declared:

"Today the Axis peoples are fighting for the liberation of the Arab people. If England and America win the War, the Jews will dominate the world. If, on the other hand, the victory is carried off by the Axis, the Arab world will be freed. The Axis is befriending us. Fight for its victory."

The Mufti stayed on in Berlin; he occasionally reviewed an Arab legion, as well as some German regiments, to whom he gave the salute à la Hitler. But, for all his broadcasts, the Arabs could not be roused into the holy war.

Admiral Canaris fretted with impatience. Marshal Rommel was defeated in Africa and things were going from bad to worse. The Mufti was letting time slip by. Canaris suggested that he take a plane to Arabia and drop by parachute onto King Ibn Saud's territory. Here he could use his personal force to organize an Arab army revolt.

But the Mufti refused the assignment. He remembered a casual remark of the king's: "Every fifth columnist found in my land will have his tongue cut out." The Mufti informed Canaris that he did not care to become a Rudolph Hess of the Near East. "It is beneath the dignity of a Mullah to be dropped by parachute," he said. He would sit the next round out.

And so a long lull descended on Canaris's undertaking to rouse the Arab world to violence against the Allies in the Near East.

On May 8, 1945, the *New York Herald Tribune* published a United Press report that Hai Amin, together with two German officers and two companions. had landed at the Bern, Switzerland, airport in a German plane. The German officers were interned, but the Mufti and his companions were deported.

Finally Hai Amin was arrested by the French army, to be turned over to the British.

CHAPTER XXI

"On to Delhi"—the Slogan of
India's Quisling

IN SPITE of the downfall of Admiral Canaris's elaborate plans for a Moslem uprising, the Japanese were not discouraged. In fact, Japan was spurred on the more, since here was an opportunity to make a good showing, to acquit herself brilliantly where Germany had failed. The Japanese chose for their arena, not the Moslem, but the Buddhist world of India and Malaya. Nevertheless, the pattern followed closely the one that had been fabricated in Bendlerstrasse.

Ten thousand Indian troops had put up a desperate fight in the malaria-ridden hell of Ipoh in Malaya. Veterans of the Battle of Burma, many of them had been captured in the jungles of Tonjong Malum. They had witnessed scenes of indescribable horror, Japanese atrocities which a pacific people like the Indians could scarcely believe possible. Indian prisoners were beaten and tortured, and many of them died in consequence. Those who survived were put on a prison diet limited to a handful of rice a day, and their ranks were still further reduced through starvation. Only the hardiest of the Indians bore up under it.

By the end of 1943 Japan had already felt the blows of the Allied Air Force. The prisoners began to be exposed to Japanese propaganda and overtures of friendship. They were told that the Japanese were fellow Aryans, and were promised release on condition that they join the Japanese army. The prisoners turned a deaf ear to these temptations. A group of them attempted a prison break and were shot down in cold blood.

The remainder knew that their situation was desperate. They could not long survive under the conditions of the prison camp. They would either die singly by being shot while attempting to escape, or be forcibly inducted into the Japanese army.

To these doomed men, however, came an unexpected reprieve. One morning a stout, bespectacled man visited the camp at Ipoh. The prisoners were holding burial services for some of their dead comrades. This portly visitor, a white-turbaned Indian, joined the worshippers. Later he spoke to the prisoners in their native tongue. His address proved him a well-educated man and a persuasive orator.

"I am Subhas Chandra Bose," he introduced himself. "I have come to save your lives. Do you wish to linger here until you die as these unhappy comrades have died? What hope is there for India when her best sons rot away as prisoners? What hope is there for India when her best sons consent to die for England? India will not be saved by the prayers and fasts of Mahatma Gandhi. Freedom is never a gift; freedom must be fought for.

"I have formed a new Indian army, stationed in Burma. It will be the liberator of India. We have to accept the help of Japan, for a country like ours cannot hope to win freedom unaided. As long as Britain and Japan are at war, we know with whom our cause is linked. This War will bring about the liberation of India from the British yoke. Join my army and free India, fighting side by side with our Japanese friends. The time has come for the colored races to win self-determination. Should you elect to join up with me, I am authorized to offer you freedom. You may act, be free, be instrumental in India's liberation—or you may stay here to die, in the ignominious role of British prisoners. You yourself know how few of you will be able to survive this camp. Come to me; I am the flag-bearer of Indian freedom."

Not many of the Indians joined Bose. Though Indians were and are sharply critical of England, they were nonetheless aware of the implications of Japanese rule. China's sufferings were very vivid to the Indian mind. But about fifty of the prisoners accepted Bose's offer. It was an act of self-preservation. They were immediately released and given decent clothes, food and a little money.

Bose interviewed these men and questioned them on their

family situation and military experience. He asked them what they knew about British troop concentrations. After six weeks' preliminary training, he selected twelve men for special work.

These twelve were to be the first unit of an Indian Secret Service financed and aided by the Japanese Intelligence Office. They were now to be sent to Japanese spy schools, where the curriculum followed the classic lines laid down by the Germans.

The twelve agents were trained as wireless operators. They studied deciphering and decoding. They learned the principles of harbor espionage, industrial espionage and independent selection of pertinent espionage goals. The complete course, which Bose supervised closely, took about a year.

In February, 1944, they left Penang in a submarine, which was to land them somewhere on the coast of Beluchistan. The twelve were given the equipment for their task. Bose solemnly emphasized the importance of their mission for the liberation of India. The glory of the cause compensated for the risk they ran. Besides, they would be royally rewarded; they were assured high positions in the New India. Before embarking, they took an oath of allegiance to Bose.

Their appointed tasks involved the demolition of certain industrial plants, the sabotage of the railroad system and the dissemination of nation-wide revolutionary propaganda, which would oppose Gandhi's non-violence movements as well as British sovereignty.

The twelve knew that their adventure was a leap into peril. Even their landing was complicated by dangers. The Japanese submarine happened upon some British merchant vessels and veered from its course to pursue them. The merchantmen defended themselves with depth charges, which nearly hit the submarine. Then, in its turn, the submarine was pursued by British warships and British planes, but managed to escape.

Finally, on the dark and moonless night of March 17, 1944, an attempt was made to land the twelve spies in two collapsible rubber boats on a lonely point of the Beluchistan seashore. The boats were lowered and the submarine commander had them towed to within a few miles of land. But the speed of the submarine made one of the frail boats capsize and its occupants narrowly escaped drowning.

The Japanese captain was furious, for the equipment which had been packed into the boat, including some small radio sets, was now at the bottom of the sea. The men of the other small boat rowed closer and rescued their comrades, who on clambering into the boat overloaded it. Soon they were all in the water, struggling for their lives. The submarine finally picked them up.

A few days later they prepared for another landing. This time they were brought within four miles of the shore. The commander declared that he dared not go any nearer, for fear British coast guards would detect the expedition. Some spare rubber boats were produced and lowered onto the high waves. To their dismay they found that the spare boats were damaged. Large rents admitted the water. They could not possibly be used.

The submarine commander was at the end of his patience. The twelve Indians, their mission a fiasco at the very start, saw themselves put back into the prison camp. However, the Jap commander roughly made a suggestion. He would stop some fishing boats, kill the fishermen, and let the Indians pilot the boats to shore. The twelve objected that the piracy would be discovered and the British apprised of their landing. Finally, they prevailed upon the Japanese commander to cruise for a week, while the Indians used the time to mend the damaged rubber boats.

On March 24, the landing was accomplished. They embarked in the newly repaired boats and rowed for about four miles. Dawn broke; they saw before them a lonely stretch of coast. Dragging their boats, they waded to land. The leader of the expedition was a former officer in the British Indian army, Jemader Yusef Khan. No sooner had he and his men touched native soil than he ordered a conclave. They sat down on the wet sand. The morning air was still sharp, but their excitement grew as they listened to Jemader Khan's words.

He put it before them plainly. They were what they had been, captured members of the British-Indian army. Not one among them wanted to become a quisling. Did any of them dispute that? Had any of them forgotten their dead comrades, the atrocities they had seen, the starvation to which they had been subjected? He would make a motion, on which they would all vote. His proposal was that they give themselves up to the authorities and tell their story.

The men listened with pounding hearts. They did not dare look at each other. Had some of their comrades been transformed into traitors? Had Bose succeeded in turning Indians against Indians? Were Indians capable of working as quislings and spies, of selling themselves to Japan, whose only concern was the defeat of England, Russia and the United States? Had their characters been perverted by the propaganda? In some respects this vote was more than a vote of the twelve. It was a plebiscite for all India. Shall we buy freedom by selling ourselves to Japan? What then will become of India? Everyone knew the answer. India would fare far worse. The men were silent, as they meditated on their national future.

The conditions of the vote were democratic. The ones who wanted to continue on the mission would be exempt from mention. Those who wanted to make a clean breast of it would nevertheless protect their comrades. Everyone was given a strip of paper. They were to write "Yes" or "No"—it was voting for or against India's quisling Bose.

Jemader Khan disclosed the decision. There were twelve votes of "No"—twelve votes for Britain, twelve votes for India. They were all of the same mind. The erstwhile spies and saboteurs burst into joyous laughter. They marched in the best of spirits to the nearest Indian village, which turned out to be Pasni, in the Kalat state. They presented themselves before the Zamindar and explained how they had come and why they had been sent. The Zamindar was very sympathetic about their trials. He fed them, and reported their arrival to Karachi. Arrangements were made to send the party to military headquarters.

Finally they arrived in Delhi, where they told their story in full detail. They described their training course and handed over their radio equipment and T.N.T. They also surrendered the money with which they had been provided. The money was supplemented by some diamonds, locked in a little casket, which were to be used in emergencies.

The military board which conducted the hearing plied them

with questions. Who were Bose's accomplices in India? Were there German instructors in the Japanese spy schools? What code was to be used for their radio messages? Who were the agents in Thailand?

The twelve answered to the best of their abilities. For the first time the British got an insight into the workings of the spy system in this region. From this knowledge devolved many military advantages.

The alleged spies were now set to work. The British Secret Service outfitted them with the necessary materials. They were to short-wave Burma, and give misinformation on the location of American troops, misinformation about the departure of certain ships. Japanese subs, prepared to act on these tips, would be waylaid by Allied ships and sunk.

The twelve men had to put up a good pretense. To further the illusion, a few had to be arrested, while the remainder continued operating. It was a neat bit of counter-espionage and it worked perfectly.

By and by Bose sent a new order: the diamonds were to be converted into cash, with which the agents were to start a newspaper against the British. The newspaper was founded; other agents of Bose turned up to join the staff, and Indian extremists were attracted to it as flies to honey. The British Secret Service watched developments with great interest. The louder the paper waxed in its denunciations of the British, the more pleased were Bose and his Japanese masters. They little suspected that the articles written for the paper came from the pen of an ingenious British journalist. The paper certainly hoodwinked the Japs. It even took in Mahatma Gandhi, who spoke out in criticism of this radical and violent sheet. For Gandhi clung to his ideal of non-violence and strongly condemned the policy of terrorism which the paper advocated.

The Japanese were well aware of Gandhi's prejudices, but they thought they could circumvent them and use him for their own cause. They thought of many subtle ways to ensnare the great Gandhi, who was very far from agreeing with Bose. The Japanese influenced him through a personal contact; a Japanese Buddhist monk, Father Kai Shoo, lived with Gandhi's family for years in his home at Sewagram. The Japanese monk

learned Hindu and went about the streets audibly repeating
his morning devotions. He was a very gentle, very devout man
whom Gandhi loved for his beautiful character. Gandhi was
wont to say, "If the Japanese resemble Father Shoo, the Japanese must be a good people."

But this is exactly what the Japanese wanted to plant in
Gandhi's heart. As a matter of fact, the monk was staunchly
in favor of the Japanese war party, an opinion he never mentioned to Gandhi. Of course, he wished for the defeat of England and the domination of Japan over India. For these reasons the British arrested Kai Shoo at Gandhi's home.

But the real Judas of India remained Subhas Chandra Bose.
Quislings may start off in great style—as they did in Norway,
Palestine, France and India. But there are not many who will
flock to them. Vidkun Quisling, for example, never had more
than one per cent of the people behind him. The Grand Mufti
had less; and Bose was totally isolated. Strutting before their
masters, these quislings exaggerated their power and influence.
Their lofty careers generally dwindled into that of master-spies.
They all started off with the titles of dictators or prime ministers, and ended as simple informers who were not even trusted
to organize a spy system on their own responsibility, but were
subordinated to the master-minds in Berlin or Tokyo.

Subhas Chandra Bose pretended to be the head of the "Free
India government." He represented a government without a
country, commanded an army without soldiers. But, though his
pretentions were ridiculous, his activities were nonetheless in-
sidious.

Like most of the traitors of this War, he was a shrewd statesman, a man of education and good background. Bose was a
genius at intrigue. He would serve the highest bidder or the
cause which promised the easiest entrance into power.

"On to Delhi" was his battle cry. Estimates put his quisling
army at three hundred thousand. In actuality, he never commanded more than sixty thousand, recruited in more or less the
same way as the twelve saboteurs. Hence their loyalty could
not be considered heartfelt. Later on Japanese officers were
put in charge of them, to enforce a rigid discipline and prevent
repetition of the double-cross put over by the twelve.

Behind forty-year-old Bose lay a brilliant career. He was born in Bengal, of an Indian family high in the British service. Young Bose was sent to Cambridge, where he became an honor student. On returning to India, he was offered a high civil service post, like that of his father. But his ego demanded more. He joined Gandhi's movement and helped organize the first great resistance movements against the British. Gandhi was struck with the talents of the young man and asked him to serve as his secretary.

But there was a clash of temperaments. Bose rebelled against the pacifist stand of Gandhi. He cried for a violent revolution, for terrorism and sabotage against everything British.

Bose was imprisoned as a dangerous agitator, which increased his popularity with the masses. Released, he was elected Mayor of Calcutta. In this role, Bose interceded for imprisoned Indian Communists. He discovered his social conscience and dubbed himself a radical socialist. He looked to Russia to help redeem India. Secretly, he joined the Communist Party and hotly condemned Fascism and Nazism. "Their racial ideas are abhorrent to a proud Indian," he declared. "Hitler's despotism far surpasses that of England" was another of his conclusions which he was soon to contradict.

A great many extremist Communists broke with their party and turned Fascist, as Bose was to do. Their ideals went by the board. The will to power was paramount with them.

At this time Russia was more concerned about the coming European War than about the liberation of India. Since Bose could get no assistance from this quarter, he had to look elsewhere. He established contact with the Nazis. British authorities began to find traces of collusion between Goebbels' propaganda bureau and the Indian leader. They suspected that Bose had made application to some groups close to the German Secret Service, but the charge was dropped for lack of definite evidence.

Shortly thereafter Bose was arrested on the charge of anti-British sabotage. He was not held long; the British released him on account of bad health. (This was a mistake the British were continually making. They released the Grand Mufti of Jerusalem, who led them a merry chase between Istanbul and

Palestine. Right in the midst of the War, they released their biggest native Fascist, Oswald Mosley.)

History has shown that a strong people can afford to be merciful, even to its direst enemies. Bose was beyond a doubt an incorrigible. In 1934–35 he was busy in Berlin, Vienna and Rome. He met Hitler and Mussolini. He listened carefully and proceeded with the utmost caution. But he followed in the footsteps of his master, and wrote his *Mein Kampf,* which he entitled *India's Struggle.* He expressed hearty approval of Mussolini's carnage in Ethiopia. He made Indians who volunteered to fight with Emperor Haile Selassie's troops the butt of furious vituperation. As a climax to his European jaunt, he founded the German-Indian Society.

One of the honorary directors of the new club was none other than Admiral Walter Wilhelm Canaris. Bose was granted a long interview with that gentleman, who expressed his warm friendliness toward Bose's dream of an independent India.

In Berlin, Bose altered many of his ideas. He had completely dropped his pro-Russian feelings. Now he became race-conscious. A stately figure in his Oriental robes, he went on conducted tours through Berlin. His guide was an attractive maiden of the Hitler Youth, named Ingeborg. She showed him the later-bombed-out Pergamon Museum, the Staatsoper, the Potsdam Drive. They conversed on the Nazi theory of the superiority of the Aryan race. India, after all, was the cradle of the Aryan race. Bose was well pleased with this idea. India rightly belonged to the Aryan-Axis group of nations. It was a new slogan and would speed the struggle for freedom. Of course, the nordic maiden who introduced him to the idea had received instructions from Canaris on the topics on which to touch. But that scarcely mattered.

The Nazis put him on the air. Bose addressed the Orient from radio stations in Zeesen and Koenigswusterhausen. He roundly condemned Great Britain, and announced the formation of the Aryan Axis. He extended friendship to Japan. When his supporters in India and his fellow leaders heard about this new policy, they could scarcely believe it. Friendship with Japan was unthinkable. Did Bose wish to make

India another China? They were perplexed and incredulous. But apparently this was precisely what Bose wished.

Bose broadcast his new-found cult of Aryanism to India, Indo-China, Afghanistan, Thailand and Iran. He commended the work of the Grand Mufti, who was agitating along lines similar to his. The two had met in Berlin and discussed a common race policy for their peoples.

Their meeting had been a noteworthy one. Both men became so involved in etiquette that they could not find sufficient words of compliment for each other. Their first problem had been to settle on the language in which they would converse. Bose could not speak Arabic, nor the Mufti Hindu. Anglophobes as they were, they were reduced to speaking the English language.

Quislings without a country, they united in their race war and assured each other of mutual assistance. They would regard each other as allies. A slight difficulty cropped up. It was but natural that the Moslem leader should look upon the Moslems in India as being in his province. But Bose, though he did not agree, treated the matter diplomatically. He contended that these details were for later settlement. The need of the moment was unity. However, the ghost of this disagreement could not be laid. The only positive arrangement they made was an exchange of espionage information. This achieved, Bose returned to India.

Even though his Nazi connections were known beyond a doubt, Bose was elected to the presidency of the Indian National Congress. Gandhi demurred, but his protest was overridden. Bose's cry for unqualified independence evoked enthusiasm. Bose also minced no words in his disgust for the old-fashioned mysticism of Gandhi. He urged an immediate showdown and the use of "direct action." His platform was extremely popular. No one wanted to believe the accusation that Bose, the forceful leader, was on the pay roll of the Nazis. They called that a British smear, but the truth of it was soon to be brought home to them.

Bose * prophesied the approach of the War. "That War will

---

* Bose died suddenly in 1945 and never saw the end of the War.

be our chance. War will cost some ten or twenty million lives. Revolution is no worse than war. And without war and revolution there can be no progress. I am going to liberate India, even though that too costs ten or twenty million lives."

Then, in 1939, the War started. Bose promptly made a journey to Berlin, where he met Goebbels and the Grand Mufti again. His next steps were dictated by the Canaris office. He was to fight against British control in India and against the influence of Gandhi. Gandhi, the great prophet, emphasized that he had no grievances against the British people, but only against their government. He ardently opposed Japan's designs on India, and warned Japan that she was not to think of profiting from a British defeat. But Bose harangued his followers in another vein: "The Axis will give us independence. Let us join with Japan in chasing the British out of India."

In 1943 Bose met dictator Hideki Tojo in Tokio. A Japanese submarine then brought him to the site of Britain's most humiliating defeat, Singapore. Bose recruited his army, raised the flag of "Free India." He concluded alliances with other quislings in Thailand and Burma. "On to Delhi" was still his slogan.

He referred to himself as the saviour of India. "I, your leader, have millions of pounds of rice ready to be shipped to famine-stricken India. But the British, our implacable and pitiless enemies, have stopped the shipment. They would rather let you starve than accept the succor which is contributed by our friends and allies in Japan."

Bose spoke long and loud. He circulated incendiary pamphlets, but all in vain. Traitors are despised by their fellow countrymen. Gandhi earnestly warned against his hypocrisy, and Gandhi's warning was heeded. In Bose's person, the Japanese and German Secret Services were given the cold shoulder. The Arab world, too, had rejected them. The Nazis failed to understand the Anglo-Saxon character. They failed also in understanding the Oriental mind. The Moslem and Buddhist world would not sell itself for gold or diamonds.

Four years of failure slightly dampened the confidence of Bose. Nevertheless, he went on giving a daily broadcast from Burma, and repeating to the Indian people,

"I know of no instance in history where freedom has been won without foreign aid in one form or another." Bose apologized for his treason and begged his people to understand his motives aright. "I have not been bought by Japan," he testified. "But I have recognized that Japan and India have the same interests."

But of what use are broadcasts from Burma when India's vast millions own only two hundred thousand radio sets? Bose's voice was unheard, and he was condemned as traitor and spy.

Though his career has been a disappointment to them, the Axis spy organizations did get some service out of Bose. He established a harbor espionage system in India, by which the Japs were enabled to sink British convoys. Although in course of time his boasted influence among the people shrank to nothing, nevertheless the fact is undeniable that Bose proved himself worth his keep, for the Axis continued to maintain him. His story is now over.

CHAPTER XXII

How America's Code Fell Into Germany's Hands

WHAT impelled the Mufti of Jerusalem to become an Axis agent? What forces make a spy? Is it patriotism, love, money or adventure? Is it hate? All these motives may operate. One motive, that of hate, has undergone a modern metamorphosis and has taken on a Fascist cast. Hate has become Nazi fanaticism, with its savage abhorrence of a class or a race.

The Mufti was spurred on by blind race hatred against the

British. The Filipino, Dr. Takis, and the Hitler of Harlem, Robert Obadiah Jordan, were obsessed by their resentment against the white race. Their smouldering hatred was fanned to a blaze by Nazi race theories. The same thing happened to a young American white man. His was a tragic case which reveals more clearly than any number of sociological treatises the effect of race hatred, in this case Nazi-inspired anti-Semitism, upon a young American of exemplary character.

He was a straight, tall, clean-cut young man. When he was a boy, he loved baseball and football. Tyler Kent had a fine education; he attended Princeton and went later to the Sorbonne in Paris, to the University of Madrid, and to George Washington University in Washington, D.C. His father had been a successful career diplomat. His mother was a sensitive, sweet woman to whom the predicament of her son came as a complete shock. She could not understand how it had come about, and hence refused to believe it. All she knew was that he was her son, and she gave him all her tenderness and sympathy. The widowed Mrs. A. H. P. Kent could not doubt her son's integrity.

Her son, an only child, was born in Manchuria where Mr. Kent was attached to the U.S. Foreign Service. Tyler grew up a promising, brilliant, charming boy. He entered the American diplomatic service when he was only twenty-two years old. Following in his father's footsteps, he worked first at the U.S. Embassy in Moscow and came, in October, 1939, to London as a code clerk at the American Embassy.

It was shortly before the War, and in those tense days the position of code clerk was given only to an absolutely reliable man. Tyler Kent was liked by everyone. He filled the demands of his post satisfactorily. Kent had acquired several foreign languages, including Russian, French, German, and Italian.

After he had been in London but a short while, he started to attend political meetings, for he wanted to understand the political developments of those troubled days. He was gravely concerned about the possibility of war.

Tyler Kent hated war and he listened to those groups in England who wanted to avert it. They were not the cronies of Neville Chamberlain or admirers of Chamberlain's tragic missions to Munich. No, they were quite another crew. Kent heard the siren song which Greta Kainen, the beautiful pacifist, had chanted in Scandinavia. He listened to Nazi-inspired peace talk. Kent began to attend the mass meetings and the small closed meetings of the Mosley Fascists. He met Captain H. M. Ramsay, a member of Parliament, who like Mosley was a violent anti-Semite.

This same group of British Fascists had connections with the Anglo-German Fellowship, an organization that contained such prominent British sympathizers with Germany as former Admiral Sir Barry Domville. Sir Barry, who later was interned, had previously been the director of the British Naval Intelligence Service.

Tyler Kent listened to the venomous propaganda that the Jews were responsible for the coming War. It was the familiar cant: the Jews and plutocrats in Europe and the United States were greedy for war profits; international banks were all run by Jews and they were already plotting for war.

Still, Kent's behavior at the American Embassy was normal. Now and then he made some anti-Semitic remarks which shocked his associates. But he continued to do good work.

Then the Second World War started. Soon after its outbreak, on May 18, 1940, a representative of the London police headquarters at Scotland Yard came to U.S. Ambassador Joseph P. Kennedy and told him a disturbing tale which the ambassador was reluctant to believe. It was a matter of great delicacy. The ambassador learned that Kent had become the object of attention by Scotland Yard through his doubtful association with a group of persons suspected of conducting pro-German activities under the cloak of anti-Jewish propaganda.

The Scotland Yard man told the ambassador that Tyler Kent had been shadowed to a girl who had later been arrested for espionage. Anna Wolkoff, the arrested girl, was a naturalized British subject of Russian origin. She was the daughter of a former Czarist admiral and worked with the Mosley Fascist group.

Miss Wolkoff had resided in Great Britain since the Russian Revolution, had been hospitably received and had made a considerable number of friends among London society.

After the outbreak of World War II the British police had become interested in Miss Wolkoff's activities. They believed that she had a channel of communication with Germany and was sending Intelligence information to the Axis.

Tyler Kent had been observed by Scotland Yard as having been in frequent contact with Anna Wolkoff and also in touch with others of a group known to her.

Scotland Yard knew, among other things, that Kent and Anna Wolkoff were even sharing an automobile, and they were also convinced that Anna Wolkoff was receiving confidential information from Kent. The officer told Ambassador Kennedy that he considered it highly desirable to search the rooms occupied by Kent.

Confronted with this charge, the ambassador had to waive Kent's diplomatic immunity. He authorized the Scotland Yard officers to search Tyler Kent's apartment and promised to cooperate to the fullest extent. But he hoped that they were altogether mistaken. Ambassador Kennedy and another American official accompanied the Scotland Yard men as witnesses of the search.

The investigators went to Kent's London apartment. The gasburner in the fireplace, the comfortable chairs, the tall windows admitting the grey afternoon light were commonplace and reassuring. But the Scotland Yard men found what they were after.

Scotland Yard and the U.S. State Department revealed that Kent had in his possession copies of embassy material totaling more than 1500 individual papers. He also had two newly made duplicate keys to the index bureau and the code room of the American Embassy. After this evidence was found, Kent admitted that he had had these keys made so that, in the event that he should be transferred from code work to another section of the embassy, he would still have access to the code room.

And there was still more evidence. Scotland Yard finally found in his possession two photographic plates of embassy documents believed to have been made by confederates for the purpose of transmitting prints thereof to Germany, and certain printed propaganda material which was prejudicial to the British conduct of the War.

The U.S. State Department bluntly stated, "The police also established that some of the papers found had been transmitted to an agent of a foreign power."

Later on, the State Department revealed that this foreign power was Germany, and they also told the surprised mother of Tyler Kent that an examination of the documents found in Kent's room indicated that he had begun classifying the material by subjects. The documents covered practically every subject on which the embassy was carrying on correspondence with the State Department and President Roosevelt.

The State Department admitted that these papers "included copies of telegrams embodying information collected by the embassy which otherwise would not have been permitted to leave Great Britain without censorship." They contained information which has been "useful to Germany."

This was a terrific blow to the American Embassy in London. The shocking discovery made Ambassador Kennedy turn white as a sheet. He asked in great agitation,

"Why didn't you notify me earlier?"

The British officials explained that they had wanted to get the complete picture, to trace the whole spy ring, before they broke the news.

This was the story: Cables from America were coming in daily, and Scotland Yard suspected that they were being relayed to Berlin in some manner. Their suspicions lighted on the code clerk. They shadowed him and traced him to the house of Anna Wolkoff, who was already under suspicion. The friendship between the girl and Kent increased and the two became careless. They began meeting each other for luncheon in town. After such meetings, Anna Wolkoff would not go home. Instead she would take a bus to a small photographic studio on a London side street.

Scotland Yard deduced that she left Kent's decoded cables at the photographer's shop and that the proprietor reduced the messages to microfilm. They ascertained with exactitude what was going on in this photo studio. A few days later, they arrested Miss Wolkoff, as well as the photographer, who was maintaining direct contact with Rome. For many months secret documents of British-American diplomacy had been going to

Rome, whence they were passed on to Berlin. And all this time the American Embassy had not the faintest suspicion of this traffic.

Kent was dismissed from his post and was instantly arrested for violation of the Official Secrets Act. He petitioned that he be sent to the United States to stand trial. In reply he was told that he had first to serve his seven-year sentence in Britain. After that he would be deported to his native land, where he might face new charges.

His accomplice, Miss Wolkoff, received ten years' imprisonment. But she had the satisfaction of knowing that her work had been extremely beneficial to Germany. For all this happened in France's critical forty days and during that time of crisis the American Embassy was without a code. There was a complete blackout between Washington and London. The old code could not be used, since the Axis held the key to it. Several weeks were needed for the perfecting of a substitute code.

* * *

In New York a mother wept for her boy. She asserted that her son had not violated his trust, that there was some terrible mistake. Years passed, but her belief in him did not flag. In fact, she started a crusade on his behalf which reached such proportions that the Kent case became a political issue in the United States. Mrs. Kent wrote hundreds of letters, to Congressmen, to church leaders, to delegates to the Democratic Convention. She demanded justice for her son. She begged that he be given a trial in the United States. The English hearing, she maintained, had been a frame-up. Her son, a prisoner on the Isle of Wight, was innocent. Then it happened that her outcries were augmented by those of the anti-Semitic elements in this country, as well as by the friends of the British Fascists. They represented young Tyler Kent as a martyr.

Their version was that the Kent case had been a gigantic conspiracy, a plot between Churchill and Roosevelt, both of whom were interested in liquidating the young man. The rumor went about that Tyler Kent knew too much. The Kent sympathizers alleged that the cables were amazing documents which showed that Churchill had been intent on dragging the

United States into the War. There were accusations of secret agreements and commitments. Tyler Kent became their hero and their "own" case.

Former isolationists and political opponents of both Roosevelt and Churchill defended Kent. Perhaps further searching into the facts of the Kent case would reveal the existence of secret pacts between the two statesmen which would expose the late President. Isolationists hoped that Roosevelt would be fatally compromised, especially in view of the 1944 presidential election. Congressmen who in the old days had voted against Lend-Lease seemed to feel that the Kent case was right up their alley. They took up his defense and had the case brought before the Supreme Court.

Mrs. Kent claimed that her son was a pacifist, who had wished to prevent the United States from being drawn into the War. This had been his motive in copying the cables. He had shown the messages to friends. (Among the friends was Captain Ramsay, M.P., an anti-Semite and pro-Fascist. Ramsay, too, had been arrested and detained until the fall of 1944.)

Nineteen-forty-four was election year in America and the story was definitely political fodder. But the plot thickened. As more evidence was produced, it began to look as if Mrs. Kent might be right in her accusation of secret agreements. Churchill and Roosevelt might have given each other some assurances, the nature of which could not be revealed until after the election in November.

Was it true that the two government heads were concealing something? Mrs. Kent could not rest until she knew the truth. She financed the trip of an impartial investigator. Ian Ross MacFarlane, a news analyst on Station WITH in Baltimore, was sent to England to learn more facts about her son.

In England he met John Bryan Owen, son of the former U.S. Minister to Denmark. Owen knew a lot about the Kent case, material which was strictly confidential. The news commentator persuaded Owen to come to the United States. He was to see Mrs. Kent, for whom he had some real news. But the fateful meeting never took place. A few days after Owen reached the United States, he was found dead in his room in

Greenwich Village.   The cause of death was diagnosed as an
overdose of veronal.   The mistake had cut off his life before
he had a chance to go to Washington for the meeting with Mrs.
Kent.   Was it an accidental death?   The police classed it as
suicide.   But stories were told that "the administration" had
chosen this way to get rid of a dangerous witness.   Native Fascists zealously spread this tale.   The mystery is still unsolved.
Mrs. Kent and American anti-Semites like Gerald L. K. Smith,
who have made themselves defenders of Kent, still speculate
about Owen's death.

The mother hoped to win her case.   The political mysteries,
the sinister coincidences, were in her favor.   But a decisive step
was taken that wrecked her hopes.   Certain persons decided
to put an end to the irresponsible and slanderous rumors which
were flying about.

The case was brought into the open, to banish once and for
all the gossip of secret pacts, framed-up trials and murders.
The State Department and Ambassador Kennedy spoke up, and
they told the whole story.

* * *

That night in May, 1940, had been one of the most staggering
in President Roosevelt's career.   Tremendously overwrought,
Ambassador Kennedy had called the White House.   He told
the President that America's secret code was now invalidated.
The whole confidential communication system of the United
States had been betrayed.   The entire cipher and code system
had been rendered useless.

Furthermore, the Germans, the Italians and the Japanese
were informed of every problem and every decision pondered
by the State Department and the White House for a period of
eight months.

A worse scandal, or a more severe blow, could not have over-
taken American diplomacy.   The Canaris espionage office had
been deciphering official American messages for eight months.
They laid their hands on cables to nearly every embassy and
legation in the world.   One young man had laid bare the entire American code system; had given the clue to many secrets

and disclosed important plans for future foreign policy; had with one gesture revealed significant statistics, production data and Lend-Lease shipments.

The secrets of British and American counter-espionage were decoded at the Bendlerstrasse. The original American cables matched against their decoded meaning enabled the Canaris office to reconstruct the code system, which could have been done without the knowledge of Tyler Kent.

Every single government dispatch is delivered to embassies and legations via commercial cable and wireless offices in the various countries. As they stand, these messages are completely open and are available to anyone in the cable office. Nothing was easier than for Canaris to station a clerk in each office, who would forward copies of the messages to the Canaris Intelligence Office in Berlin, where the Germans had reconstructed the code.

The American government, like all other governments, used several codes, both easy and complicated. One "unbreakable" code was reserved for high secrets. Kent had knowledge of them all, including the "unbreakable" code.

When the treachery was discovered, the United States was forced to abandon the codes immediately, which interrupted the communication system with countries like China for about a month. But the past could not be redeemed.

Perhaps the code clerk never fully realized until the last the consequences of his acts. Yet even after it was represented to him, he remained cold and impassive. He spoke not one word of remorse.

Reporters asked Ambassador Kennedy what had made Kent betray his own country. Kenney tried to analyze it. A copyrighted article by Henry J. Taylor, appearing in the *New York World-Telegram* of September 5, 1944, quoted the ambassador as saying:

"I don't think money figured in his actions. I can only explain it in this way. Somewhere along the line, Kent seems to have built up a terrific anti-Semitic complex. I am convinced that this attitude was the driving power for his behavior in London. When Kent was arrested I asked him how on earth he could have broken trust with his country, and what had he imagined would be its effect on his mother.   Kent never batted an eye.

"His only response was a tirade of intense anti-Semitic feeling; he showed no repentance whatever, except in respect to his mother.   As far as he himself was concerned, he told me just to forget about him."

The ambassador broke off his account and bowed his head. "It's a tragic story," he said.

Kent's mother wept bitter tears over her boy.

In her desperation and sorrow, Mrs. Kent did not object when such an outstanding pro-Fascist, isolationist and anti-Semitic figure as America-Firster Gerald L. K. Smith published "the most sensational story of the century," an account of the Tyler Kent affair which makes Kent out to be America's foremost hero and martyr.

Gerald L. K. Smith wished the American public to believe that young Tyler wanted to prevent the United States from becoming embroiled in World War II, and therefore revealed President Roosevelt and Prime Minister Churchill's secret preparations for Lend-Lease.   He claims that young Kent violated no confidences, stole no official documents; that, like all other pro-Fascist isolationists, he was a true patriot. . . .

The Kent case is one of the most tragic affairs in America's history.   It should serve as a living warning to youngsters who might listen to the gentle, peace-loving politicians who, in the name of patriotism, of Christ, of America, of all the most noble ideals, tell them that American democracy has been sold out to the foreign-born, the Jews and the Communists.

We shall hear more about the Kent case.   For example, in May, 1945, counsel retained by Mrs. Kent started action in the U.S. Court of Claims to recover the salary and foreign living allowance which her son would have received between the time of his arrest and the present.   Tyler Kent's sentence will expire in 1947, and he might then be brought to the United States for trial.   His supporters will undoubtedly make the most of the occasion.

CHAPTER XXIII

Fake Refugees

On the whole Tyler Kent had been lucky. The British dealt more gently with him than with others.

The War had made London a city of conglomerate nationalities. Uniforms of all the Allied countries were seen—Canadian, Mexican, Brazilian and Norwegian—as well as the trim uniforms of nurses from many nations. There was a daily influx of refugees. Many were patriots from the Continent who had made daring escapes in small fishing boats. They were all subjected to very thorough hearings, and their statements were checked by the various governments-in-exile, and confirmed by messages from the underground patriots at home. No one was admitted into the country casually.

Nevertheless, there were bogus patriots and refugees who evaded the investigations and the watchfulness of Scotland Yard. The Nazis were quick to recognize that the refugee game could be given a novel twist. Canaris's newest agents wore the mask of refugees. England had shown good will and good faith toward Europe's refugees. Exiles of Europe's underground were treated as brothers and they found British hospitality a heart-warming experience.

Admiral Canaris decided to exploit this good will. Dozens of refugee spies were to be smuggled into London. The "escapes" were planned from the ground up. An extraordinary amount of care and cleverness went into the stratagems.

There was a twenty-seven-year-old Belgian, Joseph Jan Vanhoven by name. He had always been a firm patriot who shared the common dislike of his countrymen for the Germans. A waiter in Brussels' Hotel Cosmopolitan, he had to serve the arrogant German officers who made the hotel their official dining spot. Vanhoven concealed his enmity from his customers. He was an exemplary waiter. For some reason he became the pet of one of the officers. One day his patron, a smart German

lieutenant named Eilenburg told him a way of getting some
meat for his family. "You go to the camp's quartermaster, ask
for Heinrich and mention my name to him. He'll give you
meat and cigarettes."

Occupied Belgium was starving; the Nazis had pillaged what
they could; they had confiscated blankets for their troops in
Russia. They had seized fishing boats, trolley cars, clothing,
crops and livestock. The country was stripped bare. Vanhoven felt a rush of gratitude toward the lieutenant. His old
father and mother had not eaten meat for many months. He
followed the lieutenant's directions. At the camp he was given
some packages of meat and about a dozen cartons of cigarettes.

The next day the waiter approached the German and thanked
him humbly. Eilenburg laughed gaily and asked him if he
would like such presents more often. He could go on getting
the stuff if he would undertake to sell some on the black market, and split the proceeds fifty-fifty with Eilenburg.

The lieutenant thought he was being bountiful in offering
Vanhoven such a high share. "We Germans are always fair,"
he assured his pawn. Vanhoven became a black market pur-
veyor. The lieutenant urged him to sell more and more.

The black market traffic went on for months. Eilenburg
made some fifty thousand francs on the trade. He went down
to Paris, where he bought a mink coat and some latest-model
frocks for his girl in Germany. In so doing, however, Eilenburg came under suspicion of the German Secret Service.
Canaris's agents wondered where the lieutenant had obtained
the money. They commenced investigations, and were disposed to believe that the lieutenant was involved in espionage.

Eilenburg was called to a hearing and questioned about the
money. The hearing was under military auspices. His commanding officer, two Secret Service agents and a Gestapo official
presided. They asked him bluntly: "Are you working for the
British? Or have you any connections with the French Maquis?"

Eilenburg, caught unawares, trembled in his boots. This
might mean execution. He broke down under the questions,
and while he protested solemnly that he would never betray his
Fatherland, he confessed that he had made money on the black

market. He was driven to do it by an ill-fated love affair. Some dancer in Munich with whom he was desperately in love demanded expensive presents.

The espionage case against Eilenburg was dropped. But retribution came in the form of a transfer to the Russian front. As for poor little Joseph Vanhoven, he heard nothing about it until one morning he was arrested. Three men called for him at the hotel. In his waiter's black frock coat he was marched off to Gestapo headquarters.

They told him that they knew about his black market dealings. The examining officer was a certain Hans Junglau, who roughly told the Belgian: "We might shoot you for it. You've been stealing army food."

Vanhoven pleaded for his life, stammering out that he never realized what he was doing. "I am only a poor man," he told the Nazis. "I did what the German lieutenant told me to do." He begged to be given another chance, in return for which he would do whatever they wished of him.

These were the circumstances that pushed little Joseph Vanhoven into the career of German spy. Dead, the sallow, insignificant waiter was of no value to Germany. On the other hand, the Germans had need of agents in dangerous places. The Nazis therefore worked out a plan. A few days after his arrest newspaper notices appeared, naming the waiter of Hotel Cosmopolitan as an infamous black market dealer and thief of army food. The newspapers said that Vanhoven was being hunted all over Belgium, for the crafty fellow had disappeared just before being arrested.

In the meantime Vanhoven was put into a German car and driven to Paris. There he busied himself looking up acquaintances in the underground. He showed them the clippings of the Belgian papers and explained that he was fleeing for his life. The French underground accepted Vanhoven as a fugitive from the Nazis. They took him in charge and whisked him from refuge to refuge. Finally they smuggled him over the Pyrenees, with the co-operation of professional auto-tire smugglers. Vanhoven then made a beeline for the German Embassy in Madrid.

There he was received by Herr Eberhard von Stohrer. Stohrer, the German Ambassador to Spain, had always maintained a sprightly interest in his sideline of espionage. As previously mentioned, he had filled the same position in Spain during World War I, when he had acted as Canaris's superior.

Stohrer enjoyed a reputation as a witty conversationalist. Diplomatic dinners and tea parties were convulsed by his well-turned jests. The ladies too adored him. He had been a close friend of Marshal Pétain when the latter was French Ambassador to Madrid. Stohrer knew Mussolini and Hitler personally. He had acted as procurer for the Canaris office, to which he introduced many Spanish agents.

The ambassador spoke to the timid waiter in French and with marked kindliness. Vanhoven was quite overwhelmed at having to report to the high official. The ambassador begged him to relax. Vanhoven had done very well so far. He deserved a small vacation. The ambassador gave him money to take one. Berlin would soon send word of his forthcoming assignment.

Vanhoven was to employ his time with the writing of a detailed report of his experiences with the French Maquis; he was to give names of the underground workers whom he had encountered.

The ambassador found Vanhoven's report very much to the point. Vanhoven exposed some members who had helped stranded Allied fliers return to England. He provided facts on secret radio operators. The report was forwarded to Canaris, with a strong recommendation by the ambassador.

The new orders duly arrived. Vanhoven was assigned to England. He was to run a secret radio transmitter, for which he was coached by an intensive radio course. A list of his espionage tasks would be handed to him in London.

The way was circuitous. First Vanhoven was to join the crew of a Spanish boat which delivered oranges to Sweden. Vanhoven complied. On arriving at Stockholm, he jumped his boat. As a fugitive patriot and member of the Belgian and French underground, Joseph Vanhoven presented himself at the British Embassy at Strandvägen. The British listened intently, for this man had seen a lot. He brought out his Belgian certificate and told his story, which was borne out by the newspaper clippings. The waiter who had stolen food from the Germans to give to his starving countrymen was a bit of a hero. It was no wonder that the Germans had placed a price on his head. Vanhoven told the British that he frequently wished to go to England to join the Free Belgian army.

Both the Belgian government, which was consulted, and the British thought highly of this newest recruit. He was secured a place on a courier plane and flown to England.

But Scotland Yard did not like the story. It was too smooth, too pat, a little odd that the man should have all his papers. They handled a great many refugees, the great majority of whom were honest patriots. But honesty was not taken for granted.

The German Ambassador had given Vanhoven one address in London. He was to contact the owner of an East End pub. After a few days in the city he drifted down that way. He strolled into the room, drank a few beers and asked as casually as he could for Mr. Pearson.

They answered that there was no Mr. Pearson here. He must be in the wrong place. But before he left, someone tapped his shoulder and invited him to another drink.

This somebody said that he knew Mr. Pearson. He drew Vanhoven to a dusky booth for their beers, and there muttered that the order was for Vanhoven to work among the Belgian sailors. He was to try to join a Belgian merchant marine crew.

As a matter of fact, there was no Mr. Pearson. It served as a code word. This pub had been used as a "message box" over a period of years. Scotland Yard agents knew all about it, but forbore to close the place for the very good reason that it tipped them off to the arrival of a new spy, since the spies were all sent to this pub for instructions.

Vanhoven, too, was left unmolested. He worked among the Belgian seamen, but his espionage assignment was abruptly terminated when, after three months, he and a few aides were arrested. Vanhoven was sentenced to be hanged at the Wandsworth prison. He made a full confession before he died and asked for a mitigation of the death sentence. He implored the British to understand that he had been forced into espionage. But their verdict was adamant.

Nearly every spy masquerading as a refugee has been arrested. The reason is simple. The refugee who enters a new country will be more strictly investigated than an ordinary citizen. Agents who were cleverly trained to avoid all the pitfalls were nevertheless discovered. They had, it is true, a longer time in which to work their mischief.

The outstanding case of a spy "refugee" was that of Willy Kernig, a thoroughly unscrupulous rogue who would do anything for money. He was forty-five years old, a smallish man, scarcely five feet five inches tall. He wore an earnest look, smiled much, was exceedingly polite. His manner, nevertheless, was subtly unpleasant.

He was a German of some notoriety. Before Hitler came to power, Kernig had been the director of a birth control clinic of unsavory repute. As a secret sideline, he ran an abortion mill. He had been imprisoned several times. He was a confirmed pervert with a fondness for young girls under fourteen. Of course, he claimed to be pioneering for sexual reform. He fled from Germany after Hitler came to power.

Willy Kernig came to Prague, the beautiful Bohemian capital. He applied to every refugee aid committee. He had a hard time making ends meet, and was often quite penniless. He wrote pamphlets on the theme of sexual reform and cultivated the acquaintance of elderly wealthy ladies. He had a knack for that sort of thing. The ladies found him agreeable and interesting, and one woman was so impressed with him that she made marriage overtures.

But Kernig felt that marriage was too slow a way of furthering his career. He took immediate steps to improve his fortune. One night he had an assignation with a pretty Czech girl, whom he seduced and whose purse he stole. The theft was reported to the police. Kernig was apprehended and sentenced to a year's imprisonment, with the additional penalty of deportation at the completion of his sentence.

Kernig had to look about for another asylum. He elected to go to Sweden. There the weary round started again. Kernig besieged the refugee aid committees, and bewailed his plight before them. He developed an excellent technique for panhandling; he would make a personal call on every minister and rabbi in the country. There was hardly one who did not give him a five-crown note out of pity for the man.

However, the Swedish police found out that his character was rather doubtful. They obtained his criminal record from Czechoslovakia, on the basis of which they decided that he was an undesirable alien. He was deported to Norway, but was there only a week when the Norwegians sent him back to Sweden. They would have nothing to do with him.

Here was a typical case for the social worker. A stranded person, a refugee hounded by the police, certainly needed help. There are Good Samaritans in every country. A Methodist minister undertook to solve the problem. He was willing to provide Kernig's fare to Turkey. In Turkey, the girls matured at the age of thirteen, which made it a safer environment for a man of Kernig's peculiarities.

The minister invited the refugee to come and talk it over. He was all gentleness and mercy. "I understand your problems," he told him soothingly. "You will be happier in Turkey. Don't fear for the future. Tomorrow I'll have your ticket ready for you, and a little extra money besides. You will begin life anew in Turkey."

Kernig expressed his gratitude. He had been worried over the deportation order, and this seemed a good way out. But "there's many a slip 'twixt cup and lip." Kernig made a terrible blunder. He forgot his briefcase at the minister's home. The minister's wife opened it to find out to whom it belonged. She dropped it like a hot brick. That such a thing should come into a minister's God-fearing home! The briefcase was full of pornographic pictures and lascivious pamphlets. Kernig, the dealer in erotica, had exposed his own racket.

The minister withdrew his offer. Now Kernig had no choice but to submit to deportation to the country from which he had come, Czechoslovakia.

Kernig's bad conduct did not help the cause of other refugees. However, in six months the incident was almost forgotten, and a small plump man entered unchallenged into Sweden. He was a Czech citizen, who wore a fur-lined coat and smoked expensive cigars. He gave his name as Bedrič Jaderny. He stopped at an elegant hotel at Stockholm's Vasagatan. Not much was known about him; he seemed to be a business man, who made a few telephone calls from the hotel and received a few visitors in his room. That was all.

He was no other than Willy Kernig, better fed and in disguise. He had become a member of a Secret Service and now had plenty of money. Soon every other day a letter containing two hundred dollars in American currency arrived for him at Stockholm's General Delivery office. He broached an idea new to the refugee world. He wanted to organize the refugees into a gigantic spy network. It was for the right side, he said, with a portentous air. He invited three refugees to the hotel and unfolded his plans. He said he was working for a Czech newspaper. He needed information on German shipping. He wanted to know how many Swedish Bofors guns were going to Germany, and any other fact on Sweden's trade with Germany or Russia.

Kernig-Jaderny seemed to take delight in mystifying his visitors. For example, he never said definitely what country he was serving. He hinted that it was a combined outfit of Russian, French and Czech interests.

The refugees whom he invited to collaborate with him did not know what to make of it. Before they came to any decision, however, they were all arrested, together with Kernig. The Swedish police found Kernig in possession of a code, several maps of the Bofors works and statistics on industrial production. It was clear evidence of industrial espionage, accomplished by a person posing as a refugee. Kernig was liable on several charges: espionage, re-entry into a country from which he had been deported and the use of a faked passport.

Nevertheless, the Swedes made an offer to the malefactor. The Swedish proposal was of this nature: Kernig would be deported unpunished if he would tell what he knew and confess the names of his paymasters. If he persisted in his silence, he would be imprisoned as a spy.

Kernig weighed the alternatives and decided to make a clean breast of it. The bulk of his confession was kept secret, and will be kept secret for twenty years. But this much leaked through: Kernig's boss was a Czech police official. He had

hired Kernig for the Secret Service after the latter's deportation
back to Czechoslovakia.

But, for all Kernig's frankness, the case remained obscure.
The Swedes could not understand Czechoslovakia's motives for
spying on Sweden.

After the conquest of Czechoslovakia a flood of light illumi-
nated the Kernig case. The paradox was solved. Kernig's
police chief turned traitor, became a quisling. He was a member of Canaris's Secret Service and had been for years.

Kernig had labored under the illusion that he was working
for the Czechs and the Russians. His reports on Swedish industry and Scandinavian shipping had gone straight to Berlin.

After Kernig's confession he was deported to Finland. During the hard times of the Finnish-Russian War he tried to escape to Estonia, but was caught by the Russians. His subse-
quent fate is unknown.

* * *

Despite initial failures, Admiral Canaris liked the scheme of
employing fake refugees. It seemed to be a method especially
suited for espionage against England. That gallant island had
become more of a stake: the Americans were stationed in England; commando raids were being organized from British bases;
bomber formations took off from there; supplies were being
amassed in England for the invasion troops. There was urgent
need for hundreds of spies to infiltrate the island and keep the
Canaris office informed of developments.

Canaris's agents had to speed their pace and sharpen their
wits. A directive went out to the contact men in England: they
were to pave the way. The situation called for mass espionage,
for individual espionage had proved ineffectual and slow. Fore-
seeing the end of Hitler and Germany, Canaris had become
desperate and ripe for recklessness.

The Allied Secret Services guessed to what lengths Canaris
would resort. They took an even more guarded attitude toward heroic escape stories. Not even confirmation from the
underground was conclusive. Nothing was taken on faith.

In 1943 a Scotland Yard officer listened impassively to the
following story. The narrator was an escaped patriot from

Belgium named Eugene Timmerman. He sat in front of the officer's desk and gave a brief summary of his life. He was a young fellow, a native of Ostende. He spoke a very respectable English, which he had picked up as a ship steward. For years he had been a worker in the Belgian underground, whose leaders vouched for him. He had made the Channel crossing in a small fishing boat. The Belgian government-in-exile welcomed him and stood sponsor for him before the British authorities.

The courage shown by the young man commanded the respect of the Scotland Yard officer, though he took care not to show that. He cross-questioned the boy keenly.

Eugene Timmerman was spokesman for three others who had made the escape with him. Their adventure was perhaps the most daring that Scotland Yard had heard recounted. Eugene and three comrades were due to be deported as slave laborers to Germany. All four agreed to escape. The underground leaders knew about the plan, of which they warmly approved. They collected warm clothing and food for the boys to take along.

The four knew the countryside well. Without incident they reached a small coastal village, where a fishing boat was waiting for them. In the boat were concealed fishermen's clothes, which the boys donned as disguises. A short way out to sea, they were stopped by the Nazis on a routine harbor patrol. The four were accepted as ordinary fishermen out for the day's work.

The North Sea was rough and the little boat provided for them would not, it was obvious, weather the run to England. So Eugene and his friends decided to sail to one of the little islands off the coast. They lived there for three weeks in the role of fishermen. Nobody bothered them at all. Every day two of the group would stroll over to the nearest village to see about a boat which could take them to England. What they learned about the possibilities was depressing. The Germans had requisitioned thousands of Belgian fishing vessels. All remaining small craft had to be registered with the Nazis.

But the four did not give up. Their neighbors were on the lookout for a likely boat and in the meantime brought the adventurers food and money. Good patriots all, they would never

have given the boys away. At last a boat was available. It was
a smallish fishing boat, built in 1910; its engine was very old
and its bottom was rotten. It measured eighteen feet in length.

The group needed gasoline. They needed provisions, but
were without ration coupons. Above all they needed a compass
and some information on the Nazi minefields. By hook and
crook they amassed what they needed. The gasoline was stolen
from a German army camp. Fishermen contributed food and
information which they had gathered from their sea trips on
the location of the minefields. Finally the boat pushed off
from shore.

None of the boys was a trained navigator, but all knew how
to handle boats. Eugene acted as captain, and the others were
assigned to look after the motor, the rudder and the sails.

The night was cloudy, dark and cool. The minefield lay
outside the three-mile territorial water zone. Within the three-
mile zone, fishermen could come and go unrestricted. The
four were frozen with consternation when the boat was stopped,
still well within the zone. Happily enough, commented Eugene, it was so dark that the Nazis could not see how pale and
nervous they were. It was a Nazi torpedo boat, whose officers
ordered a search of the vessel. No damaging evidence was
found; released, the four boys had to pretend to be doing nocturnal fishing. The Nazis kept them under observation for
four hours. Naturally they could not move toward England.
When morning came, German patrol planes gave them a signalled command to stay inside the three-mile limit. They had
to cast anchor again and waste another day at mock fishing.

The following night Eugene decided to venture the escape.
They started seaward again. They had to go very slowly,
threading their way through the minefields, whose details they
tried to memorize for communicating to the British.

By the next morning they had come a long way from the
coast of Belgium, but they were still far from England. The
old boat showed a decided tendency to leak, so that they had
to man the pumps often. Their supply of gasoline was low,
which forced them to depend on the sails. The weather was
balmy, but the wind did not come all day.

During the night the wind came, and came with a vengeance.

A terrific North Sea storm arose. The old boat could hardly stand up against it, they thought, and in short order the drifting anchor cable was snapped and the main sail was damaged, while billows poured over the deck. Worst of all, the wind was blowing them back to the Belgian coast, to the Nazis, and they could not do a thing about it.

They saw themselves arrested, shot. Finally the wind shifted. But it was only partial relief. They might not be sacrificed to the Nazis, but to the waves; the boat capsized three times. Each time it miraculously reverted to sailing position. This was probably the effect of the substantial iron ballast Eugene had had the forethought to place in the bilge. Each time the four were thrown overboard, but they had tied themselves to the mast with a long length of rope, and they were able to regain the deck.

The boat filled with water and the pump broke down. The bottles of drinking water had been smashed, and the seawater ruined all their food except for a few tins. Four days the storm raged while the boys struggled for their lives. In the midst of all their troubles, they saw several drifting mines, one of which passed only five yards away.

When the storm finally ceased, the boys, half-dead from exhaustion and exposure, started to repair its ravages. Their chief dread was that they had been carried close to the German coast, but without instruments and sea maps there was no way of knowing where in the world they were.

Then came the next shock. They saw a bomber overhead and realized that it must have spied them. If the plane were German, it was all up with them. Terrible moments intervened, until they saw the red-white-and-blue circle of the RAF. It was a Hudson bomber, and the boys went into a wild dance.

They quickly manufactured a white flag with which they gave the SOS signal. The plane responded with light signals promising to send help. An hour later they were picked up by a British destroyer, which the bomber had directed to the little boat.

The four patriots were fed, warmed and bedded until they got to England. Their story made a sensation. The Belgian government was prompt in offering Eugene Timmerman a place in the Congo Department. The information the boys gave on the minefields was very valuable. Eugene became a hero. He met old comrades of his, other escaped patriots who frequented the Belgian club, all of whom applauded him as the pluckiest of their company.

But one day when Timmerman was lounging at the Belgian club and telling his heroic escape story to some novices, a new visitor dropped in. He paused at the doorway to the room. He was an officer of the Belgian army and he gave Eugene Timmerman, who was unconscious of his presence, a long hard look. He remembered Eugene Timmerman, remembered having seen him when he worked as a translator for the Brussels Gestapo. The officer turned on his heel, left the club and went straight to Scotland Yard.

At six o'clock the next morning Timmerman's apartment was raided. A secret radio was found, a transportable type which could be fastened around the waist like a belt. Crystals and other radio equipment were discovered, as well as a bottle of invisible ink and specially prepared paper for its use. Timmerman had secreted in a drawer four hundred and seventy-five dollars in American currency and ninety-seven pounds ten shillings in English.

The spy had slipped past the guardians of the island. He had reported on American troop movements and on preparations in the Belgian Congo. Timmerman had maintained correspondence with Canaris's agents in Portugal, Spain and France. He had sent them copies of Belgian government documents and given them the location of British ammunition dumps, airdromes and naval installations.

Among his letters Scotland Yard found one instructing Timmerman to "contact the British people where they are most themselves—as in busses, trains and public places."

The perilous escape had been made with Admiral Canaris's connivance. The storm, of course, might have drowned the just with the unjust, for the curious part was that Timmerman's three comrades were honest patriots. They too had been allowed to pass by Canaris. The honest ones provided camouflage for the spy. He had managed to worm his way into England, but there he was eventually hanged.

CHAPTER XXIV

De Gaulle Agents in Africa

THE time was 1943, the year when the tide of war turned, and the scene was a quaint Alsatian hamlet in the Jura Mountains. Sunday bells rang out over the clear air to summon hundreds of small farmers to church. It was close to Christmastide. War seemed remote indeed from this quiet spot. The Nazis were considerate enough not to intrude on the people's church services.

The organ was played by the talented musician of Arbois, twenty-one-year-old Henri Koepfler. His character was gentle and quiet, like that of most of the natives of Alsace. He was small and dark-haired, with lively eyes in his still-childlike face. He accompanied the singing of the choir. He introduced his own variations on the old hymns, sometimes interweaving themes from the forbidden "Marseillaise." That trick never failed to please the congregation.

But the routine of the Sunday service was rudely broken. Outside, on the road running past the church, was heard the roar of Nazi motorcycles and cars. Some underground leader was being pursued. When would there be an end to it? The congregation silently offered up prayers for the liberation of France.

Then something went amiss inside the church. Right in the midst of a hymn the organ stopped. The people looked around them, and peered up into the organ loft. After a little flutter, however, they took up the hymn again, without the organ. But in the organ loft Henri Koepfler let his hands fall from the keys in astonishment. His old friend Jean had appeared, Jean Peroux, his classmate. He had been sentenced to death by the Nazis, and had escaped to England. Now he was here, a mysterious apparition indeed. He had been dropped by parachute.

"There's no time to lose," said Jean. "Come out where we can talk." Jean and Henri left the church by the steep little

243

staircase reserved for the organist. There was no time to renew old friendship. Abruptly, Jean came to the point. "I've come from General de Gaulle. Henri, you are in terrible danger."

"Have the Nazis discovered my part in helping the escape of General Giraud?"

"It is not that," Jean said hurriedly.

Henri, the gifted young organist, had been in the underground for three years. He had been one of the first to pledge allegiance to General de Gaulle. His avocation as a Secret Service agent had caused him many sleepless nights, and sent him on many daring adventures. Henri had organized the smuggling of refugees from Germany into France. Slave laborers, escaped prisoners of war and stranded Allied fliers were spirited to safety. The game had gone on for years, and then circumstances required that the direction of that traffic be reversed. Hundreds of Allied agents were smuggled into Germany. By degrees the persons involved had built up a flawless courier system. Henri Koepfler so distinguished himself that he was entrusted with the rescue of General Giraud from the fortress of Koenigstein. The young boy had ushered the General safely through the two hundred miles between Koenigstein and Switzerland. The entire story of General Giraud's rescue cannot yet be revealed, but Henri's skillful organization employing the boy scouts for "frontier-work" and underground Maquis as couriers through the mountains is an historic fact.

Henri the organist was one of the key men in the underground of that region. This was the reason that Jean Peroux had come to warn him. Henri had helped Belgians, Dutchmen, Norwegians—persons of all nationalities—to flee the Nazis. But the secret was out now. Jean told of the spy, Eugene Timmerman, who had been caught in England. The spy did not explicitly know Henri's name, but he knew of Belgians who had passed through Henri's underground railroad. It was certain that he had informed the Nazis of this. It would therefore be advisable for Henri to disappear as soon as possible. Jean himself would be flown back that night. The two young men shook hands and quietly separated.

Jean vanished as suddenly as he had come. Henri decided to waste no time; he would say his good-bys and leave that same afternoon. He was in the midst of packing a few necessities when he heard a car coming down the road. He jumped out of the window of his cottage and made for his bicycle. But he was too late. The men in the Gestapo car surrounded him. He was brought to headquarters in Dijon.

During the ride of several hours Henri did not say a word. He thought of what defense he could put up, what alibis he could invent. Finally, with a sigh of relief, he thought of the proper maneuver. He smiled confidently. Nothing would happen to him.

The Gestapo prison at Dijon was a gloomy old fortress steeped in legends of the Dukes of Burgundy. Henri was taken before the German colonel, whose name he did not learn.

"So you are the man who helped Giraud escape!" snarled the colonel. "You are, aren't you? You had better confess and not waste our precious time, and confess."

Henri, standing before the colonel, felt tired, and with no more ado sat down in a convenient chair.

"Steh auf, Du Schwein," cried the colonel. "Get up, you swine." An adjutant slapped Henri in the face; but he smiled and remained seated. He said: "Gentlemen, since you already know it, why do you ask me? Yes, I have had the great honor of helping General Giraud."

The Germans were dumbfounded. Prepared as they were for a lengthy hearing, the spontaneous confession disturbed them. Perhaps this was not the right man. The colonel, confronted by this baffling conduct, did not know what to do. He dropped the question of Henri's sitting down. "Well then," he said somewhat uncertainly, "tell us how it was done."

Henri sat and smiled angelically. "I'll tell you. It was easy. I had this knife here—" and Henri drew a knife out of his pocket. "A Gestapo man got suspicious and drew his revolver, and so with this knife I cut . . ."

And, as he diverted their minds with the incoherent story, Henri in a flash drew the knife across his wrists. A fountain of blood gushed out. The colonel and his men rushed for a doctor. Henri was bleeding at an alarming rate when he was rushed to the Dijon hospital.

A few days later, though his condition was still critical, Henri was able to escape. He was aided by one of the nurses of the hospital. Henri went into hiding. Cared for by patriots, he remained sick for three months. His friend Jean Peroux was kept informed of his whereabouts. Jean, the parachute courier, visited his friend about a month after his recovery. Henri, for all his claim of being perfectly fit, was still pale and weak.

"If I had known you were still so sick, I would never have brought you this new assignment," Jean apologized.

"Oh, I'm all right. Tell me what I can do. It's about time that I left off being an old invalid and saw some action."

Henri was transferred to Africa. He was to work on his own initiative there. The work bristled with difficulties. He would have to procure new papers under another name. He would have to enlist with the Fascist groups and play the part of a quisling. Henri couldn't say that he liked the assignment. He felt himself too young for such a task. Nevertheless, he was thrilled that General de Gaulle had judged him worthy of the responsibility.

Jean outlined the job to be done. The African atmosphere was thick with intrigue and double-faced diplomacy. An agent's work in Africa was necessarily solitary and dangerous. There were few who could be trusted, and dead bodies were never discovered in the vast spaces of the desert. There were several secret addresses of friendly persons in Casablanca and Dakar, but Henri was to avoid using them unless it was absolutely imperative.

Henri was being asked to conduct a single-handed fight against the Canaris machine in North Africa. The German Armistice Commission was well entrenched on that continent. Secret airfields were being built, and the French were being compelled to finish the Trans-Saharan railroad with maximum speed. For the Germans had a special motive for desiring the completion of the line between Oran, Colomb Bechar, Segou and Dakar. The Nazis still dreamed of using air and naval bases in West Africa for the invasion of the Western Hemisphere.

Ten thousand slave laborers, as well as the soldiers of the once-proud Foreign Legion, were toiling to complete the railroad line. There was a drive on to recruit ten thousand more workers from France. The conditions of the work were horrible beyond words. The work gangs, concentrated at various points along the line, had to work ten, twelve, fourteen and eighteen hours a day. Human lives received less consideration than the steel with which the tracks were laid. The overseers used whips to drive on the lagging columns of men. Airfields were to border on the railroad to protect it. Dakar was to be fortified with submarine bases. Truck highways flanked with gasoline depots were to be laid. Henri was to report on what progress was being made.

Henri listened in bewilderment. What headway could he make in this area where the Nazis held sway? He did not even know how to gain ingress into Africa. No suggestions were put forward by de Gaulle, though a promise of adequate financial backing was made.

It occurred to Henri that he could enter Africa by enrolling as a volunteer for the labor battalions. However, the young recruit learned from the Vichy authorities that registry for an Africa labor battalion could only be made from one's legal residence, with the certification of the local authorities. For Henri it was a decidedly risky procedure to return to Arbois, where he might be betrayed to the Nazis. However, there was no other way. Henri made the attempt, counting on some of his old friends to get faked papers for him. The very first day he recklessly indulged his nostalgia to the extent of walking up and down the familiar streets. He was seen and recognized by a Nazi officer, who wasted no time, but shot at him immediately. Three bullets entered his body and two his head. The young man died instantly. The mountain of flowers on his grave included one wreath which was sent by parachute, a tribute from General de Gaulle. But all the flowers could not restore the brave boy to life.

However, war left no time for long mourning. Jean, Henri's friend, volunteered for the assignment. Two months later Maurice Mercier, alias Jean Peroux, appeared in Colomb Bechar, the hottest place in Algeria. He wore the uniform of a Legionnaire and he was one of the thousands who worked at the railroad.

It was killing labor. The temperature averaged 130 degrees

Fahrenheit. The workers were provided with no tents and had to sleep on the bare sands of the desert or the gravel of the railroad bed. No sanitation had been installed. The drinking water was impure and unpalatable, filled with calcium chloride. Men fell prey to dysentery, typhus, paludism and tropical fever. Even the sick were goaded on to work. Groups were transported from one location to another by day-long treks. Many died by the wayside. Their comrades had no time to dig graves; sand was hastily scraped away to the depth of fifteen inches and the dead were laid in these hollows.

Maurice Mercier's lot was indistinguishable from that of the other slave laborers. He realized that he could not stand it long. The officers of the Legion, who acted as their overseers, were as brutal as any described in novels. They punished desertion by death. The officer in charge of Mercier's group was one Captain Linak, a German by birth, though he had spent the last twenty years in the Foreign Legion. His inhumanity outdid that of the other officers.

Maurice watched his captain narrowly. There was something amiss with this German captain who spoke French with an atrocious accent. Linak was often away, and Maurice learned that he piloted his private plane to the great cities of North Africa—Casablanca, Oran and El Hajeb.

Linak was hated by the men. Officers were exempt from the long marches, from the gruelling labor. Linak whiled away the time with liquor, and the more he drank, the harder was the life of the men under him.

None of the men had ever been in Linak's tent, and Maurice wondered what secrets it contained. Many visitors were admitted into the tent, concerning whose errands Maurice grew curious.

The construction went on, monotonous, never-ending and deadly. Maurice, a slave like the others, had no opportunity to pursue his mission, and felt himself disintegrating under the hardships of his life. Was he to die, like the thousands of others who had perished for the sake of the Trans-Saharan railroad?

There was one tactic which would avail him, though Maurice shrank from it with distaste and shame. It was one of the lowest practices of modern espionage. It was based on the psychology of the German officer class. Many German officers have by and large kept to a tradition of homosexuality. They could not be overcome by woman spies, but by men. Inversion was well-known to be a German malady, and Maurice had observed his captain keenly enough to recognize him as an example of it.

Maurice was sickened at the need for self-defilement. The precise details are too ugly to describe, but the ruse was successful. Maurice became the German captain's minion.

The captain had the power to ease the lot of his new boy friend. No more hard labor for the captain's boy. Maurice was sent to work in the field kitchen, and fulfilled the duties of orderly and servant to the captain. Later on he was advanced to be supervisor over the work gang.

Linak was guarded in his speech and did not immediately bestow his confidence on his new boy friend. Nevertheless, he decided that Maurice was compliant and reliable. When he learned that Maurice came from Alsace, spoke German and had always felt himself more German than French, his last reserve evaporated.

Maurice had been away for a week in the desert with a work gang. When he returned, the captain greeted him warmly. "We know each other so well now that I am going to offer you this new job," Linak began, and invited Maurice to become a full-fledged member of the Canaris Secret Service. Maurice demurred at accepting such a post, but Linak jollied him along and would hear no denial. He told the young man to go to Casablanca, where he would meet one of the directors of German espionage in Africa, a certain Herr Schultze, with whom he would discuss future operations. Schultze was a paymaster and used an assumed name. The more prominent figures in the Canaris machine were known by either a number or a faked name, since they were afraid of future exposure and retaliations.

* * *

Schultze was awaiting Maurice at the Hotel Alfa in Casablanca. They sipped *apéritifs* on the terrace overlooking the crowded exotic streets. Schultze made no mention of the object of their meeting. At last he asked Maurice to follow him to his room. There, where they could not be overheard, Schultze was very frank. He said that Linak had recommended Maurice very enthusiastically—but that he himself doubted whether the young man was fit for the job, or even whether he was to be trusted.

Maurice defended himself. "I don't expect you to trust me on anyone else's say-so. You may be afraid that I'll betray your orders to de Gaulle or the damned British. I understand your caution. But I've thought of a way of guaranteeing my good faith."

Schultze listened, already half won over by the direct business-like manner of the boy. "This is my idea," Maurice continued. "If I were a member of the de Gaulle Secret Service, what would I be doing? I'd be doing my damnedest to spy on German airfields in Africa, on the Trans-Saharan railroad, on naval installations and on the secret broadcasts between Africa and other countries. At least, that's how I see it when I try to put myself in the place of such a fellow. However, it so happens that I'm not a French agent, but a German investigator. As such, I can think of no better plan than to concentrate on the same objectives as they—to hang around German bases, make friends with suspect persons—in short, to undertake counter-espionage. Perhaps I could nab some of these de Gaulle agents. I could even go so far as to pretend to be one of them, to join the French underground in Africa and forward you extensive counter-espionage reports.

"In this way you can use me without committing any of your plans to me. You see, I will be in no position to compromise you or your secrets. But I'll report once a month."

It was a deal. Schultze gave Maurice fifty thousand francs and secured him passage on a plane bound for Dakar the next week.

First, however, Maurice returned to his friend Linak to notify him of the arrangements they had made, since he had expressed deep interest in how it went. Captain Linak was overjoyed at the success of his boy friend. The German captain was an ambivalent character; a fanatic Nazi and brutal beyond description to those in his power, he was nevertheless tender in love affairs and friendships. His motives become clearer when it is learned that his dominant trait was a greed for money. From covetousness he sold the tents provided for the sheltering of the slave laborers, and let the men sleep exposed on the desert sands swept by the cold night winds. His benevolence to his boy friend was no less motivated by covetousness.

"Now I can be open with you," Linak simpered. "You must know that I am working for Schultze, too. It's a kind of side-line for me. But I haven't enough time for investigations, since this damned railroad keeps me busy. I get paid for each separate report that I turn in. If you gave me some of your material and random findings, I could get more money, and split with you, of course."

A more welcome suggestion Maurice could not have heard. This was the best possible break for his secret mission. With studied nonchalance, he replied that he would be glad to co-operate with his friend, but that Linak would have to tell him what sort of material would interest him.

Linak told him they were hunting for French agents who were sending messages to Europe by short wave. The agents were using a mobile radio set and their locus of operations was somewhere around Dakar.

"But I don't know much about radio work," Maurice objected. "I'd have to be put in touch with German radio outfits who can train me for that kind of work."

Linak, eager for the rewards and promotion that would attend the capture of the French radio spies, hastened to assure his friend that that could be managed.

By this device Maurice obtained the address of secret Nazi radio operators in Dakar, as well as an introduction to them.

He went to Dakar. According to his agreement with Schultze, he posed as a de Gaullist—a masquerade which naturally he found easy to carry off. He met de Gaullist agents in whom he confided and then attached himself to the Nazi radio spy ring in Dakar. He won their confidence by dint of providing them with valuable material about the French underground—which material was, of course, prepared by the underground for Nazi consumption. Linak and Schultze were both highly satisfied, and drew up impressive reports for Admiral Canaris.

It was not long before Maurice was a capable radio spy. He

was in charge of communicating orders to South America. One of the first messages he radioed was:

"Investigate U.S. air bases in Colombia and Venezuela, as well as flights via those places to West Africa; airplane types, movement dates."

Concurrently, the FBI and the British and French Secret Services got the same message; Maurice gave it to his secret friends in Dakar.

Another message Maurice was able to forward to the Allies was a question put by Admiral Canaris:

"Can you place suitable men for us among Chilean students going to the United States for air training?"

Maurice became an invaluable agent for the Allies. What the secret agents in Dakar had labored long and vainly to accomplish he had done in a few weeks, thanks to the recommendation of his homosexual benefactor. Radio counter-espionage soon became a two-way channel. For Dakar was a center where the Nazis received information that was transmitted from the Americas. Low-powered radio sets operated in easy stages from the United States to Mexico, from Mexico to Costa Rica, from Costa Rica to Argentina, whence the messages were finally relayed to Dakar. Maurice was the receiver of these messages. Some of them may now be disclosed.

One read:

"Our people can no longer enter Canal Zone. Consul X. in Panama allegedly can be bought. . . ."

Another:

"Chilean Tolten loading here for the USA." (She was waylaid and sunk by a submarine.)

And another:

"Will send two or three large armed English ships to the bottom without any suspicion falling on us. . . . If the business is of interest expect payment after sinking, nothing in advance. . . ."

This information was a precious gift to the FBI, Naval Intelligence and Scotland Yard. But Maurice's valuable activities were abruptly cut off. It was not that anybody suspected him, but Captain Linak became lonely. He wanted his friend back. Maurice had to return, the official reason for his recall being the fact that the construction on the Trans-Saharan railroad was going poorly. Many slave workers had escaped, and hordes had died. Moreover, supplies were not coming through. Thousands of tons of steel were lacking. The cement factories in Casablanca had to transship their entire output to France, where the Nazis were building thousands of fortifications along the coast, in fear of the invasion.

Maurice was to help reorganize the railroad work. But he definitely did not want to do it. The climate affected him badly, for he was still sick with illnesses contracted during the period of hard labor. Moreover, he had accomplished his mission, as far as it was in his power to do so.

Again he outwitted Linak. "We need more workers. If you give me authorization, I'll go back to France, and will recruit ten thousand men, or as many as I can get. I don't imagine any more can be recruited from Africa."

Linak knew that it was impossible to recruit ten thousand men for this project. But he said, "If you bring me three thousand, I'll count it a job well done."

Maurice was allowed to leave for Marseilles, and he was never seen again. But shortly thereafter Jean Peroux, alias Maurice Mercier, visited the British Embassy in Lisbon. His reports were useful for forestalling Nazis crimes in Dakar. The railroad work was almost at a standstill. The Nazi spies, Linak and Schultze, were shot as enemy agents when the liberation of Africa became a reality,

CHAPTER XXV

Member of the Jockey Club

Canaris's agents searched every corner of Spain and Portugal for the vanished Maurice Mercier. What a capital blunder they had made! Mercier left in his wake a whole series of reverses for the Germans. The African venture, doomed in any case, had suffered a terrible setback. But such setbacks were almost inevitable; they were inherent in the system of mass espionage. The Allies avoided the danger of untrustworthy agents by employing a smaller number of carefully selected and well-trained agents. Canaris, with his thousands of agents and sub-agents, could not hand-pick every one of them.

Because of this fundamental weakness in the system of mass espionage, Canaris always went out of his way to punish betrayal. He wanted his underlings to know that death was the inescapable penalty for treachery to him and his Fuehrer. Every traitor who got away unscathed imperiled his entire system. Hence, Mercier must be punished.

The Admiral fancied he knew how Mercier could be reached. One of his cleverest woman agents was sent to Lisbon to discover the Frenchman's whereabouts. Where a young man of French blood was concerned, romantic bait was sure to catch the fish; that was the Admiral's standing conviction.

The agent he sent was well known—as a voice. One of the few remaining mementoes of Berlin's pre-war gaiety was the weekly concert of the Hungarian operetta diva, Marikka Roeck. She had a wonderfully magnetic voice, and her repertoire ranged from Lehar to Gilbert and Sullivan. Inside Nazi Germany alone she had a radio audience of millions, and her voice was broadcast by long wave throughout Europe and by short wave to South America. To this vast audience it was a well-known fact that she broadcast from the Berlin radio station every Monday. But what these millions did not know was that the songs often emanated from records. Marikka Roeck was frequently absent from the German capital for months. It was she who was sent on a "special mission" to Lisbon. The mission was the Mercier case. In the Portuguese capital she went under many names, sometimes calling herself Mary, sometimes more coyly, Muckie or Liebling. She spent money freely. It had all been earned in German motion pictures, she explained. She professed to be a high-spirited Bohemian with a checkered career behind her; she had been a circus performer, she said, and while still very young had gone on the stage in Vienna. Unlike many of Canaris's agents, she made no secret of her fondness for the Nazi regime. After all, she thrived under it.

Marikka visited Portugal's Palm Beach, the Casino de Estril, which boasts of a famous gambling house. There the tourist was informed that the Windsors were habitués of the place, that this or that South American diplomat spent all his spare time there, for the Casino de Estril is a meeting ground for Germans and Russians, Americans and Italians, Frenchmen and Turks. It is a common hunting preserve for agents of the Gestapo, of Canaris, of Laurenti Beria, and of the British and American Secret Services.

Marikka had as traveling companion a girl named Hildegarde Frick. She too was a singer who worked at the Berlin radio station. Hildegarde could speak Portuguese fluently.

The two girls were not only extremely good-looking, but very sociable. They were eager to make friends. They would dance with strangers, drink with the diplomats of any country. They naturally reported the names of their new acquaintances to Canaris.

But for all their traveling, for all their fraternizing, for all their staying at luxury hotels, they could not find a trace in all of Portugal of Jean Peroux-Mercier. For Mercier had escaped in an airplane from France and had gone to England to report to General de Gaulle.

Besides the Mercier case, Marikka and Hildegarde had a few subsidiary tasks. They were in touch with agents working in Mozambique and with special agents who were setting up spy nests in Spain.

Neutral Spain, under its Fascist dictator, consistently seized any opportunity to help the Axis cause. While records of Marikka singing *The Gypsy Baron* were being played over the German radio, Marikka herself was in Spain, receiving reports which were to be transmitted to the Admiral. What these reports pertained to we shall never know, but one man in the United States had made a guess as to their subject. This man is famous for guesses that hit the mark. He is Walter Winchell. It was he who revealed that a Nazi mystery ship dropped anchor in the Bay of Vigo, on the northern coastline of Spain.

The ship was a submarine camouflaged to look like a Spanish fishing boat. No one knows what the mission of this mystery ship was. Was it taking on fuel, or landing special agents, or was there a secret submarine repair station on the coast of Spain? In any case, the British found out about it and bombed the submarine.

Walter Winchell wrote a public exposé of this breach of Spain's "neutrality." "German subs enter Vigo's Rios Chapella port at night, where they refuel, rearm and refill their food and water lockers...," Winchell wrote. "Vigo has two yards which repair Nazi subs damaged by British and American forces in the Mediterranean. And two Nazi warplants, including 'La Artistica' works which turn out bomb shells for the Wehrmacht."

Winchell also gave the location of certain air bases that the Germans had acquired in Fascist Spain. Marikka Roeck must, of course, have helped to tip off the commanders of these secret bases on incoming and outgoing boats and planes. We know, at any rate, that, although the hunt for Mercier was a failure, Marikka Roeck became Germany's most important harbor spy in Spain and Portugal.

She did not long escape the watchful eyes of the Allied Secret Services. They kept her under observation, and as a result were able to discover that the Italians were helping the Nazis to organize an espionage branch that specialized in the "Latin touch."

There was a special Italian branch of the German Secret Service, headed by Dr. Eugenio Moreale. Moreale was one of the old-line politicians of Europe, a man who may well be considered a member of the diplomatic underworld. For years he was Mussolini's personal friend, emissary and financial administrator. After Mussolini was arrested and then, thanks to the blunder of the Allied Secret Services, snatched away by the Nazis, Moreale became Mussolini's secret representative on the Iberian peninsula. His official job was to watch the Italians in Portugal and Spain and to report their connections with Allied nationals. His agents followed Italians into the cafés on the Avenida de Liberdade and into the restaurants of the Place Don Pedro IV.

Suave, over-courteous Moreale did not content himself with remaining in the employ of a fallen Caesar. He found himself a bigger and better boss, one who promised to outlive Mussolini. Before the outbreak of World War II, Moreale had been involved in huge armament deals. Now he used the connections he had then established to keep open an avenue of retreat for himself. That avenue led to the dictators of Latin America, and more directly to Argentina. For in the capital of that great South American nation lived Buenos Aires' most fashionable and newest citizen, Fritz Mandl—Argentina's Munitions King.

Espionage often has its obscure connections with munitions traffic and secret armaments.

Marikka Roeck, Hildegarde Frick and Dr. Moreale were interesting personages in themselves. But they were merely links in a chain of intrigues that had its origin in Argentina's most modern arms industries, founded and owned by Fritz Mandl.

The dimout over Buenos Aires had deepened the mysteries overhanging the self-assured and prosperous capital of Argentina. Mysteries were rife in this country, which then insisted on maintaining a policy of isolation and kept itself aloof from Pan-American unity.

Argentina was cold toward her neighbor Brazil and still colder toward the United States. Her system of honest democratic elections became a thing of the past.

Let us look inside Buenos Aires of the period we are writing about. One sign of the War is the thick black smoke issuing from the hundreds of new factories in the vicinity of the capital. But the Calle Florida is gayer than ever. Its smart shops are splendid to behold. It is a veritable modern Babylon, with Spanish, German, French, English, Portuguese and Italian all being spoken. The coffee houses are jammed. As in Paris, people sit at outdoor tables all day and discuss the good life and the beauty of women. And somewhere in this mysterious city grave political problems are threshed out. Somewhere plans were made to help interned prisoners from Nazi battleships to escape.

Aristocrats, high political figures, wealthy refugees from Spain, France, Austria and the Balkans sip long drinks at the bar of the Plaza and gossip about the latest developments in the government.

Buenos Aires is a hotbed of rumor, riddles and intrigue. It is in these war years the world's liveliest spy center.

Argentina was a neutral country until 1945 and like the other neutrals has enjoyed a great boom as a result of the War. The Avenida Corrientes, Buenos Aires' Broadway, is under a dimout. Along it stroll thousands of soldiers who have nothing to do but to give their allegiance to the winner of the most recent revolution. The city is also thronged with visitors—tourists, "scientists," diplomats of all nations, paid propagandists and a variety of foreign agents. In many ways the atmosphere resembles that of a Klondike boom town. The dance bands of the night clubs blare out hot rumbas. The night clubs' best customers are the army officers.

Recently a new guest has begun to frequent the night clubs, a tall and extremely handsome man, whom the women look at with interest. The men glance at him with curiosity and distrust. He has become the subject of many anecdotes. Rumors cluster around him and he is universally regarded with respect tinged with fear. He wears civilian dress and he is always seen in company of some member of the government. When he enters, his name is whispered about: "There goes Federico Mandl."

In a short time Mandl has become a name to conjure with. He is only forty-three years old and looks even younger. He speaks Spanish with the heavy sing-song intonation of the Viennese. It is well known that no Argentine government can survive without the output of these industrial enterprises.

Mandl's last official title was "economic advisor to the Argentine government." This title is noncommittal. At any rate, it does not explain that he is the father of an Argentine armament industry which has sprung up overnight. He is providing Argentina with weapons, since the United States, for very good reasons of its own, has refused to send any.

Federico Mandl, the Munitions King of Argentina, was close to the controlling spirits of the G.O.U., or the *Grupo Officiales Unidos*, the undemocratic clique of the ruling officers. The G.O.U. has set up and deposed well-nigh every one of the governments that have come into power in Argentina during the preceding three years.

Mandl, having converted bicycle and motor factories into top-notch munitions plants, has direct control of the means of power. Generals and party leaders whom he approved he provided with weapons. And those who have the weapons are the ones who seize power and keep it.

The Munitions King of Argentina is very well known to the American authorities. There are hundreds of letters and reports on him in the files of the Alien Property Custodian. About one million dollars of Mandl's funds in the United States have been frozen.

* * *

Mandl had long been closely watched by the Allied Secret Services. Once upon a time his name was Fritz, not Federico. In those days he had an Austrian passport and made a great show of wearing the colors of Independent Austria—red, white, and red.

As for Fritz Mandl, he was one of Europe's principal armament merchants, a well-known dealer in the instruments of death. Like other such merchants of death he sold indiscriminately to all sides. Mandl had connections with most governments in Europe. He played host to the Austrian Fascist leader, Prince Ruediger von Starhemberg. He knew King Carol and his cabinet members and had dealings with them. He also sold weapons to the Rumanian Fascists who wished to overthrow King Carol. He was a frequent guest at the home of Hungary's War Minister, the late Dr. Julius Gömbös. He arranged to provide Dr. Gömbös and Admiral Horthy with equipment for their hunting parties. Gömbös needed such a variety of weapons to shoot game that he succeeded in secretly rearming Hungary from his private stock.

Mandl was also an intimate friend of Mussolini and used to attend soccer games with him. As friend to friend, Mussolini used to tip him off as to what Balkan governments were in need of weapons. Moreover, Mussolini, who had decorated Fritz Mandl, was willing to finance any Fascist group that sprang up in the Balkans. The only stipulation was that the group declare itself ready to oppose Jugoslavia.

Hungary and Rumania had their traditional enmity. Bulgaria and Greece were in constant disputes. They fought it out with munitions bought from Fritz Mandl. There would have been more stability and far less bloodshed in the Balkans but for the stock-in-trade of Fritz Mandl.

In Spain, both Franco and the Republicans waged war with his weapons. And Mandl had outfitted Hitler's SA and SS storm troopers before they took power in Germany.

Nineteen-forty-five marked the beginning of Mandl's fifteenth year in the armament business. In 1931 he had inherited the business from his father. He was then thirty years old. The business was only a small one. Before the First World War the plant at Hirtenberg, Austria, had belonged to the Kreditanstalt, one of Vienna's largest banks. But with the war's end the armament business was hit by hard times. The peace treaties of Versailles and St. Germain forbade the production of any armament in Austria and Hungary outside of hunting rifles and police revolvers. Since the Viennese bank was not interested in doing business on such a small scale, the plant was offered for sale.

Mandl's father bought it and in due course it passed to his son. Fritz Mandl proved himself an excellent business man. First he converted the plant into a thoroughly efficient and modern munitions plant. Then he began to devote his energies to European politics. He associated himself with various nationalist organizations which were at this time beginning to be more and more Fascist in character. He undertook to finance the Austrian Home Guards, the *Heimwehren,* which was led by the young playboy prince, Ruediger von Starhemberg. Starhemberg's group, while anti-German, was thoroughly Fascist. Such a group had to have weapons, and Mandl provided them. Starhemberg later revealed that the group was also financed by Mussolini, who before 1938 bitterly opposed the *Anschluss.*

Still, Mandl had to surmount grave obstacles. The peace treaties prevented him from going ahead and producing bigger and better weapons. He and his lawyers looked about for some legal way to circumvent the treaties, and found one. Switzerland had a famous munitions factory, the Solothurn Munitions plant. Mandl organized a Swiss holding company for trading in armaments. He held the controlling shares in it, but he was clever enough to include some reputable British and French industrialists in the firm. The holding company could order weapons of all calibers from the Swiss factory. Mandl obtained everything he needed from the *Solothurner Waffenfabrik* and exported the contraband goods to Bucharest, Budapest, Vienna, Madrid and Buenos Aires.

During the nineteen-thirties the armament business became an enormously lucrative racket. Although it was illegal, the only governments that had the power to stop it would do nothing. The war ministers of these governments pretended not to see what was going on. And so the arms for a new world war were accumulated. Later on, Hitler's invasion armies found vast stores of weapons, bearing the imprint of the Hirten-berg plant, in every Balkan country. It is estimated that Mandl made some sixty million dollars from this traffic.

* * *

The successful munitions manufacturer had other interests besides complicated political intrigue. One day in 1933 his eyes fell upon one of the world's most beautiful women. He saw her as the star in a Czech moving picture. He promptly declared to his friend, Prince Starhemberg, "I am going to marry that woman."

Her father was an executive of a Viennese bank. Through his banking acquaintances Mandl arranged to meet her. She was young, seductive and highly intelligent. Within a few months after their meeting they were married. The name of the girl was Hedy Kiesler. Now she is known the world over as Hedy Lamarr, the exotic and fascinating Hollywood star.

Mandl soon ran into trouble. His wife Hedy had acted in an outstanding Czech picture *Ecstasy*, under the talented director Machaty. This highly artistic film had several shots of Hedy completely in the nude. It was an artistic film, but Mandl felt that his wife was put in a compromising position by it. He attempted to buy up all copies of the film, but it was a hopeless task. Some copies even reached the United States where, however, the nude scenes were cut out of the picture. Mandl started to offer fabulous prices for the copies of the picture still outstanding, but it was no use. He told his friends, "It's easier to sell munitions to the poverty-stricken Kingdom of Albania than to corner the market on *Ecstasy*."

* * *

In the meantime storm clouds were gathering over Europe. War seemed imminent. The Balkan countries were arming and even placid Austria knew that the *status quo* was doomed. Fascism grew stronger within Austria. Mandl's friend, Prince von Starhemberg, became a member of the Austrian cabinet and rose to be vice-chancellor. He handed Mandl a monopoly contract for equipping the Austrian Home Defense storm troopers. Starhemberg wanted his storm troopers armed to the teeth, but Austria could not pay the high cost of modern weapons. Mandl suggested a plan that was feasible only in the diplomatic underworld of the Balkans and the Danube basin.

Not long before Hitler was to march into Austria, Mandl and the prince paid a visit to the Italian Embassy in Vienna. There they had a talk with Mussolini's personal representative, none other than Dr. Eugenio Moreale. Moreale was then the director of the Stefani News Agency and bore the official title of Press Attaché.

Mandl and the prince proposed to Moreale that they buy one hundred thousand rifles in Italy's possession. These rifles, the former property of the Imperial Austrian Army, had been given to Italy in 1919, as a reparations payment. The Italians had simply stored them because the Italian army was accustomed to use rifles of different caliber. Mandl and Starhemberg asked for a low price, since the arms were no good to the Italians. They intended to resell sixty thousand rifles to the Hungarian War Minister, Gömbös. They would charge him what the whole lot had cost. Because such rearmament on Hungary's part was illegal, a very high price could be got for the weapons. In effect, Mandl and Starhemberg would be getting forty thousand rifles for nothing. These would be retained and distributed among Starhemberg's storm troopers. Old though the rifles were, they had been well made and were still highly serviceable.

The deal would be profitable for Italy in two ways. First, the War Department could realize something on useless weapons. Second, it would be a way of outfitting the Austrian Home Defense without the expenditure of any money. The Austrians would be armed for defense against Hitler. At that time Mussolini was determined to keep Austria independent, for he was in mortal terror of having the Germans at the Brenner Pass.

This, then, was the offer that Mandl and Starhemberg made to Moreale, or rather, through Moreale to Mussolini. Mandl guaranteed that the Hungarians would pay, and Vice-Chancellor Starhemberg guaranteed that the Austrian railroads would transport the arms to Hungary without anyone's being the wiser. Moreale was given to understand that he would not be the loser for his part in the negotiations.

Such outright conniving between the heads of states may seem too brazen to be true. Nevertheless, there are documents, and the memoirs of Prince Starhemberg, to prove that the Austrians were actually involved in such a deal with Mussolini and Gömbös. The documents came to light as the result of an absurd mischance, the kind of trick of fate which even the best of plotters cannot foresee.

It was a hot summer day in the little village of St. Gotthardt (not the famous Swiss railroad tunnel, but a town on the Austro-Hungarian frontier). Some railroad workers in St. Gotthart, their work over, wanted to hitch-hike home. As was their custom, they rode home on one of the freight trains. They opened the door of a box car and got in.

The box car was labeled "machine parts." What was their

surprise when they found it filled with thousands upon thousands of rifles! European workers are a political lot, and these workers saw to it that the story reached the newspapers. It became the greatest political scandal that had hit Austria for many years. Even the League of Nations began investigating. Who was smuggling arms between Austria and Hungary?

Mussolini had reliable accomplices who did not betray him. And Mussolini was very anxious not to be betrayed. He did not want Hitler to know that he was giving weapons to Starhemberg, nor did he want Czechoslovakia to know that he was helping Hungary rearm.

Fritz Mandl had the whole thing hushed up and provided plausible explanations all around. He pointed out that he owned the majority share in the Swiss holding company. It was a respectable firm, was it not, with several British and French directors? He said that the weapons belonged to it and the sale was wholly in accordance with Swiss law. The Austrian newspapers got hold of the documents proving that Mandl, Starhemberg and Mussolini had been involved in a crooked deal. They even published correspondence between Fritz Mandl and Il Duce. But Vice-Chancellor Starhemberg put a stop to newspaper publicity. Soon the case was forgotten. And shortly afterward Hitler marched into Austria and took over the very rifles which Mussolini had sold to the Home Defense as a bulwark against the Nazis.

The atmosphere of Balkan intrigue and underworld tactics was not a suitable one for Hedy Mandl. Her marriage was unhappy. She alleged that her husband was cruel and she wanted a divorce. But this was not easy. Mandl had been able to hoodwink the League of Nations. He could certainly see that the Austrian courts act in his favor. Nevertheless, she filed suit for separation.

The Austrian press carried headlines on the Mandl-Lamarr case. It made quite a sensation. Mandl's political opponents seized on it and made much of it. But in a short time this case too was hushed up and forgotten. Hedy Lamarr went to the United States to begin her miraculous career in Hollywood.

It is said that, though Mandl had never been a sentimental man, he was heartbroken when Hedy left him. But political events were moving so rapidly that there was little time for private feelings.

The Austrian Chancellor, Kurt von Schuschnigg, was summoned to Berchtesgaden in February, 1938. In the interview, Hitler treated him like a schoolboy. A few weeks later Hitler made his triumphal entry into Vienna. The blue Danube was stained with blood let by the Nazi hordes.

Starhemberg and Mandl made their escape. They fled to the haven Mussolini could offer and lived in Italy for quite a while. Hitler's conquest of Austria was a terrible blow to Mussolini's power. He was now definitely in second place within the Axis, but he tried to do his best for his two friends. Without his aid it would have been impossible for Mandl to get his wealth out of Austria. American authorities have estimated that his fortune came to about forty million dollars.

Hitler confiscated all of Mandl's armament works. Hard though it is to believe, he actually paid Mandl for them in cash. One million pounds were remitted to Mandl. Hitler, reputed never to forget past favors, remembered that in the old days his storm troopers had been supplied by Mandl. Moreover, Mussolini probably put in a good word and asked for fair treatment for a friend of his. Another point was that the Hirtenberg plant was owned by the Swiss holding company, whose French and British shareholders had to be kept satisfied. There are probably other reasons behind this unexpected generosity on the part of Hitler. The fact remains that Mandl saved the bulk of his investment in occupied Austria. Otherwise he would never have been able to carry out his new production plans in Argentina.

There are indications that these plans were both far-reaching and prepared well in advance of Hitler's invasion of Austria. For, even before the *Anschluss*, Mandl had shipped millions of dollars out of Austria. He had to resort to illegal measures to do so, for Fascist Austria, like Nazi Germany, prohibited the export of currency. It is known that Prince Starhemberg helped him to evade the Austrian law and send money to the United States and Argentina. Mandl himself then left Austria and went to live on the French Riviera.

It is difficult to determine to what extent Mandl was a tool

of the Nazis and to what extent he was using the Nazis to further his own financial position. At any rate, he seemed to feel
most comfortable when he was out of their direct physical
reach, though not necessarily out of touch with them.

He worked for a while from his villa on the French Riviera,
collecting the funds he had spread over all of Europe and trying to get all the assets from his factories in Europe. In this
endeavor he depended largely on the efforts of his friend, Dr.
Guido Schmidt, the Austrian quisling and former Austrian
Foreign Secretary.

Then, quite unexpectedly, Mandl decided to take a pleasure
trip to Argentina. Whether he did so upon his own initiative
or acting upon a hint from some of his Fascist and Nazi friends,
we do not know. At any rate, his pleasure trip was a splendid
opportunity for him to look over the field and decide whether
Argentina was a good place to continue his business.

He was well acquainted with a number of Argentine army
officers, military attachés who had been his guests in Vienna.
His talks with them were highly satisfactory; he received the
assurance that the Argentine government would be delighted
if he set up a new armament industry and would reward him
with Argentine citizenship.

As a matter of fact, Mandl never had much occasion to worry
about being "stateless." When he returned to France, he was
equipped with new citizenship papers—those of Paraguay—and
the resounding title of Paraguayan Consul to Monte Carlo.
For a multi-millionaire such titles are easily acquired and they
grant them diplomatic immunity as well as many travel privi-
leges. He had previously sold weapons to the president of
Paraguay, General Estigarribia. Mandl returned to France and
then visited Luxembourg, where he arranged about patents and
other business matters with the Luxemburg owners of Argentine steel factories. There is no doubt that this "refugee from
the Gestapo," as he characterized himself, also negotiated with
German steel manufacturers and let them know about his plans
for Argentina. While in Paris Mandl also met with Laval and
a number of other French Fascists.

In October, 1938, Mandl again appeared in Buenos Aires.
This time there was no doubt that he seriously intended to set

up in business. He bought a cattle ranch and a rice plantation, and transferred huge sums from France and Switzerland to Argentina. He deposited fifteen hundred and forty pounds of gold bullion in the Central Bank of Argentina and another fifteen hundred and forty pounds with Lloyd's in London. Finally, he deposited about two million dollars in one of the best-known banks of New York City.

Following the pattern he had employed so successfully in Switzerland, Mandl founded a holding company for all his assets, the *Sociedad Anonima Financiera Industrial Argentina*. His name was not mentioned at all, but the incorporators had given him the power of attorney. Incidentally, this refugee from the Nazis included in his firm one of the leading Argentine Nazis.

He entered all sorts of businesses, bought stocks in leading Argentine corporations, went into partnership with old, well-known, conservative firms, invested in textiles and cement, plastics, synthetic rubber and artificial silk.

Evidently he was counting on huge war profits from Argentina's *ersatz* industries. He also went into the shipping business, buying the Dodero La Plata Line. There is documentary proof that he bought merchant vessels and sold them to Japan. But, if there were not other evidence, this alone would certainly not serve as an indictment against him, for in this period many American business men were selling oil and scrap iron to Japan.

In the winter of 1939–40 he visited New York and Washington and had many conferences with Wall Street bankers in connection with a scheme to purchase a large number of merchant ships. These vessels were to sail under the Argentine flag. They would probably have been used to ship goods either to Japan, or from Argentina to Germany by way of Portugal, Spain and occupied Ethiopia. Some American agencies hold the view that this was a scheme for getting munitions into Argentina from Germany.

Fritz Mandl quickly discovered that Balkan intrigues could not be put over in this country. The bankers he approached refused to have anything to do with the proposition.

Mandl was also interested in creating an independent iron and steel industry for Argentina. In fact, this interest was far keener than his interest in a merchant marine. He wanted a loan of one hundred and fifty million dollars for this project. When this was made known, the Foreign Funds Control and the Alien Property Custodian and Military Intelligence Service began keeping a sharp eye on Signor Federico Mandl. They traced all his activities in the United States.

One thing they discovered incidentally was that he apparently could not forget his former wife, Hedy Lamarr. He tried repeatedly to get in touch with her, but she refused to see him. Apparently with the vague idea of somehow competing with her, he entered the movie business. In 1940 he organized the Gloria Motion Picture Corporation, with offices at 729 Seventh Avenue, New York City. The company produced one picture called *New Wine*. The project turned out badly and was one of the rare losing propositions in Mandl's career. However, it was a mere bagatelle for him—his total investment in it was about two hundred thousand dollars.

When Mandl came to New York, he already had his future plans for Argentina pretty thoroughly outlined. He intended to re-arm Argentina and give the Argentine government all the military equipment, steel and steel products it needed.

The FBI and Military Intelligence Service know that Mandl met in New York a Nazi steel expert who was connected with the Nazi Rheinmetall Works. The German agreed to help Mandl by supplying patents and technicians.

Mandl purchased machinery in the United States and materials for a bicycle factory; he started negotiations for a brass mill and bought huge quantities of machine tools.

Advised by his Nazi expert, he made a contract with a firm that had helped to build the Hermann Goering Works in Germany and a steel plant in England. He hired this firm to come down to Buenos Aires and draw up the necessary blueprints for his new steel plant.

Mandl's New York visit culminated in a marriage. Before he left for Argentina, he wed the Austrian Baroness von Schneider. She was the niece of the notorious Dr. Rintelen, who helped to assassinate the Austrian Chancellor, Dolfuss. They are still married and live in Buenos Aires with their two pretty children.

After Pearl Harbor the Alien Property Custodian was more interested in Mandl's business transactions than in his private life. The former were far from innocent. As soon as the United States government found out that he had gone into the armament business in Argentina, it decided to freeze all his assets in this country. Federal agents discovered funds of his kept with two private banking firms. The accounts had been opened in 1939 with an estimated sum of over a million dollars in Latin American stocks and some United States securities. The accounts were in the name of his Argentine holding company. The Argentine government made efforts to obtain the release of the funds, but was informed that Mandl's activities in Argentina were looked upon with suspicion by the United States. It was no wonder, for the Allied Secret Services had by now amassed countless charges against Mandl. Despite his claim to be a refugee from the Nazis, they had ample evidence that he was collaborating with Nazi Germany. His connection with Dr. Moreale in Portugal was only a minor cutout in the jigsaw puzzle. His financial manipulations, which could only have taken place with Nazi sanction, were part of the evidence against him. But above all there was a fatal cablegram that Mandl had been indiscreet enough to send to Germany.

That cablegram fell into the hands of the Allied Secret Services. It was a blueprint of Mandl's plans for Latin America. The time was after Dunkerque, when there seemed every reason to believe that Hitler had won the War. Mandl apparently felt that there was no longer any need for caution, and cabled Germany to offer the Hermann Goering Works his fullest cooperation. He was willing to produce steel and munitions in Argentina for the Nazi High Command. Mandl bluntly asked for Nazi patents of the famous Krupp Works for his production in Argentina. He also offered orders from the Argentine government to the Hermann Goering Works. What these offers amounted to was a plan for Germany, with Mandl's aid, to store weapons in Argentina for use in an attack on the Western Hemisphere. A German army landing in South America would then not need to be supplied over long lines of communication. Its supplies would be waiting for it in Argentina.

If Mandl's plans had been carried out, Germany would have

transformed Argentina into a great military base for the invasion of North America, as the United States transformed England into a great base for the invasion of the European continent.

Berlin replied by cablegram that Mandl was to get to work at once. And this cablegram too fell into the hands of Allied Intelligence.

In a few years Mandl's ingenuity won him the position of chief financier and industrialist in his adopted land. He knew how essential shipping was in wartime. The United States might refuse to sell ships to Argentina; nothing daunted, he bought up the old Argentine Mihanovich Line of river steamers. They were a multi-million-dollar transportation monopoly which linked Argentina, Uruguay and Paraguay, and they might prove very useful.

Mandl's bicycle plants were in reality plants for producing tanks, caterpillar treads, steel armor, gasoline motors, turret guns and anti-aircraft guns. He had factories for bottle-top manufacture ingeniously converted into war plants for producing car couplings, guns, explosives and light rifles.

The new armament industry in Argentina was not built up without some unfavorable publicity. On August 27, 1941, in *Accion Argentina* there appeared a full-page illustrated article on Mandl's new bicycle factory. The author remarked that the new member of the Jockey Club had a fair chance of securing monopoly in the bicycle field, but that perhaps he was not interested in this, for the factory could be converted into an ammunition plant in forty-eight hours.

The phrase "new member of the Jockey Club" was a dig that most Argentinians understood. For Mandl had joined the Jockey Club, Argentina's most exclusive club, in spite of the fact that many leading families in Argentina refused to have any dealings with this munitions king and mystery man. He had at first been blackballed by the club, but Colonel Juan Peron, one of the new dictators, had finally ordered his membership.

Colonel Juan D. Peron, Vice-President and former Undersecretary of War, is head of the G.O.U. officers clique which introduced Fascism into Argentina. Peron is the man who overthrew two of the three presidents the country has had since the New Order was started in the Casa Rosada.

Juan Peron's record was a black one. It is not surprising that our State Department refused to recognize his government for so many years. Peron organized espionage against Chile in 1940 when he was in Santiago as a military attaché representing Argentina. He was aided by one Lieutenant Carlos Leopold Haniez, who spirited away secret documents and information from the Chilean army and sold the material to Peron. The espionage was discovered; Peron, protected by his diplomatic status, was recalled from the country, but his accomplice was sentenced to fifteen years' imprisonment.

Mandl and Peron, old bosom friends, established their own war plants. Peron's G.O.U. has the power to remove presidents and all who displease them. They removed the Argentine Foreign Secretary, Albert Gilg, from office. They have fomented revolutions in Bolivia and other South American countries.

Mandl began to acquire quite a reputation. Never before had anyone succeeded in importing such quantities of finished war materials and raw materials to Argentina. Contracts were drawn up for Chilean copper; steel was imported from Sweden. It was Mandl who made it factually possible for Argentina to harbor an undemocratic government and to oppose the United States in all Latin American affairs.

The Fascist Revolution of June, 1943, brought Mandl to the pinnacle of his power. His friends were on top; there were no longer the slightest checks upon his activities. A few months after this revolution, therefore, he bought up an old, established Argentine firm, the IMPA. Now he was able to produce airplanes, gliders, cars and trucks, as well as weapons. President Edelmiro Farrell and Colonel Juan Peron attended the opening ceremonies at the new plant.

IMPA and the other plant, Cometa, were transformed into up-to-date arms factories. Today there is no longer any doubt that Admiral Canaris and the German General Staff knew what they were doing when they permitted Mandl to rescue his fortune from Europe. This plan for a modern arms industry in Argentina unmistakably bore the stamp "Made in Germany."

Early in 1944 Federico Mandl was awarded a government

contract to the amount of fifty-six million pesos. A contract double the size of this was promised as soon as deliveries began on the first. Mandl began supplying everything Argentina's army required, from arms to trucks and field kitchens. His business expanded into the greatest arms industry he had ever possessed. In addition, he helped to set up a government project in Argentina, the Cordova Government Arms Factory. For a while he had almost daily conferences with the Argentine War Materials Commission.

When at last Fritz Mandl was placed on the Allied blacklist, he indignantly declared: "This step is not directed against me. America is worried about Argentina's military power and native industry."

Mandl never attempted to conceal his sympathy with the Fascist principle of government, in spite of his persistent claim that he was a refugee from the Nazis. In a statement on Latin America he said:

"The heads of all the Latin American countries owe their position directly or indirectly to the military. Military men like deeds, not words. In all my experience I have never known a Latin American country to cancel an armament contract, no matter what the political changes."

The celebrated French journalist, Pertinax, asserts that Mandl must be the administrator of Nazi underground funds; that he has been entrusted with the care of the secret funds of the Nazi leaders who will try to escape to Argentina after the War.

In one respect, certainly, Fritz Mandl was only one of the pieces in Admiral Canaris's wily chess game. Canaris had planned to use Argentina as a base for attacking the United States. His men were already in Dakar; there were plenty of quislings planted in Argentina. Fritz Mandl was to supply these German advance guards with arms.

The Allies choked this enterprise at an early stage. But Mandl will never give up. Argentina in 1945 remains undemocratic, though the country finally has broken with the Axis. A few days before the first United Nations Conference at San Francisco, Argentina expressed her desire finally to join the concert of Pan-American unity—just a few weeks before the Russians captured Berlin.

And, to do a thorough job, the Argentine government finally arrested the munitions king, Federico Mandl, confiscated his blacklisted armament plants and with this step saved the war industries for Argentina and from the Allied blacklist. Of course, Mandl's imprisonment was only temporary, and his plants under new management are again working full blast for the Argentine army.

Nothing has changed basically. Argentina is still chockful of foreign and native Fascists; although defeated Nazi Germany has lost her game in Argentina, the Werewolves, the Nazi underground, have found there a well-camouflaged refuge. Mandl's friends are still helpful. And where should a man like Admiral Walter Wilhelm Canaris, who has so far escaped the War Crimes Commission, find refuge? In Japan? In Ireland? Inside Germany? In Spain? In Argentina? Perhaps Canaris plans to take up one of his old aliases again—maybe even that of Moses Meyerbeer, the violin dealer. There are many Fascists left in Argentina. Will they grant asylum to the greatest spy of our time? They deny it. But who knows? Who knows?

CHAPTER XXVI

The Secret Plan for a Nazi Underground Movement

No one would ever have suspected that the man was an investigator or a member of a Secret Service. Everyone who met up with Agent B5 considered him a hypochondriac and a screwball, or at best a man with a weird assemblage of crackpot ideas. Both food and liquor in Argentina are generally good, but B5 never touched liquor and studiously avoided the dishes that restaurants offered on their menus.

A tall, bald American, he affected a straggly beard. He lived in a small boardinghouse run by a young German widow who was a good cook and a clean housekeeper. It was a pleasant *pension*, whose clientele consisted mainly of Germans and Italians. The Germans always avoided political discussions. The boardinghouse was eminently respectable, and Agent B5 in no way detracted from its respectability.

He was a very sick man—all his fellow boarders could vouch for that. At breakfast he would take a jar of diabetic marmalade out of his pocket; he would order hot water and with it concoct his private caffeineless coffee, a box of which he carried in another pocket. Then he would eat his special white bread. He would chew each piece for several minutes and then pause for a while, as though he had to wait for the bread to be digested. This unfortunate invalid would spend at least an hour and a half over breakfast every morning. The other guests watched him in astonishment; and behind his back many laughed at his habits. The hypochondriac was only too eager to describe his ailments to anyone who would listen to him. In Spanish, German or English, he explained that he had only a few years to live and even those few years depended on his following his rigorous diet. He recounted his symptoms with the greatest delight. Obviously he was too sick to work; all he could do was to sit idle and wait for the end.

He must have suffered from some kind of throat infection, for he gargled five times a day, and at regular intervals he sprayed his throat. His sprayer he also kept in his pocket.

Despite his hypochondria, however, he was rather well liked. He was pleasant enough when he could be led to talk about other matters. Then he would tell interesting stories about his younger days, or about the more remote corners of Argentina —for he seemed to know the country quite well. He also made a first-class fourth at bridge.

Some of the boarders were quite sympathetic toward this "doomed" man, although a few of them took no stock in his illness, for he looked perfectly healthy. The consensus of opinion was that he was not quite sane, but was otherwise quite easy to get along with.

Although Agent B5 took life easy, his activities were not so limited as they seemed. He saw many doctors about his diabetes and his throat disease, but these doctors were very frequently Argentine army doctors who gave him information about the Argentine army or about the escaped officers and crew of the pocket battleship, *Graf Spee,* which the Germans had scuttled. These officers and men were interned in Buenos Aires. Moreover, some of his doctors sent him to technicians who gave him X-ray and short-wave treatments. It is well known that these do not relieve diabetes, but after all the man was so fearfully hypochondriac that he could be expected to try the most absurd cures and to go to all sorts of quack healers. B5 didn't mind ridicule, for the technicians, nurses and quacks he visited seemed to know much more about the munitions factories of a certain Federico Mandl than they did about X-rays.

The poor invalid remained under the care of his doctors for many years. He had saved money in the days when he was hale; he could afford expensive medical treatment. An occasional subsidy from his present employers might have helped. For this curious boardinghouse character had for years been one of the Allied powers' best agents; for years he had been supplying vital and exact information on Argentina's Fascist army and on the country's budding munitions industry.

But even the most careful agent is subject to human error and eventually loses his effectiveness. For years Argentina's Secret Service and Admiral Canaris's office sought the Allied "message box" in Buenos Aires. They were desperately eager to find the agent who had succeeded in supplying Washington and London with the key to the German-Argentine code and who seemed to know all about Herr Mandl's activities.

Agent B5 was never unmasked—he was too clever. But there were weak points in his scheme—the fact that he had no regular employment and that he was a foreigner. Why was he in Argentina? Why did he not pursue his cure in Florida or in California?

It was this slight discrepancy in his story that led the Argentine Secret Service to suspect him. But there was certainly no reason to deport him from Argentina, for there was no evidence at all against him. All his acquaintances were professional people. Some of them were not in the favor of the undemocratic government of Argentina, but most of them were not interested in politics at all. Both the man and his acquaintances seemed utterly harmless.

B5 would have been able to continue his secret investigations for many months if he had not overlooked a few small details. It is always the small details that trip up the best of spies.

B5 was very fond of a woman agent—let us call her Anne. She had done significant service for the Allied cause, not because she believed in democracy or the Allies, but because she hated her husband, a high-ranking Fascist officer of the Argentine army who was very friendly with the new munitions king, Federico Mandl. Her husband had married her for her money and was spending it freely in gambling halls and in outfitting storm troopers.

Anne met B5 at a tea given by one of her friends in the army medical service. She liked him from the beginning and soon discovered that when he was with her he quite forgot his illness and the fact that he was "doomed" to die in a few years. A sincere friendship sprang up between them, for Anne was a lonely woman. Her husband took no interest in her; to him she was a mere chattel. Her role was to look pretty, to manage a large house and preside over its entertainments and to get more money from her millionaire land-owning parents. Unhappy as she was, she was attracted to the kindly, gentle invalid. She needed him quite as much as he needed her.

In the course of time the platonic friendship became a romance. It went on for many years, and rumor has it that the American wanted to marry her. The problem was how to obtain a divorce from her Fascist husband, for divorces are hard to get in Argentina.

The couple's desire, however, was never realized. Husbands are a suspicious lot, and hot-blooded Argentinians are, perhaps, even less tolerant of unfaithful wives than are husbands of other nationalities. This particular husband had a professional background as an Intelligence officer, and therefore had more than the usual resources at his command.

After her husband began to suspect her, Anne was shadowed for three months. Her telephone was tapped and records made of her conversations. In November, 1944, she and her American friend arranged to meet in one of the most fashionable hotels of Buenos Aires. They intended to discuss divorce plans, as well as the Argentine Fascists' newest schemes. Two plainclothes men and two uniformed policemen broke into the hotel room, where they confidently expected to find the two lovers in an embarrassing situation. What was their astonishment to find the two, looking like a long-married couple, sitting decorously at the tea-table!

The police arrested B5—on moral grounds. He was charged with disrupting a marriage. "A fine thing," said the leader of the police, "sitting here unchaperoned in a hotel room with a married woman!" The officer's indignation went the Boston Watch and Ward Society one better. "We in Argentina have high morals; we don't stand for any kind of free love."

Anne broke into tears. To her this man represented more than a sordid affair; he was the sole hope of her otherwise barren life.

B5 cautioned the police that he was a very sick man who had to be treated carefully. He was led off by the police. Anne's husband prevented any newspaper publicity about this scandal. But he managed to get B5 deported as a foreigner who had not respected the lofty morality of a clean country like Argentina.

From that day on, B5 with his diabetic marmalade and his curious potions was never seen again in Buenos Aires. His reports on Argentina were read by several foreign secretaries and Military Intelligence heads, and these gentlemen found them instructive in regard to the coming Nazi underground after World War II. But B5's mission in Argentina was over.

B5's report commenced in 1939. On December 16, 1939, the harbor of Montevideo became the cynosure of all eyes. The Nazi pocket battleship *Graf Spee,* battered and pursued, had come there seeking sanctuary. It was ordered to leave within twenty-four hours, or ship and crew would be interned by Uruguay.

The story of the scuttling of the *Graf Spee,* and the suicide of her Prussian admiral, is well known. The further destiny of the interned sailors and officers of the ship is not well known. It is significant that a large proportion of them have managed to escape from their Argentine internment camps.

According to Argentine records, there were no deaths among the nine hundred and sixty-five internees. Nevertheless, B5 reported not long after their internment that there were less than eight hundred and forty-five German prisoners of the *Graf Spee* left. All of the internees had given their word of honor to remain in neutral Argentina; their officers were even allowed to walk around in freedom. But just as the Germans broke their word to Holland, Norway, Denmark, Czechoslovakia and Poland, they broke it to Argentina. After all, the concept of "word of honor" is a mere nothing to the Nazi.

One hundred and twenty men from the *Graf Spee* escaped to form the first German underground in Argentina. B5 reported all the details of the escape, as later did Ray Josephs, the courageous American foreign correspondent. Among the hundred and twenty were six captains, twenty-one lieutenant-commanders, three radio operators and twenty-six skilled mechanics—all experts who could be used by Admiral Walter Wilhelm Canaris and his Nazi espionage apparatus.

Admiral Canaris, who himself had escaped from an internment camp during the First World War, mustered enough accomplices among the hundred and eighty thousand organized Germans in Argentina (the official Nazi figure of 1940) to pull this escape coup, the greatest in modern history.

The men escaped by the most thrilling techniques. Some fled by night, scaling walls with rope ladders. Some escaped in broad daylight by pretending they were going to church services. Some were spirited out of the country by Nazi submarines; some remained and assumed other names, with the aid of fake passports or fake Argentine birth certificates. Some were ordered to insure their safe assimilation by marrying Argentine girls. Some posed as German Catholic refugees and asked to be admitted to monasteries. A few posed as profes-

sional football players. One became a church organist. All
had the direct backing and financial help of Admiral Canaris's
office. A few technicians who were needed at home in Germany
were planted on Spanish freighters. They were equippd with
alternate sets of papers—Spanish and German. Should the Allies stop the Spanish boat, the Nazis would show their Spanish
papers. In Spain, however, they would produce their German
papers; the Nazi Embassy would take them in charge and send
them to Berlin by a Lufthansa plane.

By these channels each of the six captains was rescued from
captivity and given command on a new Nazi submarine, assigned to duties in the waters off Argentina. They stood by to
receive espionage information from their men within the country. One of these escaped officers was Jürgen Wattenberg, who
came into the news when he torpedoed a Brazilian merchant
vessel and landed finally as a prisoner of war in the U.S.A.

The German naval attaché, Herr Dietrich Niebuhr, and his
boss, Baron Edmund von Therman (who later fled to Japan),
were responsible for organizing the escapes. The Argentine
equivalent of the Dies Committee on un-American activities,
the so-called Taborda Committee, unearthed a transcript of a
message sent to one of the interned sailors:

August 16, 1942

To Kurt Ridzevski:
You are instructed to present yourself on Thursday, August 20, 1942, at eleven o'clock at the office of the German House, as the undersigned wishes to hand over to you
an official communication that will be of great value and
importance to you in your future life.

The communication was, of course, the program for his escape. A special "Political Bureau" of the German Embassy,
headed by stiff-necked Herr Rupert Weilhermer, handled all
the details of the escapes. It is not known at present whether
it was Agent B5 or one of the investigators for the Taborda
Committee who finally got the goods on Herr Weilhermer.
The embassy official was exposed by an anonymous investigator

who chose to call himself "a dove of peace." This investigator obtained a highly compromising message which Weilhermer had sent to one of his most trusted agents. The Taborda Committee published the text of it:

Dec. 28, 1943

My dear friend,
The Fuehrer expresses his gratefulness and recognition to you and all your collaborators for the services you have rendered this year to the American continent. The Fuehrer also expresses his hope that next year each of you will continue using his ability and sacrificing his properties, even his life, to contribute to a realization of what has been ordered, namely, a break of the Pan-American front through maximum help to all revolutionary, anti-Allied, anti-Semitic elements in South American countries, and to hinder as much as possible the supply of materials to the principal enemies of the Third Reich. . . ."

Not long after the publication of this message, Argentina officially broke off relations with Nazi Germany. This by no means implied that the Nazi underground disappeared from Argentina. Curt Riess, author and foreign correspondent, claims that the German underground in early 1945 had some four hundred cells organized throughout Argentina. There Canaris's men may lie low for a few years, living under assumed names, supplied with funds from their cache of jewels, gold and American dollars. And there they may try to organize the new war of revenge, World War III. They still hope to make Argentina the center of a revived German Nazism.

One thing is certain: Admiral Canaris clings desperately to his plans for world conquest. Germany has been beaten twice. Now after this War she is a country of ruins, her industries destroyed, her people starved, her young men dead or maimed. She has become utterly isolated, hated by the rest of the world and without hope of mercy or forgiveness. In such a situation, what course is open to a man of Canaris's stamp? We must remember that Canaris is but a symbol of the Junker caste, the group that has run the German military machine. He is the symbol of the hateful clique of "supermen" who have gaily launched wars because war and political intrigue are the sole aims of their lives, and who will never change. What other course can the Admiral follow if he should chance to survive the defeat of Germany and escape the fate meted out to the war criminals? (And he denied being one of them!) And what can the others do, those thousands of others who belong body and soul to the Nazi military machine? Their only solution will be a vow of hatred unto death toward the rest of the world. They will work unremittingly to prepare the way for the war of revenge, for a resurgence of conquered Germany.

Admiral Canaris is a sincere man, no doubt about that. He believes in his cause; he believes that Germany is more important than his own life or the life of anyone else. That is why he has already formed the Nazi underground. In the midst of the War, when it became clear that Germany would ultimately be defeated, the Admiral assembled his staff and issued the first orders for the new underground movement, the Werewolves and the SS elite guards.

The Admiral's plan is not so fantastic as it may seem at first glance. For the Admiral knows that Fascism as an idea will survive the defeat of Germany and of Nazism. It will still be cherished by Franco in Spain, by the Fascists in Argentina, in Mexico and elsewhere. The supporters of Fascism who talked loudly before the War will, in the postwar days, again raise their heads in the United States and England. But it is not enough for Canaris that the native Fascists will survive. They must be guided, directed, by a nucleus of German Nazis. And that nucleus will operate from a strong and strategically well-situated country.

Admiral Canaris's secret instructions for the new Nazi underground have not been published widely. But they were secured by Allied agents and reprinted in some newspapers. According to these sources, the Nazi underground after the War will operate in the following ways:

(a) Planting of able Werewolf leaders in foreign countries, where, properly camouflaged, they will have to lay the groundwork for new Nazi and Fascist attacks.

(b) Immigration of the largest possible number of young Germans to foreign countries, mainly to Latin America, and if possible to the U.S.A. They will be admitted as "expert" agriculturists, chemists, industrialists, laborers and business men (even tourists).

(c) Social invasion. Members of the former ruling families of Europe will infiltrate Latin America by getting into the society of the Western Hemisphere; there they will be assigned to special tasks of the Nazi underground (as champagne salesman von Ribbentrop was in England).

(d) Creation of a new fifth column.

(e) Forming of new clubs, sport associations.

(f) Contacts with munitions producers (à la Mandl, Juan March of Spain, Wenner-Gren of Sweden, et cetera).*

(g) Organization of campaigns of racial hatred against Negroes, Jews, Italians and other minorities, for the Fascist purpose of "divide and conquer."

The new German General Staff will direct this Nazi underground, not from the defeated Reich, but from foreign soil. After World War I the German liberals said, "The Kaiser has gone, but the Generals have remained." This time Hitler had to go, but the Nazis will remain.

This potential Nazi underground is not a mere theory of alarmists. It has been vouched for by Secret Service agents who have insistently called for action. Last but not least, there is documentary evidence.

The Canaris office has gone so far as to issue a sixty-page memorandum on the operation of this underground. This revealing document was captured in France by Allied troops. The British, American and Russian Military Intelligence Services and the respective agencies for psychological warfare have studied it very carefully.

Little has been released concerning this momentous document. Its existence might still be unknown, were it not for the

---

* Gustav Alfred Krupp von Bohlen-Halbach, merchant of death, owner of the German Krupp Works, captured by the American troops, answered when asked about his postwar plans, "I hope to rebuild the factories and produce again."

indiscretion of the French magazine *Combat,* which is published in Algiers. In the early days of 1944, when General
Charles de Gaulle and his Free French were not yet recognized
as the French Provisional Government by the United States
State Department, *Combat* printed the Canaris document. The
Free French took the document out of hiding simply to show
the world what Admiral Canaris and his Germans were planning for the postwar years. They hoped the document would
encourage the United States and Great Britain to desire a
strong France, as a counterbalance against Germany.

The magazine printed large parts of this secret document.
Here is a selection from it, as translated from *Combat:*

> Germany confused the principal adversary with the sub
> sidiary adversary—because she wanted to conquer France
> instead of throwing herself from the beginning in June,
> 1940, with all her available forces against England. . . .
>
> In the next world war, which ought to take place within
> twenty-five years, Germany must avoid making that mis
> take again. The principal adversary will be the United
> States and our entire force must be concentrated against
> this country from the beginning.
>
> It would be wrong to try to conquer Russia while leav
> ing intact the American industrial potential.
>
> For this plan to succeed, it is essential for us to hold the
> West Atlantic Coast of Europe from the North Cape to
> Gibraltar, and above all to have air bases in the west and
> south of France, and naval bases on the French Atlantic
> and North Sea coasts.
>
> Our first goal should be, from now on, to establish a
> camouflaged dictatorship in France. While appearing to
> be on friendly terms with the Anglo-American powers, she
> would be in reality our ally.
>
> Our defeat in the present War need be considered no
> more than an incident in the triumphal progress of Ger
> many toward the conquest of the world. We must inspire
> Germany, though she be defeated, with the spirit of a future
> conqueror.
>
> What does a temporary defeat matter when we have al
> ready destroyed the manpower and material wealth of our

enemies? After the War we will be able to secure a margin of economic and demographic superiority even greater than the superiority we enjoyed before 1939. For that, this War will have been useful; it will have enabled us, within the next twenty-five years, to wage another war under better conditions. Russia will need that much time to repair the destruction we have wrought. We need not fear peace conditions similar to those we might have imposed ourselves, since our opponents will always be divided and disunited.

We must strive to introduce into the coming peace the seeds of future dissensions. Our enemies are aware that the 1920 formula of "making Germany pay" is neither sensible nor practicable. We shall therefore be called upon to furnish our enemies with a few squads of workers; to return a few objects of art, plus our obsolete machinery; and we can always say that the bulk of the stolen articles they lay claim to have been destroyed by their bombings.

We must begin immediately preparing a dossier on the loot "destroyed by Anglo-American bombs." Time will do the rest. *Our enemies will grow weary before we do. We must organize a campaign of pity which will induce them to send us needed supplies at the earliest possible moment.* Above all, we must hold on to the assets we have deposited in neutral countries. . . .

The present War will thus have been victorious, in spite of our temporary defeat; it will have been a step forward toward our supremacy.

Once more we do not have to fear conditions of peace analogous to those we have imposed, because our enemies will always be divided and disunited.

We must do our utmost to sow, in the coming peace treaty, the germs of future divisions.

These are the conditions of victory.

Such is the prospectus for Admiral Canaris's underground—the postwar organization of Nazism. It does not matter whether Admiral Canaris himself survives; what matters is that he has assured the survival of his work. Thousands of his subordinates already have their orders and will go on working under those orders until a new Canaris is ready to take the Admiral's place. The organization is strong enough to create its own leaders.

Such is the ultimate significance of Admiral Canaris. This book has been written to point out the lesson of his work, that Nazism can survive without Hitler and the other Nazi leaders. Should we forget this, our children will have to face and to fight another war. Once more soldiers will perish on distant beaches and battlefields. The scene of hostilities may again be England, France, Germany, Africa and the South Pacific—or it may be Latin America and the United States.

Canaris has brought death to many men. Their faces are as many as the sands of the sea—but in the end their myriad faces are symbolized by one face. That face is the stony-eyed mute countenance of the Unknown Soldier. He wears a gray uniform, which belongs to no one army of the world—for he is the soldier of all armies.

After World War I the idea of the Unknown Soldier, *der unbekannte Soldat, le soldat inconnu,* touched the heart of the world. Monuments to him were erected from Baraboo, Wisconsin, to Liverpool, England, from Quedlinburg, Germany, to Casablanca, in Morocco. The Unknown Soldier of this War will want no more patriotic monuments. Let the monuments remind us to build no triumphal arches, to hail no conquering heroes, but to be humble and to pray, pray that it will never happen again—pray that mankind be spared another war.

Canaris, hoping to save his neck, will laugh at such an inscription. But the stony eyes of the Unknown Soldier may stare him into silence. Possibly . . . possibly . . . possibly. . . . Or will Canaris go on laughing?

INDEX